SO-ABZ-757

A GLIMPSE AT WALL STREET
AND ITS MARKETS.

BY H. L. BENNET.

Descriptions of Important Railroad and Industrial Properties.

GREENWOOD PRESS, PUBLISHERS
NEW YORK

Originally published in 1904 by Jacob Berry & Co.

Reprinted from a copy in the collections of
The New York Public Library, Astor, Lenox
and Tilden Foundations.

First Greenwood reprinting, 1968

Library of Congress catalogue card number: 68-28616

Printed in the United States of America

CONTENTS.

DESCRIPTION OF PROPERTIES.

WE transact a general brokerage business in all the leading markets of the country.

Commission charges are in accordance with the rules of the Exchange whereupon transactions are made. Our margins under ordinary conditions on the stocks usually active in the New York market are **five points.** On Philadelphia stocks under similar conditions margins of from **five to ten points** are required.

Accounts may be opened on this basis by any of the customary forms of remittance; certified check, express, postal or express order.

Funds not required as margin against transactions are subject to sight draft. Such balances draw interest at **four per cent.** per annum.

We are pleased to handle marginal or investment orders for stocks or bonds in lots of all quantities. Fractional lot accounts are accorded the same careful attention as large transactions.

We deal in **grain** and **produce futures** for Chicago and New York delivery. The customary margin on grain is **five cents** a bushel and commission one-sixteenth each way. The active wheat futures can be handled for Chicago contracts in lots of 1,000 bushels and multiples. Commission on pork and lard is **two and one-half cents** each way; margin, **one dollar** per barrel or tierce and upwards, according to market conditions.

The commission on **cotton futures** is **one and one-half** points each way, or **three points** for the complete transaction.

We are pleased at all times to receive communications regarding financial subjects of any nature.

All inquiries regarding transactions in the various markets are carefully and fully answered and may be made by mail, wire or personal interview at our offices.

JACOB BERRY & CO.

the only important exceptions being the group of Copper Mining stocks, having their central market in Boston, and which are, making allowances for the individual condition of the copper trade, subject to practically the same influences and dealt in upon the same lines as other shares; and the mass of general mining stocks dealt in all over the country also subject to so many individual influences and local conditions that they hardly belong in the present category. State and City bonds are rarely actively handled upon the Exchanges, usually being dealt in outside their limits, and, like government issues, more suited to special than general classes of investors. The securities, then, which come under this consideration may be separated by a general division into those representing the transportation business or the railroads on one hand, and the large manufacturing or industrial companies on the other. The market for the latter is confined to the home Exchanges, but many of our railroad stocks and bonds have an extensive foreign following and are dealt in heavily upon the London and to a lesser degree in the Continental markets.

Naturally it is important to the investor that he be familiar with the financial and physical conditions of the corporations whose securities he holds; but for him who places funds therein as a matter apart from his regular business, a scientific examination of the yearly and part-yearly reports of the various companies from which can be derived the different facts and figures desired, with due confidence in his own investigation, is impracticable, and requires more study and knowledge of corporation affairs and a business in which he is but a layman, than most persons can afford to devote or have time to acquire. However, through the medium of various publications which make a point of boiling down and submitting in concise form the gist of these reports, he is enabled to readily keep in touch with the information he needs by a moderate amount of properly directed reading. In this connection may be mentioned with all propriety *The Financial and Commercial Chronicle*, issued weekly, its quarterly supplement, and *Poor's Manual*, published annually, as admirably suited for examining the earning power of any corporation of prominence. The requirements of law, and what has become universally approved and expected custom in combination, compel the publication of full operating and financial statistics by railroad companies, which being analyzed for public convenience render the position of their stock and bonds readily determined.

In the consideration of industrial companies or Trusts, as they are often termed, it usually is not possible to obtain such complete data, although many and a constantly increasing number now make a practice of issuing reports similar to those of railroad companies. In the first place large industrial combinations are new as compared with transportation companies and have not yet as well established an economic position in the community ; but as they grow in this and other respects the necessity of increased publicity of their business is becoming more fully recognized and met. There has, however, always existed among them a disinclination to print publicly the results of their operations, apparently on the ground that too much information would thereby be furnished competitors. The result of this lack of public knowledge in the estimation of their securities finds very palpable evidence in the prices that they bring as compared with railroad issues paying like rates of interest. In cases where industrial companies have adopted the practice of issuing statements, a much better estimate of the intrinsic worth of their securities can of course be formed ; but the value of a statement depends very largely upon the basis it affords for purposes of comparison, and as this custom is comparatively new and many of these companies have, indeed, been operating in their present form for a limited period only, this feature is to a great extent lacking. In this connection a further point of difference in the comparison of railroad and industrial companies is that all the former are engaged in practically the same business, and among them standards of comparison can easily be formed; on the contrary, industrial concerns are occupied in almost as many different directions as there are companies to consider, each of which is subject to entirely unlike conditions of expense, profit and loss, and valuation, making it very hazardous to attempt drawing comparisons save where two or more companies chance to be engaged in the same occupation or where one has issued statements covering a sufficient number of different periods to suit this purpose. Even then a comparison of a company with itself at another time can never be more than partially satisfactory.

In cases where it has not been the custom to make reports of earnings the most tangible means at hand of judging an investment is its demonstrated capacity as a dividend payer ; obviously this, when taken by itself, is a very superficial criterion, but when taken in conjunction with a detailed report is clearly of value. This is particularly true in the consideration of mortgage obligations or bonds and preferred stocks. If, for instance, a company has been regularly paying dividends upon its junior stock issues or those last entitled to share in the profits, the extent to which net earnings must fall off, before dividends or interest upon the higher grade stocks and bonds will be encroached upon, is readily gauged. Take, for example, the case of the Northern Pacific Railway at the conclusion of the fiscal year ending June 30, 1899. Roundly speaking, two and three-quarters million dollars were required to pay the four per cent. dividend to which the preferred was entitled. Beside this about five per cent. was earned (although only three per cent. was paid) upon approximately a like amount of common stock, and the company had a set aside surplus of three million dollars to guarantee the continuance of the preferred dividends. Thus the net earnings would have to decrease to the extent of the two and three-quarter million dollars paid on the common, the million and a half surplus earned thereover and the three million surplus, or a total of seven and a quarter million before a deficit would be shown on the preferred dividend. In order to assure the permanence of a company's profits, be its business either manufacturing or transporting, it is plainly essential that a sufficient sum be expended from each year's earnings to maintain its operating efficiency. There can be no set rule governing all cases ; generally speaking, the annual requirements of a properly maintained railroad may be estimated at about $800 per mile of track ; $1,200 to $1,300 per locomotive ; $550 to $600 per passenger car, and $50 to $60 per freight car. These figures being taken from the averages of the well equipped systems of the country covering a succession of years may be accepted as pretty accurate, although they are naturally subject to variation according to the nature of country traversed and the prices of materials, etc. These particulars are given extensive explanation in the reports as now rendered. Industrial companies not having features so nearly identical as those of the railroads, similar lines of comparison cannot be drawn; but it is a noticeable and gratifying feature in the reports of such companies as they become more complete that special allowances are provided for depreciation of plant etc., in making computations of profits.

The great majority of the large corporations of the country are products of a process of consolidation. In the cases of railroads this has been more or less gradual; where the terminals of two companies have met, the common interest has often been found to be better served through a merging of the systems, and as such enlarged companies have grown in their control of the territory traversed, they have absorbed the minor lines of operating in adjacent sections. Again, when the same or allied interests have control of neighboring companies through ownership of stock and bonds, the most natural policy possible has been to profit by the obvious economies effected by a joint operation. The growth of a railroad system is like the progress of a river toward the sea. It naturally absorbs as feeders the smaller streams in its valley, and like a river a railway's traffic is always making toward an outlet in the form of some trade centre. It is the economy cf trade like that of nature to make one route suffice instead of giving each stream an individual course to the common destination. The idea of consolidation has been less gradual in its grasp upon manufacturing companies, and while the process has been quicker the ends attained are practically the same. It is interesting to note how the tendency to consolidate practically all of a given industry at one time is reflected in the titles of the resulting companies, such sweeping and imposing names as American, Amalgamated, Consolidated, Federal, National and United would hardly have been chosen with a more gradual and less complete evolution. The effect of this upon mortgage issues is that a majority of the leading corporations, railroads particularly, are sponsors for various bonds covering parts of their system only, as one operating branches and receiving profits must needs assume their obligations and pay interest thereupon before its own issues are considered. Such bonds are classed as divisional bonds, and in cases where the absorbing company agrees to pay a fixed rate of interest upon stock of the minor one, these shares are termed guaranteed stocks. The process of consolidation is often accomplished by the main company taking up the other's issues, by giving in exchange therefor bonds of its own, which being a lien upon collateral, are called "collateral bonds." This process, it may be said, simplifies very appreciably the arrangements of the finances. Another purpose for which such divisional mortgages are issued is for the construction of a branch or extension, bonds being issued covering it only, but of necessity guaranteed by the company as a whole. The term extension bonds applies to these.

Divisional and extension bonds as well as all guaranteed securities naturally form a very high class of investment, and being such are usually held at prices making the rate of interest returns a small one. In most cases they find lodgment in hands requiring the very highest class of security only, and, always barring special circumstances, the ordinary investor can obtain better all around results in securities of an order not so strictly gilt edged. Such elaborate systems of bonds are found usually with the railroad rather than industrial companies, and while interest returns must necessarily depend upon the general condition of business and money rates, these strictly first class issues rarely yield over four per cent., and very often sell upon a basis of three and one-half per cent. In a general order the next class of bonds consists of those usually termed as First Mortgages. Subject to minor issues such as those just described, they cover as a first lien practically the entire property. Under reasonably prosperous conditions of the company issuing them such bonds are a high class of investment, and there being a greater volume of them, and somewhat more subject to changing conditions than the divisional mortgages, they yield a better interest, and are a much more popular field for the ordinary investor.

Following these are second, and sometimes third mortgage bonds, which usually cover about the same property as do the firsts. The titles will not necessarily correspond exactly to these, being varied to meet the description required, and naturally it rarely happens that two companies will issue securities upon identically the same lines; often a bond will represent a first mortgage upon one part of a system, a second upon another, and perhaps a third upon another, depending largely upon the date of issue and previous obligations then outstanding. Under the circumstances this sequence is about as close a general one as can be given, and the relative position of any specified bond in a company's finances, whether it be known by one of the above titles or as a general mortgage or prior lien, can be readily determined by a cursory review of its securities. Such of this list as may be outstanding comprise the securities upon which interest is compulsory, and in event of default thereof a foreclosure is warranted.

Next in order comes the so called debenture bond, and sometimes those known as income bonds. Certificates for these usually provide for interest payments at the discretion of the company's directors, and as may be warranted by surplus profits after the claims of the senior bonds have been met, interest upon them not being compulsory. Their position is more nearly that of a preferred stock than a bond, although they are issued in the latter form, and have preference over all classes of stock in the distribution of profits. The denominations or size of the majority of railroad and industrial bonds are five hundred and one thousand dollars. In some instances they provide for registration in the name of the owner as well as being in the usual coupon form, that is with principal payable to holder, and detachable coupons representing each interest payment when due, entitling the bearer thereto upon presentation. In the case of bonds in coupon form only the option of registration as to principal is usually given. Unless there happens to be a particular reason for doing this, however, it is usually preferable to leave them in the original status, as the price of a registered bond is generally slightly lower than the coupon form by from one-half to one per cent. This is owing chiefly to the obviously greater facility with which a coupon bond is handled, and is well exemplified in the case of Government issues, where it is usua ly to be observed that this difference in the two classes of one issue exists. However, it naturally follows that in buying a registered bond the opportunity occurs of effecting this saving in price.

After the debenture and income bonds comes the stock issues, or shares which may be said to represent the value of the franchise and effectiveness of management in operating the property. In most cases there are two classes, the preferred following the bonds as to claim upon assets and profits ; and the common which completes the capital of obligations. Sometimes there are graded issues of preferred stock, companies furnishing notable instances being the Chicago & Great Western Railway and the Reading Company. In such cases they are usually classified as " preferred A " and " preferred B," or as first and second preferred, receiving dividends up to a fixed rate in order of sequence. Preferred stocks are necessarily limited as to rate of interest, fixing a point after which comes the claim of the common shares ; sometimes it is provided that if in a given year the preferred stock does not receive its full dividend the amount unpaid accrues to it in arrears and must be settled before any returns are made to the common ; such a preferred stock is described as " Cumulative." Where an unpaid dividend is not carried forward in this manner but is forfeited, the term " Non-cumulative " is applied.

Although the common shares are last in line in the division of profits it often happens that the rate of dividend paid upon them is larger than upon securities having prior claims. While bonds represent money expended in the construction of the property this is not always so in the case of stock which may represent values of various sorts. In the formation of a company, when its ultimate success is at best a matter of uncertainty, it often happens that subscribers to the bonds are given a percentage of stock as a bonus to facilitate their sale. Sometimes stock is issued for the purpose of acquiring new properties, and often dividends are paid by issuing new stock and distributing it pro rata to holders of the security so benefiting. It will thus be appreciated that at the outset of its business it is natural that a company will earn but little if anything in excess of interest upon the securities representing funds actually put into it, but as the company grows in earning power and its profits increase without a further proportionate expenditure of capital these fixed charges do not enlarge and the new profits accrue to the benefit of the stock issues. It will be readily seen that in their position as last of the capital obligations the stock issues are more subject to the influence of general business conditions, upon which the volume of earnings depends, than the senior issues, and thus being the first to be affected by any falling off in net profits, the permanence of the dividends they receive lies largely in the proper maintenance of the physical condition of the property, a point to which the investor in stocks particularly should look. The term, "watered stock," is one often observed, and its technical meaning is that stock for which there is no money expended upon property. It has become a custom to look with suspicion upon an issue to which this term is applied, but this is not necessarily justified, for as a company's surplus profits over fixed charges increases the amount available for stock dividends becomes correspondingly larger and a corresponding increase of shares is entirely proper. In short, the extent to which stock should be issued depends entirely upon the equity of earning power it may represent and the purposes it is issued to serve.

As investments, stocks are to be considered in two classes, one as to the dividends paid, which is entirely a question of the individual corporation, while the other, consisting of those not making an immediate interest return, as to prospects for a rise in price and outlook for future dividends. A purchase of the latter is in the same category as one of unimproved real estate, though if well judged is likely to bring much quicker results.

The best opportunities for making such purchases are obviously afforded by stocks representing companies which have not arrived at a complete, or practically so, development of their field of operations. As a study in possibilities the railroads offer a better field than do industrial companies, as the latter are more deeply involved in minor conditions of trade and their tendency to develop clearly more subject to interruption. A railroad builds up and settles the country it traverses, and while its business of course fluctuates with trade conditions at large it always has the traffic of its individual field, and as this progresses commercially the transportation of merchandise and passengers must show a tendency to increase. While a large part of the lines of a new company will therefore be largely unproductive at first, it is the economic purpose of the railroad to build up the adjacent country and fertilize it, so to speak ; another point of similarity between the railroad and the river.

While Government bonds are a more or less popular field of investment with people at large, there appear to be but two reasons, under ordinary circumstances, to justify this : the comparatively absolute safety as to principal and interest they ensure, their stability being that of the Federal Government, and the ready market they afford. The interest yielded to the investor is necessarily very small by reason of the high prices they bring as a combined result of their stability and the figures which National banks can afford to pay for them. These institutions having the privilege of issuing currency against them to practically ninety-five per cent. of their face value, Government bonds are obviously worth much more to the banks than to any one else, and hence the demand for them from this source puts their price upon a basis out of proportion to their value to the investor in general ; thus to place money therein, unless there is some special reason for so doing, entails a needless sacrifice of its earning power. The time for obtaining the best results through buying Governments is when they are first issued, though of course such occasions are few and far between. An excellent example of this was the three per cent. War Loan of 1898, which was sold at par entirely to subscribers in amounts of five thousand dollars and under, and which before long commanded a premium of ten per cent. Many of the original subscribers sold their allotments immediately at profits of two and three per cent., without even the formality of paying for their bonds, which was done by those who bought from them. The term "popular loan" by which this was described is very fitting, as the approximate two hundred million dollars of bonds issued at par and shortly afterward selling at 110, represented a profit of twenty million dollars to the small investors who took them.

The security issues of States and municipalities as well as those of the smaller corporations of various sorts, including the growing volume of electrically equipped railway lines being more in the nature of special investments and suited to special purposes, are obviously a class apart from the stocks and bonds of the larger railroad and industrial companies, under the glass of constant public scrutiny and handled upon the broad market an Exchange affords. Undoubtedly the issues of the electrical roads are destined to take a more active part in the markets as these companies grow in importance, as is indicated by the active interest demonstrated in the securities of such of the larger of these systems as now have representation upon the Exchanges.

SPECULATION IN SECURITIES.

The radical difference of purpose between investment and speculation in securities is that while the former seeks for stability of principal and permanence of interest returns, the sole object of the latter is to complete and close out the transaction at such a profit as may be expected to materialize within a comparatively short time. Thus the investor looks to the ultimate fate of the security, the immediate rise or fall being of secondary consideration only, as meaning a slight saving or a slightly greater expense in effecting his transaction. On the other hand the speculator looks to the immediate market movement, whether prices will rise before they fall or vice versa, and regards the intrinsic value of a property as to the extent it will be reflected by the momentary fluctuations only. Therefore while the investor makes researches into a company's soundness of physical and financial condition and prospective development, it is to the influences which affect prices but temporarily that the speculator accords closest attention. Obviously the money used for investment purposes is that which is required to yield an income with minimum risk of principal, but the money which finds a logical and proper employment in the more uncertain field of speculation is that which need not of necessity be otherwise used, and the loss of which entails no undue hardship. In other words it is money which can justifiably be risked in the endeavor to increase it largely. Speculative operations are conducted chiefly in stocks rather than bonds, as there is less certainty in the interest returns of the former and their prices more subject to changing conditions.

Like any other market, that for securities takes its tendency to rise or fall from predominance of supply or demand, and this derives its inspiration chiefly from a few fundamental causes such as the condition of general business as reflected in the earnings of corporations and the extent to which people have money for purchases of bonds and stocks; political affairs, both local and world wide; the condition of the crops and the prices they bring, and the movement of money from one financial centre to another. Upon the extent to which these factors incline people at large to increase or reduce their holdings of securities the general movement of prices depends. The man who is described as progressive keeps in touch with these things. He could not be progressive unless he did, and if his observations are clear and his conclusions accurate, the speculative markets offer the opportunity of turning them to pecuniary profit, for it should be borne in mind that they offer equal chances to both optimist and pessimist. To this facility of putting a monetary value upon opinions is due largely in turn the constant increase in the number of persons who make a point of following closely matters of finance and general business, to the obvious benefit of the understanding and intelligence of the community; and it is through the medium of logical and conservative speculation and investment that persons not otherwise in touch with the large railroad and industrial corporations of the country can profit by their development and growth as reflected in the prices of their securities. An excellent and remarkable instance of the possibilities attaching to properly directed speculation which came directly under the eye of the writer may be cited in this connection. A sum of between one hundred and fifty and two hundred dollars was invested as margin in the purchase of a small amount of Chicago, Milwaukee & St. Paul stock, and as the market advanced the line of stock was increased, the accrued profits serving as margin for the new purchases. The transaction was followed out upon theoretically correct lines, and resulted in a profit of approximately twenty-five thousand dollars, which, so far as the writer knows, is practically all retained. This, of course, was an unusually successful case, though it is one of which but few persons know, happening as it did in the famous speculation of 1898-99, when many fortunes were made. Such results could not have been achieved had not the theory and principles involved been given careful study ; not the study of years, for this was the first or practically the first transaction of this sort that the man had ever attempted, but during the six or eight months which it covered he learned and applied the truths of speculation sufficiently well to improve the opportunity and bring it to a successful conclusion. It is just because so many people will not accord the subject the study due it, or apply the results thereof properly, that there are not more cases of this sort than now occur. This study is merely one of those factors which cause market movements, and the manner and logical extent of their several effects thereupon. The commanding position the United States have acquired in the commerce and finance of the world has resulted in American markets finding the basis of their movements chiefly in home conditions, and the observation thereof is much simpler than when prices followed a foreign initiative, based primarily upon foreign conditions. Another result of American commercial growth is the repurchase of great quantities of our securities which were bought originally by Great

Britain and Europe at a time when this country did not possess the capital necessary to develop its resources. This has the two-fold effect of thoroughly domesticating the control of the interests these securities involve, and of reducing the amount of interest annually shipped abroad in the form of either actual coin or exports of our products.

The method of a speculative, or as it is often termed, a marginal transaction in stocks, is simple and in all essential principles easily understood. Stocks so dealt in are usually of a par value of one hundred dollars : that is, each share represents that amount of capitalization of the corporation issuing it ; occasionally the par value is of a smaller amount, in which case computations are so altered as to bring transactions upon an equivalent basis, this uniformity simplifying business greatly. Prices fluctuate by one-eighth of one per cent. of the par value, or multiples of that amount, each change of one-eighth being equal to twelve and one-half cents per share. The fluctuation is always based upon the par value without regard to what the market price may be, a change of one per cent. amounting to one dollar per share, whether the quotation is fifty or one hundred and fifty. A trader wishing to purchase a quantity of stock, the actual cost of which would be greater than the amount to be invested, deposits with his broker a sum of money equaling a certain percentage, usually from five to ten per cent. of the total par value. The broker then buys the stock, advancing the balance required to complete payment, his funds being protected against possible decline in price by the money deposited with him. This money is known as margin, being the margin between the buying price and that whereat a fall in value would encroach upon the broker's advance, and just as long as the trader maintains this margin to a reasonable extent above the figure of its exhaustion the broker can carry the stock. There is no time limit within which a transaction must be closed, the period of its duration being entirely at the discretion of the trader, subject to the margin holding good, it lying with him to decide when best to accept the profit or cut short the loss As the security is bought for the benefit of the trader solely, the broker advancing the balance to facilitate earning his commission only, the trader is entitled to the entire profit accruing from the advance at which it is sold, thus profiting through an investment of capital many times greater than that by which he is personally involved. When the transaction shows as great a profit as the trader deems likely to be made, he can order it closed, and is credited with the gain, less expenses, of the operation. These consist of commission for buying and selling, and interest upon money advanced, usually at six per cent. It will be seen that these computations are very simple and easily made. If, after making purchase, the market weakens and probabilities seem to favor a decline before an advance, a sale can be ordered at any time, thus limiting the loss, and whatever that may then amount to is deducted from the deposit, the remainder being free for a new deal. Stock so bought with the idea of selling it later at a higher price is termed in speculative parlance "long stock," the expression being in contra-distinction of its opposite, or "short stock." When it is believed that prices will decline and purchases can be made in the future below existing quotations, the trader or operator can make what is known as a "short sale." In this case margins are deposited in the same manner and in the same proportion to the size of the transaction as when purchasing for an advance. The broker sells the number of shares ordered, and to provide for their delivery borrows certificates for a corresponding quantity which he turns over to the purchaser. There are always more or less of the shares actively dealt in to be had for such purposes in the vicinity of the Exchanges, called the "floating supply," or that which has not present lodgment with investors, and by its use in this way the duration of a short transaction is equally unlimited as to time as is a long purchase, and like that subject only to the marginal protection provided and the views of the operator. As a short sale is made in anticipation of a fall before an advance in prices, the profit accrues when they decline, amounting to a dollar per each share sold every one per cent. fall, the proportion and in fact all computations corresponding exactly to those of a purchase for the rise. When it appears advisable to close the deal, the broker is ordered to buy the same amount of stock as that sold short, and he then delivers the certificates so purchased to the party from whom the shares were borrowed originally, thus closing the transaction. It will be seen very readily that an advancing market means a loss upon such a deal, each one per cent. rise meaning a reduction of the margin of one dollar per share, and if the sale is unclosed when the market has advanced sufficiently to render the marginal deposit inadequate to protect the broker from loss, he is privileged to close it out precisely as he is privileged to sell long stock under corresponding circumstances. There is a prevalent idea that a short sale is a more or less complicated transaction ; as soon as the mind is rid of this, and understands that it is commenced with a sale and closed with a purchase, it is mastered. It is simply a reversal of a long trade ; there is nothing complicated about it.

It must be very clear that with a volume of business aggregating hundreds of thousands of shares daily—the largest day's business on the New York Stock Exchange approximated one million seven hundred thousand—that the quantity of certificates and large checks passing from office to office would be enormous. To simplify matters as much as possible, the leading Exchanges have adopted a system of settlement through a Clearing House, composed of members of the Exchange only, whereby it is required, as far as possible, that only brokers with stocks to carry at the close of the day are obliged to handle the actual certificates. Thus if A buys one hundred shares of a certain stock from B and sells it to C, it is the province of the Clearing House to arrange that B will deliver the stock to C, and A settle his profit or loss by payment to or draft upon the Clearing House, which in turn makes settlement with the other two, the amount it receives and pays out balancing. Such an institution is patterned after those in use among banks.

It is evident that the great quantity of stocks carried by brokers upon margins amounting to only a small percentage of their actual cost, require immense sums of money to complete the payment, sums far beyond those which the capital of the brokers can furnish. These funds are obtained from the banks and the trust companies, which take the securities as collateral, and require a greater margin of difference between the amount advanced and the market price than the broker usually receives from his client. In this way the large institutions of deposit are enabled to earn interest upon the great sums in their hands, much of which would otherwise be idle. Such loans are usually needed from day to day only, which explains the great number of "call loans" in Wall Street. Such a loan is subject to the call of the lender before the close of banking hours any day, and because of this readiness with which the funds involved can be recalled and the always known value of the collateral, there is practically no risk attached to making them. The bearing of the ability and willingness of the banking institutions to make loans of this nature upon the facility with which securities can be bought and carried is easily understood. When there is a plentiful supply of such lendable money, rates for it are low and tend to increase purchases, but when for any reason this supply is reduced, rates advance correspondingly and loans are called or returned, the result being a diminution of purchases and increased sales, with the effect of advancing or depressing prices, as the case may be. The conditions of the money market are published in the papers daily, as a part of the news affecting securities, along with the tables of quotations. Every Saturday the Associated Banks of New York issue a statement of their loans, deposits, cash holdings, funds in circulation and surplus reserves, giving to whomsoever may be interested the figures which indicate the degree of elasticity of their lending power. This is chiefly a question of the surplus reserve, which is determined as follows. The banks are required by law to maintain an amount of specie or legal tender equal to twenty-five per cent. of their deposit liabilities, this being known as the "reserve." The amount of cash held in excess thereof is known as the "surplus reserve." When a bank makes a loan to a client, it simply places the amount thereof to his credit, thus increasing its deposits correspondingly, and as the funds so loaned to brokers when drawn upon, rarely go outside of the city banks, the associated institutions seldom lose in actual cash through this means. The holdings of money remaining stationary, it will readily be seen that increases or decreases in such deposits change the proportion thereof to cash holdings, thus adding or deducting from the surplus reserve. When this nears the twenty-five per cent. mark the banks are naturally obliged to curtail accommodations, but when there is an extensive surplus the loans may be extended proportionately. Naturally the reserves fluctuate with the holdings of cash, and when funds are withdrawn from New York to interior centres to facilitate the movement of crops or to supply the needs of trade, as they are at certain periods of the year, during October and November, for instance, or to the Government treasury, owing to larger revenue receipts than disbursements, or abroad in settlement of trade differences, etc., the effect upon reserves is similar to that of an expansion of loans. Of course, the flow of money to or from New York is dependent upon no fixed rules save the supply and demand, and where it is of greatest use at the moment there money commands the best interest, and other things being equal, the movement sets toward that point.

It is more in their influence upon our money markets than by their purchases and sales of our stocks that security prices here are affected from European centres, imports or exports of gold being an important factor in the home supply of money. Our European settlements are made mostly between New York and London, and are conducted by means of bills of exchange. The parity of exchange upon London is $4 867, which is the actual value in American gold of the pound sterling. When the demand for bills upon London is heavy owing to an adverse balance of trade the price advances until it reaches a point where it is cheaper to ship gold than to buy drafts, and on the other hand when the balance of trade is in our favor the price declines until gold can be shipped here at a saving. The figures at which gold can be imported or exported profitably varies slightly under different conditions, but may be put at approximately 4.89 to 4.89¼ for exports, and 4.83¾ to 4.84¼ for imports. A demand for money at

London and higher rates there than at New York naturally inclines to advance exchange and make gold exports more probable, while reversed conditions serve to favor imports. The conditions of foreign exchange are the same as those of domestic exchange in their essential principles, and both classes combined serve as an automatic means of preventing protracted periods of excessive interest rates at any centre. A point of interest as bearing upon the balance of trade and thereby upon the foreign exchange market is that the amount paid annually for shipping American products in foreign vessels is estimated at about $100,-000,000.

While the question of money is palpably a very important one in the movement of security prices it by no means follows that it is necessarily the leading influence. There are other considerations which often overrule it in bearing upon the supply and demand for stocks. The effect of general business and political conditions is perhaps still more potent. An excellent example of where these have worked results, entirely inconsistent with the money situation, was the almost steady depression of prices which occurred during the period of business depression succeeding the panic of 1893 and which lasted practically until the temporary boom of the spring and summer of 1895, although lendable money was so plentiful as to be a virtual drug on the market during the greater part of the time. On the other hand, the two months preceding the election of 1896, when the success of the advocates of the gold standard was practically assured and construed favorably to security values, witnessed a very sweeping rise in prices ; this was in the face of money rates ranging all the way from six to one hundred per cent.

The relation of business conditions to the degree of prosperity enjoyed by the country's transportation and manufacturing industries, and thereby to the value of their securities, is that of the soil to the plant. If crops are good and trade active, so much the larger tonnage for the railroads and so much greater the quantity of manufactured products the farmer and people at large can buy, particularly if the foreigner buys our products at relatively good prices. As the maker of clothing, for instance, sells more goods he must needs employ more hands to make them, and as labor finds more employment it commands better wages and buys more freely of necessities as well as luxuries, thus adding its share to the stimulation of trade; with the consequent increase in the freight it handles the greater the wear and tear upon the track and rolling stock of the railroad, which is obliged to buy more freely from the iron maker. And so on through the ramifications of commerce, business being larger and more profitable to all concerned, and resulting in increased returns in the shape of greater dividends to security holders. When conditions are reversed precisely opposite is the effect; earnings diminish and profits upon invested capital contract correspondingly. Obviously, questions of security values lie chiefly with these conditions of trade and agriculture, which thus form the primary basis of market movements. A very important factor in stimulating purchases or sales of stocks is popular sentiment. This takes its color largely from the general business situation; when that is viewed in an optimistic light people are naturally disposed to think well of buying stocks, but when the outlook is for diminishing profits the inclination is to sell. The full importance of sentiment as a market factor is not likely to be appreciated at first glance; commercial, political or monetary conditions are required for the basis of any extensive price movement, but after this is once fairly under way the very confidence begotten by a show of strength or tendency in either direction is often the cause of its continuance, the rush of buyers or sellers to participate in what appears to be an easily gauged movement creating a demand for, or a supply of, stocks that usually ends in carrying prices to an extreme limit, unjustified by actual facts. It rarely happens that a rise or fall of large proportions does not overreach what should be its natural limitation; one excellent example of this out of many was the bull movement which culminated in the spring of 1899, where under the influence of purchases, instigated mostly by the sentiment of enthusiasm, great lines of stock were accumulated at prices far above those which actual investors would pay, and when money rates finally advanced and compelled wholesale liquidation, the ardor of optimism was dampened, speculative buying ceased, and a series of violent declines ensued until a reasonable level of prices was reached and brought in a new demand.

The influence of politics bears upon price movements from several directions. In the first place its effect is felt through reflection upon general business and vicariously upon stocks, for although as a rule it may be said with full deference to their unquestioned respective powers that our political parties do not control the elements nor the growth of the crops, changes in our commercial laws certainly affect trade. Changes in tariff tend to do this. When foreign politics extend so far as military expression or threats thereof, the effect is to advance the price of breadstuffs, for war means waste, with consequent benefit to the American grower and carrier. Legislation which is likely to be of restrictive influence upon the trade of a corporation or a group of them, or which by increasing taxation and thus reducing profits, naturally detracts from the esteem in which their securities are held and induces sales, while the passage of laws opposite in intent will encourage buyers. The law imposing a franchise tax enacted by the New York Legislature of 1899 is illustrative of this point. While politics are purely a matter of personal opinion, and what one man believes in another may deprecate, sentiment plays no part in the effect of a law, and the financial community is never long in deciding what it regards as beneficial or detrimental to values, and buys or sells regardless of personal creed.

The province of the stock market is essentially that of a mirror —the affairs of commerce, finance, politics, etc., finding reflex in its changing prices. But its reflection of affairs is purely anticipatory rather than retrospective, as the keenest judgment and some of the deepest brains in the country are involved in its movements, and in making their operations will look to future conditions, as it is in conformity with those that the market must swing rather than the events of the past. A rise or fall in prices anticipatory of an expected occurrence is described by the expression "discounting," which is often used in discussions of the market situation. Therefore it usually happens that when any looked for event actually becomes a reality, it has already found expression or reflection in the price movement, and the successful operator must look into the future for a basis of his transactions. An excellent illustration of this in practice was furnished in the market movement at the time of the 1896 election, referred to heretofore. When the result of the balloting became known it was found to have been reflected or discounted by the preceding violent advance, and upon the announcement, which was accounted highly favorable to security values, prices broke heavily.

The foregoing are the natural laws whereupon movements of prices depend, but while the stock market may be very properly described as active, it is certainly not animate, and a handle or lever whereby these natural forces are applied is necessary for them to exercise their effect; precisely as all the steam in the universe could not turn a wheel without a piston. This application is attained by means of cliques of operators fostering the tendency to either buy or sell stocks which actual conditions inspire, and doing whatever is possible to help along a market movement. It is termed "manipulation." Operations of this character are conducted by powerful and influential individuals, or combinations of them, and may be confined to the shares of one company or extended over the entire stock list, according to their magnitude. Taking a case of an ordinary movement with the primary purpose of simply making a profitable deal, the manipulator will look to the merits of the situation as favoring a rise or fall in prices, and then proceed to acquire a line of long or short stock, as the case may be, without disturbing the market's equilibrium, and in such quantity as he believes the magnitude and extent of the speculation will permit of his closing out profitably. If the campaign be with the view of bulling or advancing prices, the next step is to start them upward by bidding openly for the stock as well as making transactions at rising figures by means of brokers working together in the open market upon the Exchange floor. The activity and tendency of the stock to advance thus generated naturally attracts traders at large desirous of participating in the advance, and increases the volume of purchases, thus giving the instigators of the movement an opportunity of selling at a profit the stocks they originally bought. A transaction of this sort is usually undertaken at a time when it is known to those persons most closely informed as to the affairs of a property that some particularly favorable or unfavorable development concerning it is about to transpire, and when this actually occurs the process of completing the distribution of the stock accumulated by the pool is accomplished upon the strength of it. Of course until this is done the promoters must stand ready to support the price of their stock with buying orders, and to protect it against any effort which other interests may make to turn the course of its price for purposes of their own, but after the holdings of the pool have been closed and its support withdrawn, the immediate future of the price depends upon the general and more indiscriminate buying power which has been generated, and unless this exceeds in volume the profit taking sales of persons who have bought while the rise was in progress, the pressure of the latter will naturally work a reaction. In this connection it is proper to note the sympathetic tendency to advance or decline which one stock will exert upon others. The inclination to buy or sell is apt to spread from one stock to others, particularly if conditions are propitious to a general market movement, and if a successful campaign is conducted in one part of the stock list, the chances are that like efforts will be made elsewhere. Some most remarkable instances of the gusto of public buying, fanned into flame by manipulation based upon exceptionally sound legitimate conditions, occurred in the bull movement before mentioned which followed the Spanish war and culminated in the spring of 1899. Particularly noteworthy among these were the shares of many industrial combinations formed about that time, the common stocks of which, though unduly watered, were enabled to earn and pay dividends, owing to the remarkable prosperity of business throughout the country. Large blocks of these common shares were allotted to stock operators in payment for services in floating the capital obligations, and were in turn sold in the general market at prices which were attained only through the enthusiasm of buyers whose optimism got the better of their judgment. The rise in prices became so indiscriminate that its contagion extended everywhere, advances justified by real merit exerting a sympa· thetic effect upon other shares, which consequently reached figures that could be explained by naught but undue inflation. When this at last came to an end a radical readjustment in prices followed, but not, however, until many fortunes of both large as well as moderate amounts had been made.   In all the hurrah which accompanied this famous rise the necessity of manipulation to start a move in a particular stock was clearly outlined. Repeatedly, amidst the upward rush of the rest of the list, a particular stock would remain quiet and practically stationary until taken in hand by its friends ; then its activity, as measured by the volume of business in it, would increase, and once the rise was initiated it would join in the prevalent flight, and it was necessary only to purchase, regardless of price, to share in the profits which for a time seemed unlimited. Even to a greater extent than was the case in this particular chapter of speculation is manipulation essential to any speculative movement of importance, and as it indicates the direction toward which the most powerful interests are working the advantages of following it are apparent.

In cases where manipulation has for its object a decline in prices, the effort is made to bring about as great an amount of liquidation as possible from holders of stocks, thus giving the operators conducting the movement an opportunity of making purchases to cover their short sales. With this in view it is usual that news items, based upon conditions detrimental to the value of the stocks involved, be given circulation, while the decline is accelerated by further short sales and brokers working together as in the case of a campaign for the advance, the purpose being to increase the apparent excess of supply and by the consequent fall in prices induce holders of long and investment stock to sell. To make possible as great an amount of short sales as a campaign of this nature requires, it is necessary to borrow corresponding quantities of stock to accomplish the delivery until they can be closed, or "covered," as it is termed, by actual purchases, and if the supply of stock available for such loans becomes materially reduced, a consideration, called a premium, is exacted for its use by the lenders. When such a condition of affairs arises the expense of carrying large lines of short stock is likely to become too heavy to justify so doing, or should the effort to dislodge long stock not meet with the success expected, it very often happens that traders operating upon the other side of the market will come in as buyers and bid up prices with the view of forcing the bear party to cover its sales at an advance, the bulls who have bought when prices were down then having the chance of selling out at a profit.

But there are other purposes for which manipulation of prices are used as a means of attaining than a simple speculative deal of this sort. Very often it happens that interests having in contemplation an advance in prices, or any other purpose involving the necessity of buying stocks, will precede an upward movement, or in fact interrupt one, by breaking the market and improving the opportunity so created by purchasing shares, the sale of which has been induced by the fall. When an effort is made to force certain interests to liquidate long holdings or cover short sales, the attempt is described as "gunning." Sometimes through stimulating activity in the securities of a company new parties are enabled to accumulate sufficient amounts thereof to obtain the controlling interest in its management, which perhaps could not have been done through private negotiation. It may happen that the sales which must be induced to accomplish such an end are inspired by advancing prices, thereby tempting holders to accept the opportunity of making an advantageous sale, or it may happen that prices are depressed until the desired sales are forced or made to avoid a further sacrifice.

As such operations as these are constantly in progress and orders to buy or sell always being executed, the result is in the market being the scene of many cross purposes, and the balance of supply and demand constantly changing, thus creating a more or less uncertain surface fluctuation in prices. The underlying trend of the movement, however, depends most largely upon the tendency of that manipulation emanating from the most powerful interests concerned in the speculation, which, in turn, takes its cue from the general outlook of business, political and monetary conditions. Briefly, the movement in prices so inspired, is an expression of the views or purposes of the best informed people, and to blend with it is well likened to going with, or opposing it, to stemming the tide. To manipulation is largely due the value of the security market as a market. The operations of the cliques or pools taken by themselves form a market upon which large quantities of stock can be bought or sold, while the volume of business from other sources forms the main basis whereupon the whole structure rests. Important operations or a manipulated movement in a stock are usually indicated by an increase in the volume of transactions and a more decided tendency to rise or fall than evinced previously, and a close examination of the quotation tables from day to day will disclose many such cases.

The true measure of values, which, despite such various influences as may temporarily inflate or depress quotations, is the price level at which the actual investment demand will absorb stocks, or, in other words, those figures which interests who settle for their securities in full and take the certificates will pay. This is the net conclusion derived from the popular idea of the intrinsic worth of individual securities tempered by money rates and other market influences, as well as the comparative interest returns obtainable through other forms of investment; and though manipulation, sentiment, or other factors affecting the supply and demand may, for a time, force prices above or below this level, they are practically certain sooner or later to adjust themselves to it. If prices are above such investment level, the naturally induced sales of investments and the closing of long stocks, the accumulation of which has advanced them, will carry the market down, and if below, the covering of short contracts and increased investment buying will advance them. As has been said before, the market usually being under more or less excitement, it seldom happens that prices adhere to this always changing level, which must needs be at all times a question, but the time when they do cling to it most closely is after a period of speculative activity when the inevitable reaction has brought them there and before a new movement is inaugurated, an occasion usually accompanied by a falling off in the volume of trading to comparatively minimum proportions.

It must be evident that stock speculation being a matter of supply and demand is subject solely to the opinions of men which are as free to change as the winds of heaven. It is what these opinions are most likely to be, and hence the questions upon which they are based, that offer the tangible field for study and observation. Therefore it is impossible to formulate a set of fixed rules for determining when a movement will begin or cease, but this can be best judged by the trend of the manipulation as the lever which moves prices, or an evident reluctance of the market to continue its predominating tendency which would obviously infer its turn, these being always subject to new conditions arising of a nature to work a contrary effect.

METHODS OF TRADING.

Reference has been made to following out speculative deals upon theoretically correct lines. The basis for this is in the governing principle of speculation that profits should be allowed to increase as long as the movement of prices is favorable, but when a market shows an inclination to move adversely it is conceded best, as a rule, to cut losses short and thus avoid large ones or save accumulated profits. As profits accrue additional transactions can be made, using them as margin without the necessity of closing out the original trade, and working upon this basis it is often possible to attain very large results from a small nucleus. In such cases it is the best policy to follow the market with an order to close the entire deal should the prices react a certain specified amount, which should differ according to the degree of activity of the stock dealt in, thus assuring the safety of at least a part of the gains and at the same time leaving the opportunity of further profits. Such an order is in the nature of a "stop," and is one often used in speculation. Its definition is given subsequently.

Methods of trading should differ with the activity and nature of the market, the above being practicable only in a more or less protracted move. When prices are not disposed to continue in either direction, it is best to accept moderate profits rather than increase holdings as gains materialize.

In event of the market going adversely, it is often a good policy to average holdings; thus, if a stock is bought at 90 and it declines to 88, another purchase of a like amount would bring the average cost down to 89, and render it possible to sell without loss so much sooner when the market turns.

A "stop order" is one placed at a price under the market in case of long stock, or above the market in case of short stock, to close out holdings at whatever prices are obtainable when its figure is reached.

A "market order" is for immediate purchase or sale at time of receipt by the broker, regardless of price.

A "limited order" is one to be executed at a specified price or better only.

A "day order" is one intended for execution upon date of receipt only, and if not filled then to be cancelled. Limited orders come under this description, unless otherwise specified, save those for profit-taking, when given at the same time as the instructions for opening the trade, which are kept good.

An "open order" is one to be held good indefinitely or until filled. A stop order comes under this ruling, unless the contrary is stated.

A "scale order" is for the purchase or sale of a stock at a number of stated prices, as the market rises or falls thereto. This is a form of limited order, and is held for day of receipt only, unless otherwise stated.

In giving orders, it is best to state positively whether they are intended as being "open" or good for the day only, as while the above is the customary method of treating them in this respect, different brokers are liable to have different rules.

SPECULATION IN PRODUCE FUTURES.

The markets for futures, that is, contracts for future delivery of products of the farm, ranch and plantation, make possible for those observers of crop and market conditions other than the farmer, miller, shipper, etc., participating in the opportunities of profit offered through the changing of prices in accordance with varying conditions of supply and demand. Without such markets, these opportunities would be very meager, even to those persons directly involved in the growing or distribution, and in return for the privilege of dealing in commodities, to the production of which he does not lend, the outside trader reciprocates by adding to the breadth of the market for them, and it is, in fact, to the magnitude of his dealings that the existence of a market of reasonable scope is due. It is only such a market that enables the producer to apply business foresight to his occupation, and by it the entire business of manufacturing and shipping large quantities of these products is greatly facilitated.

Defined, a transaction in futures is the negotiation of a contract whereby the seller agrees to deliver, and the buyer to receive, a specified quantity of a commodity, such as wheat or cotton, during a stated month. Thus, such a term as "July wheat" means a contract calling for the delivery of wheat during the month of July. It will often happen that a shortage of supply or a heavy demand from one source or another places prices higher than they appear likely to hold. It is then obviously to the planter's advantage to improve the opportunity which the market for futures affords, as the prices for spot staples are followed more or less closely by those of futures, by an advance sale of his crop, basing calculations for the ultimate delivery upon the minimum quantity he is likely to make. The planter who has a prospective crop sufficiently large, simply has to sell such portion thereof as he deems well in the open market, while the smaller farmer makes his sales to an inbetween man, who purchases it either upon commission orders or in lesser quantities, usually at a slight concession from the price larger lots are bringing, and is able, by selling in bulk, to secure the difference as his profit on the transaction. Of course, if at the time of planting or harvesting, prices of futures are low, it may be better policy for the planter to hold his crop until circumstances render its sale more advisable, and if he desires meanwhile to raise funds upon it, the banks will make advances to within a reasonable amount or margin of the market price upon a note in the form of a mortgage upon a minimum amount of the probable yield, or after harvest, upon warehouse receipts for the commodity deposited there, which is, of course, covered by insurance. Millers, exporters and others engaged in handling cash or spot staples, are enabled to protect themselves against loss on such purchases by sales of futures, the option or future market thus serving as a means of protection against the risk incurred through the fluctuations of prices, and is thus a most important adjunct to this branch of the business.

The United States being the world's largest producer of grain its markets are of primary influence in determining prices, and Chicago, being its chief produce centre, is naturally the headquarters of speculation in grain and provisions, although an extensive business in futures is transacted in other of the larger cities, notably New York and St. Louis. Speculation in grain futures on the Chicago Board of Trade is conducted in quantities of five thousand bushels and multiples, and on the Consolidated Exchange of New York business is done in Chicago contracts of one thousand bushels. This trade as between broker and customer is on lines almost parallel to those of stock transactions. The trader deposits a margin of so many cents per bushel, one cent being equivalent to one per cent. on stocks, and termed in either case a "point," but as the transaction is in future contracts, there are no actual goods delivered save when the contract months arrive, and consequently the broker does not have to advance a balance as in stock trading. So far as the customer is concerned, the actual termination of the deal is when he sells to close a long or buys to cover a short transaction, although the broker may be obliged to wait until the contract months arrive to settle the trade; but the usual process is through a system of clearances resembling that for stocks, and the transactions may be turned from broker to broker many times during the interval. As in stock transactions, profits accrue to the trader immediately upon closing the deal without regard to how distant the contract month may be. Transactions can be for either long or short account, and, if adequately margined, held as long a time as desired until the beginning of the contract month, when it is necessary to either transfer them to a later option or month of delivery, or else provide for receiving the actual grain and paying for it in full when long, or for delivering it if short. The process of receiving the cereal entails much detail of attention which should not properly attach to speculation, as well as storage charges, insurance premiums, etc., and as the commodity itself is subject to deterioration with time, the alternative of transferring is almost exclusively adopted among traders. It consists of simply closing the standing trade and opening a corresponding one in another active trading option.

This description applies to all the speculatively handled grains, and to hog products as well, save as to the quantities dealt in, which, with minimum amounts of fluctuations, are shown in the following table:

Commodity.	Minimum Contract.	Fluctuation.	Monetary Equivalent.
Grain	5,000 bushels*	1/16c. per bushel	$3.12½
Pork	250 barrels.	2½c. per barrel.†	6.25
Lard	250 tierces of 340 lbs. each	2½c. per 100 lbs.†	21.25
Ribs	50,000 lbs.	2½c. per 100 lbs.†	12.50

As with all speculative commodities, the basic question of prices is the relative amounts of supply and requirements. As a speculative grain, wheat commands the most widespread interest, for

* One thousand bushel lots of wheat, and sometimes other grains, are handled on the Consolidated Exchange of New York.

† Sometimes fluctuations are in one-half of these amounts, when they are described as " splits," meaning a split between the full quotations.

although corn represents a greater monetary value than any other American cereal, it does not occupy so important a position in the world's markets as does the finer grain, and an analysis of conditions affecting the price movements of the latter serves as a description for the grain markets in general. Referring, then, to wheat, the requirements to be met are the domestic food supply and the needs of seeding, both of which are comparatively regular and usually counted as practically a known quantity ; the figures are easy to remember, approximating one million bushels per day. The factor of uncertainty in the requirements, however, is the amount exported. This depends chiefly upon the abundance or the contrary of the foreign crops, through the extent to which they meet the consumption, though this is apt to vary considerably, as in certain countries the use of wheat is very much more a question of price than in America. A fair average for the world's annual consumption is 2,500,000,000 bushels, although it is apt to run a quarter billion more or less. The countries to which we export chiefly, however, are the most regular consumers, being the United British Kingdom and Western Europe. The other crops they depend on mostly are the Russian, Danubian, French, Indian, English and Argentine, so that any failures or partial failures among these are at once felt in the demand for the American surplus.

DESTINATION OF AMERICAN WHEAT EXPORTS.

	Year ending June 30 — 1899.	1898
United Kingdom	74,613,304	80,163,805
Germany	10,311,450	3,218,401
France	2,232,190	30,041,289
Remainder of Europe	41,045,883	22,124,014
British North American possessions	8,369,014	5,116,901
Central Am. States and British Honduras..	39,869	41,540
West Indies and Bermuda	899	1,384
South America	259,492	1,857,433
Asia and Oceanica	30,112	70,663
Africa	2,523,219	5,493,470
Elsewhere	7,083	102,361
Total	139,432,815	148,231,261
Total, including flour	222,694 920	174,089,094

Any shrinkage in the foreign supply of crops naturally advances prices abroad, a rise which must be reflected in the American markets not only by the increased demand for our surplus, but also as there can never exist at different centres for more than a brief time much more of a difference in price than represented by freight charges. Prices may show temporary discrepancies at times, owing to such causes as a special local demand or an unusual shortage in local supplies, but when a given article can be bought in one place and immediately sold in another at a profit greater than the cost of transportation, the volume of purchases and sales made to grasp this profit becomes a means of automatic adjustment of prices.

The supply depends upon two sources: the surplus remaining with farmers or in the warehouses, and the crop in prospect. The supply on hand naturally depends upon the size of the preceding crop and the volume of export business, its best measure being the weekly statements of statistics bearing upon the visible supply at the principal centres which are printed in the newspaper articles treating upon the cereal markets. The stocks in farmers' hands and where the statistician cannot obtain accurate figures are known as the "invisible supply." In considering the tendency of stocks to increase or decrease as shown by such data, the period of the crop year must be borne in mind; the movement of spring wheat to market, for instance, not beginning until about the end of June. The prospects of the crop are given best by the reports of the Department of Agriculture at Washington, issued on the tenth of each month, which by the opportunities they afford for comparison with corresponding periods in previous years whereof the size of the crops are known, render supposedly reliable forecasts of the probable amount of the yield, subject, of course, to damage from climatic or other causes. These reports give the comparative acreage, the condition of the plant, etc. These points are treated also from day to day in the newspaper and trade reports from the crop belt, which also state the comparative volume of grain received at principal centres. While it naturally follows that the increased supply resulting from a large crop will serve to depress prices, the volume of exports is probably a more potent factor in determining values. An excellent instance of comparison leading to this conclusion is that for the year 1895, when with a wheat crop of 467 million bushels following one of 460 million, with exports of 142 and 126 million bushels per annum respectively, cash wheat at Chicago sold at 48¾ cents, while in 1898 when the crop was 675 and that before it 530 million bushels, exports reached 222 million, and cash prices at the same time touched $1.23½. It is true that in 1898, which was the time of the Leiter corner, the market was under unusual manipulation, but prices held well above the dollar mark for many weeks and futures reached the vicinity of $1.80. It is true also that without the basis of a tremendous export trade the bull operators could not have been successful in forcing prices up as they did, which bears out the point that manipulation is the lever by which natural forces are applied to markets.

This relationship, or conformity, of manipulation to trade and crop conditions is quite as true when applied to the market for produce futures as in the case of stocks, but under ordinary circumstances it is not probable that prices are kept away from such figures as the actual situation warrants for any protracted length of time. The true reason for this conformity is probably to be found in the practically unlimited field the markets for wheat include, and the natural tendency of prices to seek a consistent level is too great for other forces to long withstand. The farmers as a body, themselves, are always pretty well posted as to the situation, and if, in their combined opinion, prices have fallen unduly, they will curtail shipments and thus reduce the amount of grain for sale, while on the other hand if the market advances to figures that seem unlikely to be maintained, those who control wheat can be depended upon to sell in sufficient volume to check the rise. Thus while prices usually respond readily when urged with good reason, the breadth of the market makes it too heavy a pendulum to be swung far from a well defined though changing centre of gravitation.

The most striking instance of manipulation in grain markets is that resulting in a violent advance, called a "corner." This is most apt to occur, when at all, near the termination of an option. when the amount of the actual product likely to come upon the market can be most easily gauged and controlled.

A corner is described as an artificial scarcity of a commodity due to holding it off the market, and to purchases of future con-tracts in excess of the quantity of the actual article available for delivery against them. The manipulators, through the control thus gained, are able to advance prices to an abnormal level, the motive being to sell earlier purchases to the shorts when the rise forces the latter to cover their contracts. Although wheat has been cornered a number of times, the operation has almost invari-ably resulted in a loss, the purchases which must be made at the top figures in order to maintain the corner, spoiling the average of the total and the volume of sales induced by the advance being too great a weight financially to be controlled. A corner is of most obvious advantage to the producer, as owing to it he obtains far higher prices than would be possible under ordinary circum-stances.

The options or future months for delivery in which speculation is conducted chiefly are May, which is just prior to the winter crop coming upon the market ; July, which is just after it ; August and September, when the spring crop is being received, and Decem-ber when the yield is known and the extent of the supply becomes evident.

Between the prices of cash wheat and of futures there logically exists, barring other influences, a difference equivalent to the carrying charges of the actual article until the month of delivery. These consist of storage, interest and insurance fees, etc., and approximate a cent and a quarter a bushel per month. In the natural process this difference dwindles as the contract month approaches, until, with its expiration, the contract falls due, and the wheat becomes the cash or spot article. While these charges always enter into the determining of future prices, there often exist other influences which operating one way serve to widen this gap, or tending otherwise, to modify and perhaps entirely obliterate it, the price of cash grain sometimes being above that of futures. These influences are most likely to be in the nature of a larger immediate supply than is indicated for the time of the futures' maturity, a condition which will serve to depress cash prices, or an urgent immediate demand, with the outlook of a freer movement subsequently, which tends to advance cash figures in a greater proportion than the price of futures.

The principles involved in this field of speculation are essentially the same as in the stock market, and methods of trading are upon practically the same lines. The forms of orders are also similar, but when an option is not specified the next following active one is understood.

SPECULATION IN COTTON.

As wheat and corn are the chief speculative commodities produced in the West, so is the position of cotton to the South. In fact, so deeply is this section involved in this crop that its welfare depends more upon the condition of the market therefor than anything else. It is very gratifying that the Southern States are of much greater importance from a manufacturing standpoint than only a few years ago even, but it is a pertinent fact that the steady growth in this direction has been almost entirely in the making of cotton products. It is noteworthy that despite the development of cotton manufacturing in this section, there has been no corresponding falling off—in fact, statistics say none—elsewhere, which is indicative of the steadily increasing quantity of cotton consumed annually. This condition is present the world over, and the increased requirements enable the Southern planter to raise profitably crops showing a steady increase in their average size. The year 1900 shows an estimated consumption of eleven million bales of American cotton, whereas prior to 1897–98 the largest crop ever made was nine million eight hundred thousand.

The relationship of the future market to the cotton planter is essentially the same as to the farmer raising grain. By its means he is enabled to improve propitious conditions for the advance sale of his product, retaining the option of holding it until picked, or longer if advisable. All the larger Southern cities naturally do a very extensive business in handling actual cotton, but the chief markets for futures in this country are in New York and New Orleans, while on the other side Liverpool and Bremen are the prin cipal speculative centres.

The American system of quoting cotton prices is in one hun dredths of one cent per pound, and transactions in future contracts are in quantities of one hundred bales of five hundred pounds each, or a total of fifty thousand pounds to the contract. Therefore, upon such a contract the minimum fluctuation of one one-hundredth cent per pound, or, as it is termed, one "point," equals five dollars ; thus one one-hundredth cent per pound per bale of five hundred pounds = 5c. x 100 bales = $5. The principles involved in cotton trading are practically the same as those in grain. The carrying charges approximate seven and a half points per month, and there are of course influences of a similar nature affecting the comparative prices of different future options and of spot cotton. Unlike the grain markets, where future dealings are practically confined to four options, cotton futures are more or less active in all the twelve months, and the chief line of division is between those months when the supply depends upon the old crop and those when the new crop will be upon the market, which begin with September. Planting of cotton is done from about March 15 onward, according to the part of the belt and weather conditions, and the crop, theoretically and in fact, usually does begin to come to market in bulk about September 1. Thus, until about the end of August, spinners and dealers must depend upon what remains of the previous crop for supplies, and to complete delivery against sales of August futures, but as the new crop movement is well under way in time for September deliveries, the very material difference of trade conditions between the months of the old and those of the new crop is apparent, and usually results in a higher range of prices for the options just prior to September than for that future. The size of the cotton crop is measured by the amount materializing between September 1 and August 31.

Coming to the influences which move cotton prices, the general parallel with the grain market continues. The demand devolves upon the needs of domestic spinners and upon export requirements, which, in turn, hinge upon the consumption by foreign manufacturers. The supply is a matter of surplus carried over August 31 and the size of the crop. Where the parallel diverges chiefly is in the pre-eminence of American influence. The yield of our Southern States is from 80 to 85 per cent. of the entire production of the world, the other countries which grow the staple to any extent being India, Egypt, Brazil and Peru. In the consideration of cotton grown elsewhere than in this country, it is a notable fact that it is to a large extent adapted to special uses only, often being blended with our own product in the manufacture of certain classes of goods. This point is well illustrated by the fact that we import on an average 80,000 bales a year of foreign grown cotton while exporting about 75 per cent. of our own crop. Under these circumstances, the foreign production cuts very little figure in the price movement. The prospects of the growing crop are best judged from the monthly Government reports, which treat upon all the agricultural products of the country, and after the movement to market begins the receipts at ports and principal interior towns are indicative data as to the amount of the harvest. These figures are published in the newspapers and trade reviews along with their reports of general market conditions.

As with the grain markets, again, manipulation of cotton prices as a general thing must adhere very closely to actual conditions, for although the control of prices lies chiefly in American hands, it is still very much distributed, and excepting where an excited speculation lends to that result, prices are not easily swung far from a basis accurately reflecting actual trade and crop conditions. Corners have been made in cotton from time to time with more or less success, and usually with the August future as a centre of operations, it being the fag end of the crop, when supplies reach their ebb, and thus offering the best opportunity for a deal of this sort. A certain purpose of manipulation, which the cotton trader may usually expect, is a persistent effort from Liverpool, the port through which Manchester and other British spinning centres import their staple, and from the Continent, to depress prices and distribute as much bearish news as possible, in order to permit of foreign purchases being made advantageously, and an equally determined and natural effort emanating from our own Southern centres to advance the market, the better figures cotton brings the better for trade there. In this case, as in war, however, the Great Power is with the side having the more artillery—artillery consisting of the factors making the basis of values, *i. e.*, trade conditions, amount of surplus stocks and relative volume of the crop movement.

The same customs of trading that apply to stock and grain transactions hold good with cotton futures, although it is particularly important to specify the desired option, owing to the number dealt in and the distinction between the old and new crop months.

SPECULATION IN COFFEE.

Business upon the New York Coffee Exchange is in contracts for the future delivery of that staple, chiefly Brazilian product. With New York, the principal centres of speculation are Havre, Hamburg and Antwerp. Rio de Janeiro and Santos are the chief Brazilian markets and ports of export.

Although coffee has never attained prominence in the speculative field approaching that of grain and cotton, when active it affords an excellent trading market, and one not entirely difficult to judge. Owing to the speculative commitments being comparatively limited in volume, manipulation is less of a market factor than with stocks, grain and cotton, and the effect of changes in the crop, trade or statistical position is more direct in its bearing, though not so sweeping, upon the price movement. Attention directed to coffee as a speculative commodity is steadily increasing, and this will undoubtedly result in broadening the market.

A general description of the market influences, movements and customs of trading would be practically a repetition of what has been said regarding grain and cotton, save as to the technical differences in form and recording price changes.

The minimum contract is 250 bags of 130 pounds each, amounting to 32,500 pounds per contract. Price changes are recorded in amounts of 5/100 or 1/20 of a cent per pound, equaling $16.25 per contract of 250 bags. The monetary equivalents of these fluctuations are shown in this table:

Fluctuation per lb.	Amount of Contract.	Equivalent of Money.
5/100 or 1/20 cent per	250 bags or 32,500 lbs.	$16.25
10/100 or 1/10 "	" " "	32 50
50/100 or ½ "	" " "	162.50
1c. or 20/20 "	" " "	325.00

As with cotton, coffee trading is comparatively active in all the twelve options. The reason why the coffee market has never gathered the numerous following that our home-grown staples have, is the absence of a producing class and the relatively smaller number of persons engaged in handling the raw article, these being confined practically to the limited number of importers, roasters, etc. This absence of a large class of people, utilizing a future market in conjunction with their business of producing or otherwise handling the actual article, illustrates by contrast the importance of such a market to trade and how essential it is to the growers, shippers, manufacturers, and warehouse people. It is to their presence and dealings in the cotton and produce markets that the latter owe their magnitude and stability, and only with a strong framework of this nature to grow upon can speculation assume extensive proportions and round out a well developed market, capable of sustaining the business needs of all classes.

Furthermore, the people who handle coffee in what may be termed its crude state, prove the importance of having a market for future contracts by the fact that they have established one.

When a cargo is engaged for shipment from Brazil, the importer is enabled to sell at once against its arrival, thus providing against a decline in price while the consignment is in transit and minimizing his risk. If the coffee roaster, the grain miller or the cotton spinner wishes to provide for future requirements of raw material at the existing price basis, he is by the purchase of options enabled to do so without fear of an advance in prices upsetting his calculations. Of course this is viewing the matter apart from a speculative standpoint, but it illustrates forcibly the importance of these markets to the mercantile community as a clearly-cut product of necessity.

DESCRIPTION OF PROPERTIES.

AMALGAMATED COPPER COMPANY.

This company was incorporated on April 27, 1899, in New Jersey. It is in the nature of a holding company, and according to a statement filed with the New York Stock Exchange in June, 1901, owns a majority of the following stocks:

Anaconda Copper Mining......................	$30,000,000
Boston & Montana Con. Copper & Silver Mining.	3,750,000
Butte & Boston Consolidated Mining..........	2,000,000
Parrott Silver & Copper Company.............	2,298,500
Hennessy Mercantile Company	1,500,000

And all of the following:

Washoe Copper Company......................	$5,000,000
Colorado Smelting & Mining Company........	2,500,000
Diamond Coal & Coke Company.............	1,500,000
Black Foot Milling Company.................	700,000

The original $75,000,000 stock of this company was offered for public subscription at par in May, 1899, by the National City Bank, New York. It was stated that the total applications amounted to some $412,000,000.

In June, 1901, the authorized stock was increased to $155,000,000 to acquire the stocks of the Boston & Montana and Butte & Boston Companies. Holders of Boston & Montana were offered for each $25 share of that stock, 4 shares of Amalgamated Copper, and holders of the Butte & Boston for each $10 share of its stock, received 1 share of Amalgamated Copper stock.

The net earnings of some of the constituent companies for the years ending June 30 have been reported as follows:

	1899.	1900.	1901.	1902.	1903.
Anaconda..............	$3,463,700	$5,365,520	$5,069,071	$1,289,610	$1,200,900
Boston & Montana....	2,882,955	3,701,510	7,042,303	1,630,695	4,053,465
Butte & Boston.......	....	....	586,053	166,136	202.408
Parrott.	472,795	336,180	510,196	577,617	439,773
Colorado Mining Co...	....	....	303,619	152,495	....
Total..............	$6,819,450	$9,403,210	$13,511,242	$3,816,553	$5,896,546

Dividends on constituent companies (shown per cent.) :

	Par value.	1898.	1899.	1900.	1901.	1902.	1903.
Anaconda Copper	$25	10	13	16	13	4	4
Boston & Montana	25	64	144	172	140	24	32
Butte & Boston	10	..	..	50	..	..	..
Parrott	10	18	39	60	35	5	..

The only bonds are Boston & Montana 7's, $400,000 due, $100,-
000 November 1 yearly to 1907, and Butte & Boston 6's, $1,500,-
000 due April 1, 1917. Dividends on Amalgamated Copper Company were : 2% quarterly (Q J) October, 1899, to July, 1901, both
inclusive; in October, 1901, 1½%; in January, 1902, 1%; May,
1902, to May, 1904, both inclusive, ½% quarterly.

The Anaconda is the principal company controlled by the
Amalgamated Company and owns one of the largest mines in the
country, its ores carrying large amounts of gold and silver as well
as copper.

During the first three years of its existence the aggregate production was 1,068,000,000 pounds of copper, 40,650,000 ounces of
silver and 135,000 ounces of gold. The company has an extensive
reduction and. smelting works at Anacorda, Mont., reported to
have cost about $7,000,000. It also owns a controlling interest in
the Butte, Anaconda & Pacific Railway Company, which road
connects the mines and smelters.

Litigation is pending with F. A. Heinze concerning mining
rights.

Officers of the Amalgamated are as follows : President, Henry
H. Rogers; Secretary and Treasurer, William G. Rockefeller,
New York. Directors : Frederic P. Olcott, Robert Bacon, James
Stillman, William Rockefeller, William G. Rockefeller, Henry H.
Rogers, Anson R. Flower, New York ; A. C. Burrage, Boston.

Main office, 52 Broadway, New York.

Annual meeting, first Monday in June, at Jersey City.

AMERICAN CAR & FOUNDRY COMPANY.

Organization, etc.—Incorporated in New Jersey February 20,
1899, as a consolidation of various car manufacturing companies.

Business consists of manufacturing freight and passenger cars, street cars, car trucks, car wheels and various parts of cars.

Plants acquired consist of—

Michigan Peninsular Car Company, Detroit, Mich.
Missouri Car & Foundry Company, St. Louis, Mo.
Jackson & Woodin Manufacturing Company, Berwick, Pa.
Ohio Falls Car Manufacturing Company, Jeffersonville, Ind.
Union Car Company, Depew, N. Y.
St. Charles Car Co., St. Charles, Mo.
The Wells & French Company, Chicago, Ill.
Terre Haute Car & Manufacturing Company, Terre Haute, Ind.
Buffalo Car Manufacturing Company, Buffalo, N. Y.
Niagara Car Wheel Company, Buffalo, N. Y.
Ensign Manufacturing Company, Huntington, W. Va.
Pennock Brothers, Minerva, O
Murray Dougal & Company, Milton, Pa.
Indianapolis Car Company, Indianapolis, Ind.
Common Sense Bolster Company, Chicago, Ill.
Jackson & Sharp Company, Wilmington, Del.

Capitalization.—The authorized capital stock of the company consists of $30,000,000 7% non-cumulative preferred stock and $30,000,000 common stock, all of which is outstanding. Par value $100.

The preferred stock has prior rights as to both assets and dividends. Both classes have equal voting power.

The company began the payment of regular quarterly dividends of $1\frac{3}{4}\%$ on the preferred stock July 1, 1899. The dividend period is however now changed to quarterly, F. M. A. and D., and such quarterly payments have since been regularly made.

On the common stock dividends were paid in 1900 at the rate of 1%; 1901 and 1902, 2% yearly; 1903, 1% quarterly, (Q F); 1904, $\frac{1}{2}\%$ February, $\frac{1}{2}\%$ May.

Earnings.—Net earnings for 10 months ended February 29, 1904, $4,172,745, as against for the same period 1902-03, $5,900,971.

Comparative income and profit and loss statement for years ended April 30:

	1903.	1902.	1901.
Earnings from all sources...........	$8,447,030	$5.503,928	$5,015,394
Renewals, replacements, etc........	1,044,399	817,275	633,926
Net earnings.....................	$7,402,631	$4,686,653	$4,381,468
New construction charged off.......	342,729	391,051	325,642
Net income.....................	$7,059,902	$4,295,602	$4,055,826
Dividends (7%) on preferred.........	2,100,000	2,100,000	2,084,075
Dividends on common.............(3%)	900,000	(2%) 600,000	(2%) 595,450
Balance, surplus.................	$4,059,902	$1,595,602	$1,376,301
Previous surplus...................	6,670,551	5,074,949	3,698,648
Total surplus...................	$10,730,453	$6,670,551	$5,074,948

Comparative balance sheet April 30:

Assets.	1903.	1902.
Cost of property......................................	$58,874,629	$59,118,183
Material on hand....................................	13,133,803	11,915,129
Amounts receivable................................	9,613,588	7,461,951
Cash on hand and in banks.........................	2,463,056	1,571,458
Total...	$84,085,076	$80,066,721

Liabilities.	1903.	1902.
Preferred stock......................................	$30,000,000	$30,000,000
Common stock.......................................	30,000,000	30,000,000
Audited vouchers....	12,930,406	12,925,793
Pay rolls.................	424,216	470,376
Surplus..	10,730,454	6,670,552
Total...	$84,085,076	$80,066,721

The Audit Company of New York appends its certificate to the report.

The plants of this company comprise: 15 freight car shops, 2 passenger car shops, 13 wheel foundries, 14 casting foundries, 14 iron forging shops, 2 pipe foundries, 2 rolling mills, 4 brass foundries, and auxiliary shops, covering altogether some 425 acres of ground.

The total annual capacity of the united companies is in round figures: 100,000 freight cars, 500 passenger cars, 350,000 tons of wheels, 300,000 tons of forgings, 150,000 tons of castings, besides bar iron and pipe.

The material on hand, judging from the current liability of audited vouchers which amount it about equals, would appear to be not more than is necessary for current requirements.

The accounts receivable are no doubt due from railroads and concerns of like standing. Of the $4,000,000 added to surplus in the fiscal year ended April 30, 1903, $1,000,000 is in cash.

Annual meeting of the company is held the last Thursday in June.

Main office, Lincoln Trust Company Building, St. Louis. New York office, 25 Broad Street.

AMERICAN ICE COMPANY.

A corporation formed under the laws of New Jersey March 11, 1899. The company was organized to bring under one management several large corporations distributing ice in New York, Brooklyn and other eastern cities, in combination with ice plants and storage facilities on the Hudson and Kennebec rivers.

The company has acquired all the stock of the Consolidated Ice Company of Maine and of the Knickerbocker Ice Co. of Maine.

It has plants for manufacturing artificial ice in New York, Brooklyn, Washington, Baltimore and Philadelphia, at which places it owns valuable docks.

The company also controls the American Coal Company which was formed in 1901 to carry on the sale of coal at retail.

The published balance sheet for the year ended December 31, 1903, compared with that of 1902, is as under :

Assets.	1903.	1902.
Property account	$36,827,110	$34,886,151
Treasury stock	1,436,700	1,616,700
Investment securities	5,150,279	6,541,751
Cash and notes	365,544	17,067
Loans	43,425	69,300
Bonds and mortgages	3,957	4,107
Insurance premiums	9,665	9,918
Ice and coal	472,805	760,029
Accounts receivable	758,316	964,627
Profit and loss (deficit)	170,924	162,492
Totals	$45,238,725	$45,032,147

Liabilities.	1903.	1902.
Preferred stock	$15,000,000	$15,000,000
Common stock	25,000,000	25,000,000
Bills payable	870,757	441,409
Underlying bonds	1,176,050	1,183,000
Collateral trust bonds, American Ice Company	2,266,000	2,508,000
Real estate mortgage	512,737	354,626
Accounts payable	404,962	520,419
Insurance fund	8,219	24,693
Totals	$45,238,725	$45,032,147

Income account is not available at this moment, but it is observed from the above that the last year's operations added about $8,000 to the deficit.

The stock authorized is all outstanding with the exception of $1,436,700 carried as treasury stock.

The preferred stock is 6% cumulative. Dividends were paid thereupon at the rate of 1¼% quarterly from October, 1899, to April, 1902, but the July, 1902, quarter was deferred and nothing has been paid since.

On the common 1% was paid quarterly from November, 1899, to February, 1902, inclusive, but nothing since that date.

The collateral trust bonds are $5,000,000 authorized. They were created in April, 1902, to relieve the finances of the company, the amount issued having been used to retire floating debt.

The directors have power to execute mortgages upon the property of the company without the consent of the stockholders.

This company has been the subject of considerable so-called anti-trust legislation, particularly in New York. It has been stated that it received valuable concessions from the former Democratic New York City municipal administration. Much dissension was caused in March, 1903, owing to reports that last dividends paid on preferred stock had not been earned.

There is every sign of effort upon the part of the directors to bring the concern, through efficient management, to a more stable basis. A plan to develop the coal department, thus using to best advantage the teaming and storage facilities in time of its inactivity, promises well.

Directors, etc.—Wesley M. Oler, President; Guy B. Johnson, Vice-President and Treasurer; Edward T. Bedford, Charles T. Barney, John A. Sleicher, John Greenough, Charles I. Hudson, Enos Wilder, William G. Crenshaw, Jr., R. M. Thompson and Miles O'Brien. Secretary, J. R. Bennett. Office, 1178 Broadway, New York.

Annual meeting in February.

AMERICAN LOCOMOTIVE COMPANY.

Incorporated in New York on June 10, 1901, to build and dispose of locomotives, etc. The company acquired properties and plants as below:

Brooks Locomotive Works, Dunkirk, N. Y.
Pittsburg Locomotive & Car Works, Pittsburg, Pa.
Dickson Manufacturing Company, Scranton, Pa.
Rhode Island Locomotive Works, Providence, R. I.
Schenectady Locomotive Works, Schenectady, N. Y.

The company also owns all the stock of the Richmond Locomotive & Machine Works, Richmond, Va., the Manchester Locomotive Works, Manchester, N. H., the American Locomotive Company of New Jersey, and the Cook Locomotive & Machine Company, Paterson, N. J., and in March, 1904, the entire capital stock of the Locomotive & Machine Company of Montreal was acquired.

The combined plants occupy about 160 acres of land and the annual capacity is about 2,000 locomotives, exclusive of the Montreal plant.

Comparative general balance sheet, June 30:

Assets.	1903.	1902.
Cost of property	$45,672,860	$45,482,293
American Locomotive Company preferred stock	900,000	900,000
Richmond Locomotive & Machine Works consols	118,000	118,000
Sundry securities	6,483	37,526
Cash	1,048,132	1,153,855
Accounts receivable	5,593,409	4,255,721
Material and supplies	3,108,497	2,187,566
Contract work	3,677,107	2,874,167
American Locomotive Company stock	200,000	200,000
Totals	$60,324,488	$57,209,128

Liabilities.	1903.	1902.
Common stock	$25,000,000	$25,000,000
Preferred stock	25,000,000	25,000,000
Bonds, constituent companies	1,512,500	1,512,500
Accounts payable	2,822,112	3,324,908
Bills payable	3,415,000	1,700,000
Unclaimed interest	820	9,985
Dividends payable in July	437,500	437,500
Profit and loss	2,136,556	224,235
Totals	$60,324,488	$57,209,128

Comparative income account :

	1902–03. (12 mos.)	1901–02. (12½ mos.)
Gross earnings..........................	$33,105,725	$26,398,394
Manufacturing, maintenance and admin. expenses.	28,052,315	23,291,217
Net earnings............................	$5,053,410	$3,107,177
Interest on bonds of constituent cos., notes, etc....	248,157	105,865
Net income	$4,805,253	$3,001,312
Dividend on preferred stock at 7%..................	1,750,000	1,750,000
Surplus	$3,055,253	$1,251,312
Additions to property	1,142,932	1,027,077
Balance..	$1,912,321	$224,235

The gross earnings for 12 months to June 30, 1903, show an increase of 25.4% over the previous 12½ months reported on, and only 20.4% increase in expenses.

It is stated that the expenses include 20% written off from cost of patterns and drawings and a charge of $484,370 for positive additions to the company's property, also that renewals, replacements and betterment charges included in expenses, amply maintain the effective and actual value of the plant. This is understood to be in addition to $1,142,932 for additions to property charged direct to the surplus.

The increase in gross earnings is said to be due to an increased volume of business, rather than to higher proportionate prices.

Development of the overhauling and repairs department is expected to be productive of good returns in future.

During recent years there has been a steady demand for locomotives of heavier type and increased tractive power. This has gone along steadily, closely following increased capacity of bridges and heavier weight of rail. Increased train load has demanded greater hauling capacity, and the American Locomotive Company report contracts on hand for deliveries up into the summer of 1904.

Dividends.—On the preferred stock the rate is 7% cumulative, and the rate has been maintained from October, 1901, to April, 1904, inclusive.

The stock of the American Locomotive Company was at one time largely held by the International Power Company. The shares of the latter company collapsed in the spring of 1902. This was due to the latter stock being one of the securities promoted by the so-called Webb-Meyer Syndicate that fell of its own weight at that time. The credit of the American Locomotive Company however was in no way involved.

Officers.—President, S. R. Callaway; 1st Vice-President, A. J. Pitkin; 2d Vice-President, R. J. Gross; Secretary, Leigh Best. Treasurer's office, 25 Broad Street, New York.

AMERICAN SUGAR REFINING COMPANY.

A corporation formed under the laws of New Jersey, January 10, 1891, to succeed the Sugar Refineries Company, which was formed in 1887, a majority of the sugar refineries in the United States being taken over and its certificates issued to represent the value of their plants. The capital issues represented in certificates was $50,000,000. At the above date the certificates of the old company were exchanged for $25,000,000 preferred and $25,-000,000 common of the new corporation.

In 1892 the stock was increased to $37,500,000 of each class to acquire additional properties. In 1901 both classes were increased to $45,000,000, to extend the company's operations in Cuba and elsewhere.

The company has paid 7% per annum on the preferred stock since the reorganization. On a part of the preferred stock the dividends are semi-annual, 3½% each, January and July, and part quarterly, 1¾%, January, April, July and October.

On the common stock the company paid 4%, half-yearly, from July, 1891, until October, 1892, when the rate was raised to 2½% quarterly. In April 1893, the rate was made 3% quarterly, until an extra dividend of 10% was paid, after which it was 3% quarterly until April 1900, when the rate was reduced to 1½%. In July 1900, 1½% was also paid.

The October, 1900, dividend was 1¾% or 7% per annum, and that rate has since been maintained.

Comparative balance sheet, December 31:

Assets.	1903.	1902.
Real estate and machinery..................... ......$35,180,057		$34,669,191
Cash and debts receivable............................ 34,683,022		30,046,750
Investments in other companies..................... 51,986,127		45,270,776
Sugar raw and refined.............................. 12,338,662		15,842,924
Totals...............................$134,187,868		$125,829,641

Liabilities.	1903.	1902.
Capital stock.......... ....$90,000,000		$90,000,000
Debts 31,922,032		24,958,321
Reserves... 12,265,836		10,871,320
Totals...............................$134,187,868		$125,829,641

The company publishes no income statement.

In December, 1896, interests connected with the company acquired control of the Woolson Spice Company, of Toledo, Ohio, a corporation engaged in roasting and preparing coffees. The object of this was to meet the competition of Arbuckle Bros., a large coffee house which was about to build and operate an opposition sugar refinery. This was effected in 1898, and the years 1898-99 were marked by severe competition, resulting in loss of profits.

At an annual meeting of the stockholders in January, 1899, a resolution was approved, transferring the accumulated profits or surplus to working capital amount.

This company originally controlled about 90% of the output of refined sugar in the United States, but was considered in 1892 to have controlled some 65%. It is now probably still less of a monopoly.

The fluctuations in the price of sugar stock have been very wide, showing a range of 40 to 50 points in most of the past 10 years, as may be seen in the table in another section of this book.

Directors.—H. O. Havemeyer, Chas. H. Senff, Arthur Donner, Lowell M. Palmer, John Mayer, W. B. Thomas, John E. Parsons. Treasurer, Arthur Donner. Transfer office, 117 Wall Street, N. Y.

ANACONDA COPPER MINING COMPANY.

This company was organized under the laws of Montana, June 18, 1895. It owns the famous Anaconda Copper Mine at Butte, Mont., together with a large undeveloped property, and a reduction and smelting works, the latter costing some $7,000,000.

The stock of the Butte, Anaconda & Pacific Railway Company is controlled by the Anaconda Company. This line is 27 miles long and connects the various properties of the company.

This company is the principal constituent of the Amalgamated Copper Company, which acquired a controlling interest in its stock in 1899.

Stock authorized and issued ($25 par), $30,000,000, is full paid and non assessable.

Dividends.—Up to 1900, the company had paid over $12,000,000 in dividends. During 1900, 16% was paid; in 1901 13%; in 1902 and since, 4% for the full year has been maintained.

No recent report is available, but the gross earnings and profits for a series of years is given below:

	Gross.	Profits.
1896	$12,057,677	$4,258,514
1897	17,419,361	5,136,048
1898	18,334,233	3,551,346
1899	....	3,463,700
1900	18,730,131	5,365,519
1901	18 128,558	5,571,816
1902	....	1,289 610

Reference is made to the vast production of the properties of this company, under the head of "Amalgamated Copper Company," elsewhere in this publication.

The reduction in profits is considered to be attributable to the lower price of copper, which in 1901 was artificially held at 17c. per pound.

Such artifice was not, however, necessary to the excellent showing of the company in previous years.

There is some dissatisfaction amongst the minority stockholders as to the management, it being considered that this property is saddled with undue burdens in the combination of interests controlled by the Amalgamated Copper Company.

THE ATCHISON, TOPEKA & SANTA FE RAILWAY COMPANY.

This corporation was formed under the laws of Kansas December 12, 1895, and acquired under foreclosure the Atchison, Topeka & Santa Fe Railroad at a sale December 10, 1895. Possession of the property was taken January 1, 1896.

Mileage, June 30, 1903:

Atchison, Topeka & Santa Fe Railway	6,174
Rio Grande & El Paso Railroad	20
Gulf, Colorado & Santa Fe Railway	1,203
Southern California Railway	478
Southern Kansas Railway of Texas	129
	8,004

The property embraces an unbroken line of track from Chicago to the Pacific Ocean and to the Gulf of Mexico, beside branches and extensions from such main line. Of the mileage operated 405 only is not owned, and 350 miles is owned but not operated.

During the fiscal year ended June 30, 1903, the Santa Fe Pacific Railroad, consisting of 875 miles, and the San Francisco & San Joaquin Valley Railway, consisting of 372 miles, were transferred to the Atchison, Topeka & Santa Fe Railway Company and operated directly. Construction of the Eastern Oklahoma Railway is in progress, but not taken over by the operating department at the above date.

Profit and loss account to June 30, 1903:

Dr.

Dividend No. 8 on preferred stock	$2,854,345
" " 9 " " "	2,854,345
" " 4 " common "	2,039,110
" " 5 " " "	2,039,110
Appropriation for fuel reserve fund	285,174
Amount written off for construction account in respect to betterments, improvements and equipment, etc.	3,000,000
Balance per balance sheet	16,853,660
	$29,925,744

Cr.

Balance forward from June 30, 1902	$16,027,415
Net income for year ended June 30, 1903	13,898,329
	$29,925,744

It will be seen from the above statements that, besides paying 5% on the preferred stock and 4% on the common, 4% additional was earned, but was chiefly used to reduce the cost of property, create reserves, and fortify the assets generally.

The funded debt per mile of road, with interest obligations for the past two years, was :

	July 1, 1903.	July 1, 1902.
Funded debt per mile of road	$28,501.20	$28,882.27
Interest charges per mile of road	1,152.17	1,167.85

Capital expenditures for the year are shown to be as under :

Construction and acquisition of new mileage and stocks and bonds of other railway companies	$6,998,002
New equipment	3,496,717
Reduction of grades, changes of line, and construction of permanent way	1,356,767
Buildings and shops	1,056,819
Second track	318,783
Ballasting	240,189
Improvements, China Basin and Mojave Divisions	878,681
Other improvements and betterments	979,893
Total	$15,325,851

Less—Charged to special betterment fund	$367,079	
Reduction in value, S. F., P. & P. Ry. securities	182,764	
" " " Petroleum Development Co	400,000	
Proceeds sale of lands	579,683	
Credit by charge to profit and loss	3,000,000	
		4,529,526

Leaving a net amount of $10,796,325

Comparative general balance sheet, June 30, 1903, and June 30, 1902 :

Assets.	1903.	1902.
Railroads, franchises, property, stocks and bonds	$431,226 691	$418,982,696
Construction and equipment current year	7,006,741	10,606,721
Investments, new acquisitions	13,205,075	10,321,618
Securities on hand :		
Company's	2,583,896	2,895,896
Other	475,817	357,067
Other investments	2,851,550	....
Material and supplies	4,532,847	3,403,027
Prepaid insurance	43,192	32,020
Union Trust Co. of N. Y.:		
Cash deposit required by mtge	....	252,976
Guar. Trust Co. of N. Y.:		
Cash deposit for fuel reserve fund	439,450	548,033
Accounts receivable, traffic balances, etc	6,255,098	6,764,884
Cash on hand and in banks	10,960,788	20,544,406
Total	$479,581,145	$474,709,344

Liabilities.	1903.	1902
Capital stock :		
Common	$102,000,000	$102,000,000
Preferred, less amount set aside for improvements, etc , $17,286,470	114,199,530	114,199,530
Funded debt :		
General mtge. 4% bonds	138,797,500	138,728,500
Adjustment mtge. bonds	51,728,000	51,728,000
Serial debenture 4% bonds	27,500,000	30,000,000
Eastern Oklahoma 4% bonds	5,645,000	....

Liabilities (continued).

Funded debt :	1903.	1902.
Chic. & St. L. 1st mtge. 6% bonds....................	$1,500,000	$1,500,000
San F. & San J. Valley 1st mtge. 5% bonds.........	6,000,000	6,000,000
Miscellaneous bonds....	759,750	828,810
Special betterment fund.............................	....	367,080
Rolling stock replacement............................	556,731	211,688
Rail renewal fund.....................................	1,325,932	366,781
Tie renewal fund......................................	227,742	....
Fuel reserve fund.....................................	439,450	548,033
Accrued taxes..	866,049	953,104
Interest on funded debt accrued, etc..................	3,724,575	3,713,435
Accounts payable.....................................	7,457,226	7,536,968
Profit and loss surplus...............................	16,853,660	16,027,415
Total......................................	$479,581,145	$474,709,344

Income account for year ended June 30, 1903 :

Dr.

Operating expenses :	
Maintenance of way and structures....................	$9,304,892
Maintenance of equipment..............	8,510,543
Conducting transportation...........................	19,023,145
General expenses..	1,598,530
Taxes...	1,758,120
Rental of tracks and terminals........................	361,204
Balance carried down...............................	21,793,962
	$62,350,396

Deductions from income :	
Interest on bonds....................................	$7,080,645
Interest on adjustment bonds..........................	2,053,840
Advances to sub. companies...........................	73,345
Depreciation of securities......	4,190
Land department account.............................	1,605
Balance net income carried to profit and loss....................	13,898,329
	$23,111,955

Cr.

Earnings :	
Passenger....................................	$13,469,985
Freight.......................................	44,622,439
Mail express, etc....................................	4,257,972
	$62,350,396

Balance net earnings...............................	$21,793,962
Additions to income :	
Interest and discount..............................	478,553
Income from investments...........................	827,313
Sundry adjustments..............................	12,127
	$23,111,955

Stock.—The preferred stock has preference as to assets and non-cumulative dividends not exceeding 5% per annum as declared by the directors out of the net profits. No other mortgage and no increase in the preferred stock can be made without the consent of a majority of all the preferred stock and all the common stock represented at a meeting. Stock issues may be seen in the balance sheet above.

Dividends.—Preferred—1899, 2¼%; 1900 ₊%; 1901 to Feb., 1904, 5% yearly (F. & A.).

Common—1901, 3½%; 1902, 4%; 1903, 4%; 1904, June, 2%.

Freight statistics :

Date.	Miles.	Per cent. operating expenses.	Tonnage.	Rate per ton per mile. in cents.	Earnings per train mile.	Average tons per train mile.
1896–7....	6,479	74.68	8,578,802	1.051	$1.50	140
1897–8....	6,946	72.69	9,979,509	1.029	1.46	142
1898–9....	7,108	68.14	8,924,678	1.019	1.64	161
1899–0....	7,341	59.53	9,893,018	.976	2.16	221
1900–1....	7,807	59.23	11,112,614	1.007	2.44	242
1901–2....	7,855	57.34	11,596,093	.988	2.53	247
1902–3....	8,004	61.65				

Annual meeting.—Third Thursday in October.

Officers.—Chairman of Executive Committee, Victor Morawetz; E. P. Ripley, president ; D. L. Gallup, comptroller; H. W. Gardiner, assistant treasurer.

BALTIMORE & OHIO RAILROAD COMPANY.

A corporation chartered by the State of Maryland, by act approved February 28, 1827, and chartered by the Commonwealth of Virginia March 8, 1827.

The road is controlled in the interest of the Pennsylvania Railroad System, and jointly with the Lake Shore Road controls the Reading Railroad. On March 1, 1896, the property was placed in receiver's hands, but was restored to the stockholders July 1, 1899, under a plan of reorganization, which was carried out without foreclosure.

The system extends from Baltimore to Philadelphia, and from Baltimore to Pittsburgh, Chicago, St. Louis and other Western points. It operates over the Central of New Jersey tracks into New York.

The total mileage leased, owned and operated in July, 1903, was 3,935 miles.

General balance sheet, June 30, 1903 :

Assets.

Cost of road, including bonds and stocks pledged with Trustees as security for Funded Debt..	$236,837,021
Real estate..	12,920,659
Gas and electric plants...	665,847
Equipment..	32,242,220
Cost of other roads owned......................................	11,830,958
New bonds and stocks held to retire old.........................	271,437
Bonds of sundry companies......................................	14,730,294
Stocks of sundry companies.....................................	28,777,637
Stock of Southwestern Equipment Company........................	9,997,553
Material on hand...	4,836,202
Current assets :	
Cash in hand and in banks...............................	15,858,691
Agents' balances..	4,609,924
Traffic balances..	1,342,587
Bills and accounts receivable...........................	6,580,114
Deferred and miscellaneous :	
Interest paid in advance................................	2,253
Cash deposit for coupons................................	15,684
Washington Terminal advance............................	695,038
Due from other roads....................................	3,246,765
Insurance Fund..	250,000
Southwestern Equipment Company loan account, for purchase of equipment.....................................	8,510,799
	$444,221,690

Liabilities.

Capital stock :	
Preferred..	$59,374 289
Common	124,262,062
Funded Debt:	
Prior Lien 3½% Bonds....................................	72,000,000
First Mortgage 4% Bonds................................	69,000,000
Pittsburgh Junction, Middle Division, 3½% Bonds.........	13,810,530
Southwestern Division 3½% Bonds.........................	43,600,000
Ten-year Gold Convertible Debenture 4% Bonds............	592,000
Pittsburgh, Lake Erie & West Virginia 4% Bonds.........	22,884,000
Ground Rent Liens (capitalized at 6%)...................	802,308
Real estate mortgages...	414,396
Old bonds and stocks not deposited..............................	147,963
Car Trust Bonds and Lease Warrants not matured.................	9,487
Monongahela River Railroad Car Trust Warrants..................	315,000
Monongahela River Railroad First Mortgage 5% Bonds............	700,000
West Virginia & Pittsburgh Railroad Co. First Mortgage 5% Bonds.	4,000,000
Schuylkill River E. S. Railroad First Mortgage 5% Bonds.........	4,500,000
Pittsburgh & Western Equipment Trusts..........................	477,749
Current liabilities :	
Vouchers, pay-rolls and traffic balances................	6,441,094
Accrued interest..	3,480,926
Dividends declared......................................	3,825,689
Individuals and companies, taxes, etc...................	4,477,270
Miscellaneous liabilities..	3,600,280
Profit and loss...	5,506,647
	$444,221,690

Comparative income accounts for years ended June 30 :

Earnings :	1903.	1902.
Freight	$47,756,251	$43,779,786
Passenger	12,520,988	11,288,537
Express	1,189,843	1,069,206
Mail	1,353,871	1,346,994
Miscellaneous	628,680	457,972
Gross earnings	$63,449,633	$57,892,495
Expenses :		
Maintenance of way and structures	$6,175,115	$7,235,389
Maintenance of equipment	8,270,156	7,384,331
Conducting transportation	23,653,780	20,946,896
General expenses	1,470,912	1,440,368
Operating expenses	$39,569,963	$37,006,984
Net earnings from operations	$23,879,670	$20,885,511
Other income from securities owned, etc	1,609,850	1,235,220
Total income	$25,489,520	$22,120,731
Deductions from income :		
Net earnings Washington Branch (included in System earnings)	$386,858	$305,125
Interest and rentals	8,934,919	10,162,832
Taxes	1,239,725	1,175,061
Miscellaneous improvements, etc	596,259	265,194
Discount and commission on securities sold	513,595	1,038,743
Total deductions	$11,671,356	$12,946,955
Net income	$13,818,164	$9,173,756

Profit and loss account, June 30, 1903 :

June 30, 1902 :   *Dr.*

Appropriation for additions and improvements	$3,500,000
Dividend on Preferred Stock, 2%, paid March, 1903	1,200,000
Dividend on Preferred Stock, 2%, payable September, 1903	1,200,000
Dividend on Common Stock, 2%, payable September, 1903	2,485,241
Dividend on Common Stock, 2%, paid March 2, 1903	2,485,241
Sundry adjustments	66,255

June 30, 1903 :

Balance per balance sheet	5,506,647
	$16,443,384

Cr.

June 30, 1902—Balance	$2,625,221
June 30, 1903—Net income for year	13,818,163
	$16,443,384

The percentage of expenses to earnings in 1902-3 was 67.03, as against 59.28 in the year 1901-2.

Stock—Common, $125,000,000 authorized, $124,262,062 outstanding ; Preferred, $60,000,000 4% non-cumulative, $59,374,289 outstanding.

Funded Debt—see details in balance sheet above.

Dividends—per cent.:

		1904.	1903.	1902.	1901.	1900.
Common	March,	2	4	4	4	2
Preferred	"	2	4	4	4	4

Executive Committee—Oscar G. Murray, Chairman, J. K. Cowen, S. M. Prevost, John P. Green, James McCrea and Samuel Rea.

AMERICAN COTTON OIL COMPANY.

This is a New Jersey corporation of 1889, formed to succeed the American Cotton Oil Trust. It owns some 50 cotton seed crushing mills in the Southern States, and numerous oil refineries, soap factories, lard plants, etc.

General balance sheet, August 31, 1903:

Assets.

Real estate, etc.	$12,433,122
Cash	1,280,493
Bills and accounts receivable	2,348,099
Products, raw material, etc.	3,571,247
Good will, patents, etc.	16,576,763
Total	$36,209,724

Liabilities.

Common stock	$20,237,100
Preferred stock	10,198,600
Debenture bonds	3,000,000
Bills payable	1,050,000
Commercial accounts	597,332
Accrued interest	11,250
Dividends	1,115,442
Total	$36,209,724

The surplus for the year ended August 31, 1903, after paying 4% dividend on the common stock and 6% on the preferred, was $108,681.

Dividends.—Preferred—June, 1892, to December, 1903, inclusive, 6% per annum (June and December).

In November, 1898, the first dividend was paid on the common at 3%; 1899, 4%; 1900, 3½%; 1901, 2%; 1902, 4% in December and

2% in June, making 6% for the year; December, 1903, 2%, and 2% declared for June 1, 1904.

The funded debt is the remainder of $5,000,000 8% due in 1900, which was extended at the rate of 4½% for 15 years.

A majority of the stock is in the hands of a committee since December, 1901, with power to sell within three years at not less than 105 for the preferred and not less than 60 for the common. This is no doubt the answer to the Virginia Chemical Company, who was understood to be quite anxious to control this valuable property.

Main office.—Guttenberg, N. J.

Annual meeting.—First Thursday in December.

Directors.—Edmond Urquhart, Robert F. Munro, William Barbour, J. Kennedy Tod, Charles F. Clark, J. R. Maxwell, Richard T. Wilson, George Austin Morrison, Edward D. Adams, Charles Lanier, Harris C. Fahnestock, Joseph Larocque, Bradish Johnson, William Nelson Cromwell and J. F. Chamberlin.

BROOKLYN RAPID TRANSIT.

Organized under the laws of New York January 18, 1896, and acquired the property of the Long Island Traction Company. In 1899 a controlling interest in the Nassau Electric Railroad Company was purchased, and subsequently the Brooklyn Rapid Transit acquired the Brooklyn Union Elevated Railroad, Kings County Elevated Railroad Company and the Brooklyn & Brighton Beach Railroad. The Kings County has since been merged with the Brooklyn Union.

The Prospect Park & Coney Island Railroad was leased from the Long Island Railroad in the same year.

The Long Island Traction Company owned all the capital stock of the Brooklyn Heights Railroad, which leased the Brooklyn City Railroad for 999 years, guaranteeing all fixed charges, etc., and 10 per cent. dividend on $12,000,000 of stock. In acquiring the first-named property the Brooklyn Rapid Transit took over this lease with its obligations.

The mileage operated, including both elevated and surface lines owned, controlled and leased, is 249 miles of double track.

Consolidated general balance sheet, Brooklyn Rapid Transit System, June 30, 1903:

Assets.

Cost of properties..	$92,488,400
Advances account construction leased companies:	
Brooklyn City Railroad Company..............................	5.479,787
Nassau Electric Railroad Company............................	1,948,929
Prospect Park & Coney Island Railroad Company...............	214,574
Brooklyn Union Elevated....................................	1,681,267
Not distributed	1 037,018
Guarantee fund..	4,005,755
Current assets..	1,842,621
Unadjusted accounts...	16,187
Total.	$108,714,540

Liabilities.

Capital stock, Brooklyn Rapid Transit Company....................	$45,000,000
Underlying companies.................................	985,655
Bonded debt, Brooklyn Rapid Transit Company.....................	12,000,000
Brooklyn Heights Railroad.	250,000
Sea Beach Railway....................................	650,000
Brooklyn, Queens County & Suburban Railroad..........	6,624,000
Nassau Electric......................................	15,000,000
Brooklyn Union Elevated Railroad.....................	23,000,000
Real estate mortgages.	337,140
Current liabilities..	3,119,905
Surplus..	1,747,839
Total..	$108,714,540

Income account of system for years ended June 30:

	1903.	1902.	1901.
Gross earnings......................	$13,557.814	$12,788,168	$12,135,559
Operating expenses..................	8,688.868	8,952.214	7,970.634
Total income.......................	$4,868,946	$3,835,954	$4,164,925
Fixed charges, net..................	3 904,068	3,732,633	3,587,122
Surplus for year...	$964,878	$103,321	$577,803

From the surplus for the year 1902-03 $168,095 was deducted for betterments, etc.

Stock.—Issued as authorized.

In March, 1902, a new general consolidated mortgage of $150,000,000 was authorized to retire outstanding liens and provide for improvements as needed from time to time.

Dividends.—None paid.

Annual meeting last Friday in January. Main office, Brooklyn.

Directors.—Horace C. Duval, Timothy S. Williams, Edwin W. Winter, John G. Jenkins, Anthony N. Brady, David H. Valentine. Norman B. Ream, H. H. Porter, E. H. Harriman, W. G. Oakman, Anson R. Flower, R. Somers Hayes, Henry Siebert.

CANADIAN PACIFIC RAILWAY.

Incorporated February 18, 1881, under charter from the Dominion of Canada, and with its charter received $25,000,000 in eash and 25,000.000 acres of land as a subsidy. The Government also conveyed to the company free of cost 713 miles of road.

The line extends from Montreal to Vancouver, with extensive branches, and operates under lease 2,683 miles.

Total mileage owned and operated at July 1, 1903, 7,748 miles.

The company also owns lake, river and ocean steamships, being the largest carriers in the Pacific trade.

General balance sheet, June 30, 1903:

Assets.

Cost of railway and equipment	$242,769,210
Steamships	11,771,133
Securities held	43,470,868
Hotels, buildings, etc	2,266,635
Deferred payments on lands, etc	13,914,480
Advances, new lines, etc	3,073,262
Material and supplies on hand	5,498,788
Miscellaneous securities and advances	1,606,902
Accounts receivable	4,918,698
Due from Dominion Government	236,688
Cash in hand	12,172,612
	$341,699,276

NOTE.—In addition to the above assets. the company owns 12,081,776 acres of land in Manitoba and the Territories (average sales past year. $3.67 per acre), and 3,759,418 acres in British Columbia.

Liabilities.

Capital stock	$84,500,000
4% preferred stock	32,500,000
4% consolidated debenture stock	67,252,253
Mortgage bonds:	
1st mtge. 5%	34,998,633
Canada Central Ry. 6%	973,333
Due Province Quebec on Q. M. O. & O. & North Shore Ry	7,000,000
Algoma branch 1st mtge	3,650,000
North Shore Ry. 1st mtge	616,120
Land grant bonds:	
Guaranteed 3½%	14,500,000
Current accounts, pay rolls, etc	7,153,478
Interest	1,772,070
Equipment replacement fund	588,543
Cash subsidies	30,229,109
Land grant, sales	37,119,562
Surplus	18,846,175
	$341,699,276

Cash will be reimbursed in the sum of $6,972,556.78 by the sale of common stock voted for increased equipment.

Income account for year ended June 30, 1903 :

Gross earnings	$43,957,373
Working expenses	28,120,527
Net earnings	$15,836,846
Additions to income—interest, etc	1,286,812
	$17,123,658

Deductions:
Fixed charges	7,052,197
Surplus	$10,071,460

Deductions:
Amount applied against cost of steamships	$150,000
Dividend on preferred stock, 2%, April 1, 1903	650,000
Half-yearly dividend on common stock, 2½%, April 1, 1903	2,112,500
Balance for year	$7,158,960

From which 2% on preferred and 3% on common, payable October 1, 1903, has been declared, but evidently not yet charged out.

Dividends.—Common—1890 to 1894, 5% yearly; 1895, nothing; 1896 and 1897, 2½%; 1898, 4½%; 1899, 4%; 1900, 5½%; 1901 and 1902, 5%; 1903, 5½%; half year, 1904, 3%.

Preferred—4% yearly since 1894, date of issue.

The preferred stock is 4% non-cumulative, and the issue is limited to one-half the amount of the common.

Operating expenses amounted to 63.97% of earnings in 1903, as against 62.44 for the previous year

Annual meeting.—First Wednesday in October.

Main office.—Montreal.

Chairman, Sir William G. Van Horne; President, Sir Thomas G. Shaughnessy; Secretary, Charles Drinkwater.

Directors.—Lord Strathcona and Mount Royal, Sir William C. Van Horne, Richard B. Angus, Sir Thomas G. Shaughnessy, Charles R. Hosmer, Wilmot D. Matthews, Edmund B. Osler, Sir Sanford Fleming, Thomas Skinner, Geo. R. Harris, Robert Mackay, George A. Drummond, David McNicoll, R. G. Reid and Clarence Mackay.

CENTRAL RAILROAD OF NEW JERSEY.

Chartered in 1849. In hands of receiver from 1887 to January, 1888, but reorganized in 1887 without foreclosure. It is owner of 409 miles of railroad, and operates under long (999 years) lease, 268 miles—Total operated June 30, 1903, 677 miles The line extends from Jersey City to Wilkesbarre and Scranton and the coal fields of this district, and with the B. & O. & Reading operates the "Blue Line" service from New York to Washington. The Reading Company owns a controlling interest in this company, and is in turn controlled by the Pennsylvania & Lake Shore jointly.

A line to Long Branch is also included in the trackage owned. The company owns $8,242,900 par value stock of the Lehigh & Wilkesbarre Coal Co., out of an authorized issue of $10,000,000 ; also three-fourths of the bonds.

General balance sheet, June 30, 1903 :

Assets.

Railroad and equipment	$60,187,295
Securities owned	21,942,070
Advances for construction	600,810
Insurance fund, bonds in hands of treasurer	100,000
Material and supplies	1,184,766
Current assets :	
Cash	2,167,929
Due from agents, individuals and companies and for traffic balances	3,179,813
Bills receivable, L. & W. B. Coal Co	2,555,408
Other accounts	46,932
	$91,965,023

Liabilities.

Capital stock	$27,415,800
Funded debt :	
General mortgage bonds, 1987	45,091,000
Equipment bonds, sundry dates	3,270,000
Convertible deb. bonds, 1908	50,000
Real estate mtg. bonds	179,100
Current liabilities :	
Vouchers, pay rolls and temporary loans	2,596,218
Interest due July 1, 1903	996,775
Other interest and rentals	32,874
Due other railroads	478,402
Due individuals and companies	507,586
Dividend due Aug. 1, 1903	548,316
Interest, taxes, etc., accrued, not due	1,479,297
Insurance reserve fund	128,773
Renewal and improvement fund	350,000
Profit and loss	8,840,882
	$91,965,023

Income account for 18 months ended June 30, 1903:

Gross earnings......................................	$26,063.831
Operating expenses..	16.649,742
Net earnings...	$9,414,089
Income from investments (not including surplus earnings of L. & W. Coal Co., $345,851.77)...	1,729,926
	$11,144,015
Deduct taxes, interest and rentals...................................	8,320,336
Balance—surplus...........	$2,823,679
Dividends—6 quarterly, including Aug. 1, '03........................	3,289,816
Net debit to surplus for the period...................................	$466,137

The authorized capital stock is $30,000,00, of which $27,415,800 is outstanding.

Of the $50,000,000 general mortgage bonds authorized, $4,909,-000 are still unissued.

The company reports heavy losses in tonnage and revenue for the period under review, owing to strikes in the anthracite region.

Dividends.—1891, 6½%; 1892 to 1894, 7% yearly; 1895, 5½%; 1896, 5%; 1897, 4¼%; 1898 and 1899, 4% yearly; 1900 and 1901, 5% yearly; 1902, 8%; 1903, 8%; 1904, May, 4%.

Main office.—143 Liberty Street, New York.

Annual Meeting.—Friday following the third Monday in September.

President, Geo. F. Baer; Secretary and Treasurer, G. O. Waterman.

CHESAPEAKE & OHIO RAILWAY.

A corporation organized under the laws of Virginia in 1868. After foreclosure proceedings the company was reorganized July 1, 1878. Was again reorganized without foreclosure in 1888. The system operated, embraces a total of 1,641 miles, of which 938 miles is owned in fee, 377 miles controlled by stock ownership, the balance being leased line.

The line runs from Newport News, Virginia, and Washington to Cincinnati, Ohio, with branches.

General balance sheet, June, 30, 1903:

Assets.

Road and equipment, etc.	$112,705,521
Bonds and stocks owned	21,248,147
Advances	1,638,769
Cash on hand	28,193
Cash for coupons, etc.	231,222
Agents and conductors	459,772
Railways	495,529
Individuals and companies.	407,161
Materials and supplies	776,375
Loan to Big Sandy Railroad	1,264,517
Miscellaneous.	197,307
	$139,452,513

Liabilities.

Common stock	$60,529,900
First and second preferred stock	9,600

Funded debt:

5% first consolidated gold mortgage bonds, 1939	25.858,000
4½% general mortgage gold bonds, 1992	34,833,000
6% series A, gold bonds, 1908.	2,000,000
6% series B and scrip bonds, 1908.	13,354
6% gold bonds due 1911	2,000,000
6% gold bonds due 1922	142,000
4% first mortgage gold bonds, R. & A. Division, due 1989	6,000,000
4% second mortgage gold bonds, R. & A. Division, due 1989	1,000,000
5% first mortgage gold bonds, Cr. Valley Branch, due 1940	650,000
5% first mortgage gold bonds, Warm Sp. Branch, due 1941	400,000
5% Greenbrier & N. R. Railroad gold, 1942	555,000
5% Kineon Coal Company gold, due 1915	200.000

Current liabilities:

Interest accrued on funded debt	909,318
Unpaid coupons including those due July 1, 1903	227,207
Unpaid dividends	4.015
Vouchers, pay rolls and traffic balances	1,847,712
Due individuals and companies	44,337
Loans and bills payable	1,000.000
Taxes accrued not due	157,964
Profit and loss	1,071,106
	$139.452,513

Income account for year ended June 30, 1903:

Earnings :

Freight traffic	$12,510,006
Passenger traffic	3.474.905
Express, mails, etc.	726,691
Gross earnings	$16.711,602

Expenses :

Maintenance of way and structures	$2,178,835
Maintenance of equipment	2,679,021
Conducting transportation	5,839,230
General expenses	355,636
Operating expenses	$11,052,723

Net earnings.	$5,658,879
Income from other sources	190,374
Total income	$5,849,253
Deductions from income :	
Interest on funded debt	$3,472,449
Interest on bonds of roads of which the stock is owned	87,500
Car trust payments	273,094
Interest, discount and exchange	89,369
Taxes	447,115
Miscellaneous.—Loss on C. & O. S. S. Line, etc	210,122
Total deductions	$4,579,649
Net income	$1,269,604

Profit and loss, June 30, 1903 :

Dr.

Discount on equipment trust certificates sold	$120,000
Sundry old accounts written off	27,013
Dividend No. 4, 1% November 26, 1902	605,299
New equipment and construction	591,012
Balance June 30, 1903	1,071,106
	$2,414,430

Cr.

Balance June 30, 1902	$1,062,325
Premium on general mortgage bonds sold	82,500
Net income for year to June 30, 1903	1,269,604
	$2,414,430

Stock, common.—Authorized $70,000,000, of which $60,529,900 has been issued.

The first and second preferred stock under the plan of reorganization is convertible into 4½% bonds and the common stock on the basis of ⅔ and ⅓ respectively for the first preferred and ⅓ and ⅔ for the second preferred.

Bonds.—The general mortgage created in 1892 is for $70,000,000 and from the unsold balance $2,000,000 are to be used each year for additions to property, etc.

The company controls the Chesapeake & Ohio S. S. Company, operating a line of steamships between Newport News and Liverpool.

Dividends have been paid from 1899 to 1903, both inclusive, at the rate of 1% yearly.

The Pennsylvania Railroad Company and New York Central & Hudson River Railroad together own a controlling interest in this property.

Statistics :

Year.	Miles.	Gross Earnings.	Per Cent. Operating.	Surplus before Dividend.	Rate per Ton per Mile.	Earnings per Train Mile.
1899-1900	1.476	$13.402,070	64.90	$1,156,580	.343	$1.670
1900-1901	1.562	15.371,541	62.20	2,001,897	.388	1.980
1901-1902	1,636	16,524.378	62 90	2,060.408	.402	2 046
1902-1903	1,878	16,713,006	66.10	1,269,604	.463	2.446

Officers —President, George W. Stevens; Secretary, C. E. Wellford.

Directors.—Decatur Axtell, John P. Green, S. M. Prevost, George W. Stevens, Chauncey M. Depew, William H. Newman, Samuel Rea, H. McK. Twombly, H. V. Wickham.

General offices, Richmond, Va.

Annual meeting, Tuesday before last Tuesday in October.

CHICAGO & ALTON RAILWAY COMPANY.

This company was organized in April, 1900, and purchased nearly all the stock of the Chicago & Alton R. R. Co.; also the St. Louis, Peoria & Northern Line between Springfield and Grove.

The "railroad" is maintained as a separate organization and is operated by the "railway" company under lease for 99 years from above date, the rental being the net earnings, after payment by the lessee of all interest on bonds, taxes, etc.

Mileage.—Including the St. L., P. & N., 58 miles, the line operated, extending from Chicago, Ill., to E. St. Louis; Bloomington, Ill., to Godfrey, Ill.; Roodhouse, Ill , to Kansas City, etc., was at July 1, 1903, 915 miles.

General balance sheet, June 30, 1903 :

Assets.

Cost of railway, equipment and securities	$65,230.517
Bonds owned	2,328.800
Advances for betterments, etc.	616.672
Current assets:	
Cash	972.845
Agents, individuals and other companies	1,253.943
Material, fuel and supplies	335.009
Unadjusted accounts	231,850
	$70,969,636

Liabilities.

Common stock		$19,542,800
Preferred stock		19,544,000
First lien 3½% bonds, 1950		22,000,000
4% collateral trust notes, 1907:		
Authorized	$5,000,000	
Unsold	1,365,000	
		3,635,000
Current liabilities:		
Loans and bills payable		2,510,000
Interest payable, July 1, 1903		457,700
Dividend payable, July 1, 1903		390,880
Interest and dividends accrued		267,095
Vouchers and pay rolls		1,307,894
Traffic balances		114,547
Miscellaneous interest, etc		3,360
Unadjusted accounts		11,674
Renewal fund		8,648
Material and supplies, under provisions of lease		606,599
Profit and loss		569,439
		$70,969,636

Income and profit and loss account for year ended and at June 30, 1903:

Earnings:		
Freight		$6,610,637
Passenger		2,908,583
Mail		241,112
Express		218,039
Miscellaneous		92,721
Gross earnings		$10,071,092
Expenses:		
Maintenance of way and structures		$1,213,365
Maintenance of equipment		1,190,832
Conducting transportation		3,983,068
General expenses		237,931
Total operating expenses		$6,625,196
Net earnings		$3,445,896
Additions to income:		
Dividends on stock owned*		1,525,622
Interest on bonds, etc		244,449
Total income		$5,215,967
Deductions from income:		
Interest on 3% refunding bonds		$1,200,000
Rentals payable by C. & A. R. R		245,021
Taxes		345,000
Net earnings of leased property*		1,544,462
Miscellaneous		7,105
Interest on 1st lien bonds of railway company		770,000
Interest on 4% collateral trust notes		97,004
Discount on 4% collateral trust notes sold		29,728
Interest on loans, etc		123,943
Miscellaneous		2,663
Total charges		$4,364,926

*The disbursement above marked represents a payment of 7% on the outstanding stock of the railroad company, of which the greater part is held by the railway company, as indicated by the large proportion shown above as a receipt.

Net income..	$851,041
Dividend on preferred stock, 4%..................................	781,760
Balance surplus for year..	$69,281
Balance profit and loss June 30, 1902...........................	500,158
Balance profit and loss June 30, 1903...........................	$569,439

The railroad mortgage securing the 3% refunding bonds of 1899, authorized for $40,000,000, may be increased to $45,000,000 by vote of two-thirds of the stockholders to provide for extensions, etc., and issued at the rate of not over $1,000,000 per annum, to the extent of $20,000 per mile.

Dividends.—Paid on preferred, January, 1901, to January, 1904, both inclusive, at 4% per annum (J. & J.).

Directors.—Edward H. Harriman, James Stillman, George J. Gould, Mortimer L. Schiff, Norman B. Ream, John J. Mitchell, Charles H. Chappell, James B. Forgan, David R. Francis, Samuel M. Felton and F. S. Winston.

Main office.—Chicago, Ill.

Annual meeting.—First Tuesday in October.

CHICAGO GREAT WESTERN RAILWAY COMPANY.

This is an Illinois corporation formed in January, 1892, for the purpose of reorganizing the Chicago, St. Paul & K. C. Ry. Co., to which property title was acquired in September, 1893, and satisfaction of the old mortgages was completed in 1902.

The line as operated at January 1, 1904, was 1,464 miles in length and covered the territory of the C. St. P. & K. C. from Chicago to St. Paul and St. Joseph, Mo., and branches, 823 miles; Mason City & Ft. Dodge, 263 miles; and Wisconsin, Minn. and Pacific 271, etc. Projected extensions will shortly give the company a through line from Chicago to Omaha and Minneapolis and St. Paul to Omaha.

The company owns all the stock and bonds of the Mason City & Ft. Dodge road, and operates the W. M. & P. under a lease of 100 years from April 1, 1901, the Chicago Great Western Ry. Co. receiving the entire net earnings above interest on bonds. The company, however, owns the entire stock issue.

General balance sheet, June 30, 1903 :

Assets.

Cost of rolling stock owned...	$7,595,165
Cost of road and terminals............................	62,057,230
Stocks of proprietary companies.....	10,671,753
Stocks in transfer lines and depot companies.......................	293,694
Bonds and stocks of other companies	222,005
Cash with London Finance Co	190
Cash in New York...	35,764
Cash in London...	119,018
Cash—Current........	352,856
Accounts receivable...	179,532
Due from agents and conductors.............................	318,374
Individuals and companies............................	887,308
Miscellaneous accounts...	129,463
Material and supplies...	1,188,700
	$84,051,052

Liabilities.

4% debenture stock and scrip, less $1,463,000 in treasury...............	$26,117,089
5% debenture preferred stock A, less $35,500 in treasury.............	11,336,900
4% debenture preferred stock B, less $21,110 in treasury.............	9,468,090
Common stock...	29,921,045
5% gold notes, due in 1904, sterling...................................	905,303
5% gold notes, due in 1907, sterling...................................	48,485
5% gold notes, due in 1908, sterling......	2,558,788
Temporary loans..	335,000
Accounts payable..	73,994
Vouchers and pay rolls	2,185,971
Interest and taxes accrued, etc......................................	131,875
Interest payable July 15 on 4% debenture stock.....................	520,880
Dividend payable Aug. 31 on 5% preferred A..............	284,310
Surplus...	163,322
	$84,051,052

Income and profit and loss account for year ended and at June 30, 1903 :

Earnings :

Freight...	$5,633,437
Passenger	1,782,218
Mail..	111,980
Express...	103,574
Miscellaneous..	65,258
Rentals	5,519

Surplus earnings proprietary lines :

Wis Min & Pacific R. R. Co.....	66,848
Mason City & Ft D. R. R. Co.................................. ..	54,355
Total......................................	$7,823,191

Expenses:

Maintenance of way and renewals..............................	$916,559
Maintenance of equipment...........	934,718
Fuel for locomotives..	840,536
Conducting transportation..	2,067,624
Traffic agencies, etc..	218,237
General expenses..	456,954
Total..	$5,434,630
Net earnings, including proprietary lines........................	$2,388,561

Deductions from income:

Taxes	203.897
Terminal rental	238.324
Dubuque bridge rental	30,000
Leased lines rental	139,819
Interest on company's proportion bonds of St. P., Union Depot & M. Tfr. Ry	13.995
Interest on loans	160.589
Total	$786,624
Balance—net income	$1,601.934
4% on debenture stock	$1.025,693
5% on preferred stock A	568.620
Balance to surplus	$7.621
Balance surplus June 30, 1902	155,701
Balance surplus June 30, 1903	$163,322

The authorized common stock was increased from $30,000,000 to $50,000 000 in February, 1903, to provide for the acquisition of the Mason City & Fort Dodge railroad.

The 4% debenture is authorized for $15,000,000, and interest is payable half yearly in gold. (J. and J).

The 5% preferred A stock is authorized for $15,000,000, and dividend is contingent on earnings. Dividends paid as under. The 4% preferred B is authorized for $10,000,000, and dividends depend also upon the earnings. No dividends yet paid on this class.

Compared with the previous year's operations, the report for the fiscal year ended June 30, 1903, shows the following noteworthy facts: Gross receipts increased 3 62%; operating expenses increased 2.84%; net earnings increased 6.03%.

Dividends.—On preferred A 1899, 4%; 1900 to February, 1904, 5% yearly (J. and J.).

Directors.—A. B. Stickney, President; A. Oppenheim, S. C. Stickney, F. Weyerhaeuser, W. Lusk, H. E. Fletcher, T. H. Wheeler, William A. Read, R. C. Wight.

Annual meeting.—First Thursday after first Tuesday in September.

Main office, St. Paul, Minn.

CHICAGO, MILWAUKEE & ST. PAUL RAILWAY COMPANY.

This company was organized in 1863 and has operated under its present name since 1874. The property has by purchase and construction reached a mileage of 6,682 miles, and traverses in many directions the states of Illinois, Wisconsin, Minnesota, Iowa, Missouri and the Dakotas.

General balance sheet, June 30, 1903:

Assets.

Road and equipment	$235,610.737
Bonds and stocks owned	3.911,425
Bonds in treasury	5,144,000
Materials and supplies	4,553,723
Cash	8,600,598
Agents and conductors	948,265
Traffic balances	1,754,662
Due from United States Government	368,005
Renewal and sinking funds	6,015,545
Total	$266,906,961

Liabilities.

Common stock	$58,183,900
Preferred stock	47,724,400
Funded debt	123,754,500
Pay roll vouchers and traffic balances	4,895,654
Reserves and sinking funds	6,043,707
Interest accrued, not due	2,805.148
Profit and loss surplus	23,499,652
Total	$266,906,961

Income and profit and loss account for year and at June 30, 1903:

Earnings:

Passenger	$9.542,201
Freight	34,797,045
Mail, express, etc	3,323,491
Total earnings	$47,662,737

Expenses:

Maintenance of way and structures	$7,347,048
Maintenance of equipment	3,893,834
Conducting transportation	16,829,796
General expenses	952,309
Taxes	1,470,187
Renewal and improvement account	1,105,000
Total expenses	$31,598,174

Net earnings..	$16,064,563
Other income	510,031
Total income....................................	$16,574,594
Interest on funded debt............................	6,101,335
Net income.....................................	$10,473,259
Dividends :	
Common, 7½%................................	$4,363,792
Preferred, 7%...............................	3,291,883
Balance, surplus for year..........................	$2,817,584
Profit and loss balance June 30, 1902...............	20,682,068
Profit and loss balance June 30, 1903...............	$23,499,652

Bonds.—In 1889 a general mortgage was executed to secure a new issue of $150,000,000 100 year gold bonds, to take up all outstanding issues and to provide other funds.

At June 30, 1903, the status of this account stood as under:

Amount in the hands of the public..................	$30,500,000
In the treasury...................................	3,896,000
	$34,396.000
Reserved for prior liens...........................	$87,655,500
Available for future improvements.................	27,948,500
	$150,000,000

Certain of the prior lien bonds were convertible into stock, which right having been used to considerable extent has left a large amount of the general mortgage bonds available for improvements instead of being necessary for retirement of such prior lien bonds at maturity. At July 1, 1903, there remained $2,953,000 prior lien bonds so convertible.

Stock.—The preferred stock is 7% non-cumulative and shares equally with the common after 7% has been paid on each class.

Dividends.—(A & O). Preferred : From 1891 to 1903, both inclusive, 7%, April, 1904, 3½%.

Common : 1892, 2%; 1893 and 1894, 4%; 1895, 2%; 1896, 4%; 1897 to 1900, 5% yearly; 1901, 6%; 1902 and 1903, 7%; April, 1904, 3½%.

The net earnings for the year ended June 30, 1903, showed an increase of $648,333 over the previous year, and the freight tonnage increased 7.14%.

The commodity statement for the year shows a slight decrease in percentage of agricultural products, whilst other commodities increased 9.55%.

The more diversified character of freight evidently indicates a higher average class of traffic, since the revenue per ton per mile shows an increase of 3%.

Over 40,000 tons of new rail was laid and charged to expenses, which is slightly less than in the previous year, and the cost of 1,284,000 new ties was charged to expenses in the year against the cost of 1,854,600.

Annual meeting in September, as directors may appoint.

Main office, Chicago.

Directors.—Roswell Miller, A. J. Earling, Frederick Layton, J. Ogden Armour, Frank S. Bond, Joseph Milbank, William Rockefeller, Peter Geddes, John A. Stewart, Samuel Spencer, James H. Smith, Charles W. Harkness, Henry H. Rogers.

CHICAGO & NORTHWESTERN RAILWAY COMPANY.

Organized in 1859 to acquire the Chicago, St. Paul & Fond du Lac Railroad, sold under foreclosure. This line was 177 miles long, but through acquisition and extension the system now operates 7,365 miles, of which 7,248 miles is owned outright and the balance controlled through stock ownership.

The line operates between Chicago and Omaha and Chicago to St. Paul, with branches and extensions throughout the States of Illinois, Wisconsin, Michigan, Iowa, Minnesota, South Dakota, Nebraska, and a short distance in Wyoming and North Dakota.

The system is considered a Vanderbilt property.

General balance sheet, June 30, 1903:

Assets.

Road and equipment	$220,376,196
Bonds, stocks and advances	19,949,488
Materials and supplies	3,678,920
Sinking funds	7,647,714
Cash on hand	8,411,102
Bills receivable	182,357
Agents and conductors	2,205,872
U. S. Government	283,838
Various persons	166,689
Total	$262,902,175

Liabilities.

Common stock	$50,674,476
Preferred stock	22,398,954
Bonded debt	162,310,500
Sinking funds	7,647,715
Current bills, pay rolls, etc.	3,994,020
Miscellaneous accounts	38,000
Coupons unpaid	143,362
Dividends declared	2,139,380
Accrued interest	1,665,095
Land income account	1,989,574
Railroad income account (surplus)	9,901,098
Total	$262,902.175

Income and profit and loss account for year ended and at June 30, 1903 :

Earnings:	
Passenger	$12,036,277
Freight	35,171,064
Mail, express, etc.	2,635,440
Gross earnings	$49,842,781
Expenses:	
Maintenance of way and structures	6,247,400
Maintenance of equipment	5,031,795
Conducting transportation	19,199,174
General expenses	973,900
Taxes	1,807,845
Total operating expenses and taxes	$33,260,113
Net earnings	$16,582,668
Other income:	
Investments	577,080
Total income	$17,159,748
Deductions from income:	
Interest on funded debt	$6,540,170
Interest on bonds refunded	5,316
Sinking fund	225,000
Appropriated for real estate, construction, etc.	5,013,418
Total	$11,783,904
Balance net income	$5,375,844
Dividend on preferred stock, 7%	$3,060,414
Dividend on common stock, 8%	1,791,600
Balance to surplus	523,830
Profit and loss balance, June 30, 1902	9,377,268
Profit and loss surplus, June 30, 1903	$9,901,098

Bonds.—A new mortgage was executed to secure an issue of $165,000,000 90-year refunding bonds at not over 5% interest

Of this amount $131,645,000 were reserved to retire underlying bonds, and the balance may be used to provide funds for extensions and improvements.

Stock.—The authorized issue of stock is $77,601,045 preferred and $22,398,955 common. The preferred stock has first right to 7% dividend, after which the common is to receive 7%; after this the preferred receives 3%, and when the common has received 3% the stocks share equally.

Dividends.—Preferred (Q. J.)—7% for many years to July, 1902, when an extra 1% was paid, making 8% for the year, which rate has since been maintained by 2% quarterly payments.

Common (J. & J.)—From 1886 to 1893, 6% yearly; 1894, 3%; 1895, 4%; 1896 to 1899, 5% yearly; 1900 and 1901, 6%, since when the rate of 7% has been paid in semi-annual installments of $3\frac{1}{2}$%.

During the year ended June 30, 1903, there was laid and the cost thereof charged to expenses 56,890 tons of steel rail and 1,592,000 ties, and about 400 miles of road was ballasted. Expenses also include the cost of 116 new steel bridges on masonry superstructure.

The gross earnings in the same period show an increase over the previous year of $1,300,000.

The rate per ton per mile earned on the freight haul shows a slight increase over previous years, as also does the earnings per passenger train mile. However, the percentage of expenses to earnings has increased from 62.85% in 1899–1900 to 66.73 in 1902–1903, which is probably accounted for in the heavy charges included in expenses for renewals.

The company has remaining from land grants some 460,000 acres of land. The sales in the year above reviewed amounted to about 38,000 acres, which realized, including town lots sold, $666,625.25.

Proceeds from land sales are not included in the earnings, but credited to the land income account, the surplus of which account at June 30, 1903, may be seen in the above balance sheet to be $1,989,574.

Main office.—Chicago.

Annual meeting.—First Thursday in June.

Directors.—W. K. Vanderbilt, F. W. Vanderbilt, H. McK. Twombly, Samuel E. Barger, Chauncey M. Depew, James Stillman, James C. Fargo, Frank Work, Albert Keep, Marvin Hughitt (president), Byron L. Smith, P. Kimball, Oliver Ames, Zenas Crane.

CHICAGO TERMINAL TRANSFER RAILROAD COMPANY.

This company was created in 1897 to reorganize the Chicago & Northern Pacific and Chicago & Calumet Terminal Railway Companies. Its property consists of passenger and freight terminals at Chicago, and a belt line around the city. It also owns about 50 acres in the business district and some 800 acres outside the city of Chicago, besides 7,500 feet of docks on the Chicago River.

Track owned, 90 miles; operated under lease, 18 miles; total operated, 108 miles.

The company has leases for use of its tracks and depot facilities with the Baltimore & Ohio and a number of other lines entering Chicago.

General balance sheet, June 30, 1903 :

Assets.

Property and franchises	$45,402,364
Cash (including for coupons)	359,592
Accounts receivable	271,468
Accounts receivable in dispute	136.187
Agents and conductors	174.912
Treasury securities	600,995
Material and supplies	114,720
Total	$47,060,239

Liabilities.

Common stock	$13,000,000
Preferred stock	17,000,000
Funded debt	15,444,000
Vouchers and pay rolls	350,592
Interest matured and accrued	283,083
Taxes accrued	81,334
Bills payable	312,000
Reserve funds, etc	228,734
Profit and loss	360,495
Total	$47,060,239

Income and profit and loss account for year ended and at June 30, 1903:

Earnings:

From railroad tenants	$629,077
Other tenants and income	123,376
Freight and switching	921,543
Passenger	72,376
Total earnings	**$1,746,372**

Expenses:

Maintenance of way, etc.	$198,195
Equipment	153,177
Conducting transportion	569,934
General expenses	102,363
Taxes	112,000
Total operating expenses and taxes	**$1,135,670**
Net income	$610,702
Interest on funded debt	597,600
Balance, surplus for year	**$13,102**
Profit and loss balance, June 30, 1902	347,393
Profit and loss balance, June 30, 1903	**$360,495**

Bonds.—The first mortgage is for $16,500,000; issued $15,444,000.

Stocks.—Preferred, authorized and issued, $17,000,000 4% non-cumulative ; common, authorized and issued, $13,000,000.

Dividends.—None yet paid.

Annual meeting, second Wednesday in October.

Main office, Chicago, Ill.

Officers.—President and General Manager, J. N. Faithorn; Secretary and Assistant Treasurer, W. T. Wisner.

COLORADO FUEL & IRON COMPANY.

A corporation formed under the laws of Colorado in October, 1892, as a consolidation of the Colorado Coal & Iron Company and the Colorado Fuel Company, and subsequently acquiring the properties of the Grand River Coal & Coke Company, subject to incumbrance.

The company owns and operates iron and coal mines, steel plants, rolling mills, coke ovens, etc.; also owns the entire capital stock of the Colorado & Wyoming Railway, 170 miles in length

In 1896 the company leased the coal properties of the Atchison, Topeka & Santa Fe Railway, with an annual capacity of some 600,000 tons.

A contest for control in 1902 was finally settled by compromise, and equal representation was accorded the contestants.

General balance sheet, June 30, 1003:

Assets.

Real estate	$17,128,642
Mines development	131,025
Royalties in advance	68,741
Equipment all departments	27,490,753
C. E. Phelps, assistant treasurer	168,000
Customers' accounts	1,274,624
Individuals and companies (net)	271,842
Bills recei-able	322,838
Stocks, supplies and materials	3,400,941
Securities—stocks and bonds	989,128
Colorado & Wyoming Railroad Company	3,398,701
Crystal River Railroad	327,299
Minn. Ld. & W. Co	666,049
Miscellaneous	151,733
Total	**$55,790,316**

Liabilities.

Capital stock:	
Common	$23,932,000
Preferred	2,000,000
Bonds	20,063,000
Bills payable	4,994,922
Unpaid vouchers	1,471,045
Unpaid freight	92,535
Unpaid pay checks	675,965
The Colorado Supply Company	203,818
Sinking funds	977,005
Funds for payment of taxes	60,000
Bond interest accrued, not due	424,891
Emergency fund	203,708
Miscellaneous	105,314
Profit and loss surplus	586,113
Total	**$55,790,316**

Income and profit and loss account for year ended and at June 30, 1903:

Earnings:

Fuel department	$9,304,427
Iron department	6,981,828
Denver retail department	364,664
Miscellaneous	3,044
Gross earnings	$16,653,963
Expenses	$14,662,981
Net earnings	$1,990,982
Taxes	$115,477
Interest on bonds, less miscellaneous income	978,785
Sinking funds, etc	613,112
Dividend on preferred stock, (4%)	80,000
Total	$1,787,374

Surplus for year..	$203,608
Profit and loss balance June 30, 1902.............................	528,640
	$732,248
Deduct:	
Net loss adjustments, fuel and iron departments, etc.............	146,135
Profit and loss balance June 30, 1903	$586,113

Stock.—The preferred stock is 8% cumulative. Dividends payable in February and August. All the preferred and common stock is outstanding to the full amount authorized.

Dividends.—Preferred: 1894, 4%; 1895, nothing; 1896, 8%; 1897, 4%; 1898 and 1899, nothing; 1900, 40%; 1901, 8%; 1902, 8%; 1903, February, 4%.

Common.—3½% in 1901; none since.

The net income shows an increase of about $500,000 over the previous year—the production of coal being approximately 100,000 tons or 25%; coke 165,000 tons or 23% greater, and the production of iron being slightly less than in the previous year.

At a meeting of directors on November 11, 1903, a plan was proposed and unanimously adopted for the provision of the company's financial requirements.

The proposition contemplates the formation of a new company which shall issue $45,000,000 convertible consolidated first mortgage bonds covering the entire property. Thus about $13,600,000 will be provided to repurchase properties formerly sold, pay for enlargements, extensions, etc.

It is proposed also to increase the common stock about $6,200,000.

The present debentures would be exchanged at par for the new bonds and a bonus of 20% in common stock, such bonds to be convertible into stock at par.

A syndicate has agreed to underwrite the $13,600,000, receiving $1,000 in bonds and $200 in stock for each $800 paid. Stockholders will be given the right to subscribe on this basis. Some $12,000,000 out of the $14,068,000 have already assented.

Main office.—Denver, Colorado.

Annual meeting.—Third Wednesday in August.

Directors include John C. Osgood, president; George J. Gould, Edwin Hawley, Edward H. Harriman and H. E. Huntington.

CORN PRODUCTS COMPANY.

This is a New Jersey corporation formed in 1902 as a consolidation of the Glucose Sugar Refining Company, Illinois Sugar Refining Company, National Starch Company, New York Glucose Company and the Charles Pope Glucose Company.

General balance sheet, February 28, 1903 :

Assets.

Cost of securities	$72,258,745
Bills receivable	115,000
Cash in banks	3,212,511
Total	$75,586,256

Liabilities.

Preferred stock	$27,376,990
Common stock	44,881,755
Surplus	3,327,511
Total	$75,586,256

Stock authorized.—Preferred, $50,000,000 7% cumulative, and $30,000,000 common.

The Corn Products Company has no funded debt, and has not assumed those of the controlled companies.

Dividends.—Preferred : July, 1902, to April, 1904, 7% yearly in quarterly payments of 1¾%. Common : 4% declared out of the earnings of 1902-03. payable in quarterly payments of 1%, April July, October and January. The March, 1904, dividend was passed because of heavy expenditures for improvements.

At a meeting in March, 1904, it was reported that the official audit for the fiscal year ended March 1, 1904, had not been completed, but that it was estimated that the earnings of subsidiary companies amounted to about $5,000,000, from which there was to be deducted $420,000 for interest on underlying bonds and $1,750,000 for re-building plant, etc.

This would leave a net income of about $2,830,000 as against $4,142,522 for the previous year.

Increased capacity afforded by the above-mentioned expenditure should be productive of better showing for the future, provided as good markets as in the past are found for the product.

Main office, New York.

Officers.—President, C. H. Matthiessen ; Vice-President and Seeretary, C. L. Glass.

COLORADO & SOUTHERN RAILWAY COMPANY.

This line operates under a charter from the State of Colorado, December 20, 1898, and is successor to the Union Pacific, Denver & Gulf, and the Denver, Leadville & Gunnison Railway Companies, whose properties were sold under foreclosure.

The company owns a majority of the capital stock of the Ft. Worth & Denver City Railway Company, a line extending from Texline to Ft. Worth, Texas, a distance of about 450 miles, and controls jointly with the Rio Grande Western, the Colorado, Midland Railway, an important line traversing the Rocky Mountains and drawing traffic from its vast mineral wealth.

The road's main line extends from Denver to Texline, a distance of 356 miles, and the numerous branches throughout the State of Colorado, extending 150 miles into Wyoming, gives it a total mileage of 1,121 miles, of which about one-third is narrow gauge.

General balance sheet, June 30, 1903:

Assets.

Road and equipment	$63,466,751
Improvements	998,506
New equipment	2,895,530
Cash	437,178
Individuals and companies	275,376
Agents and conductors	144,222
U. S. Government	19,791
Colorado warrants	574
Advance insurance	10,611
Materials and supplies	512,141
P. U. D. and railway stock	80,000
P. U. D. and railway stock	8,120
P. U. D. sinking fund	10,400
Other securities	1,176,200
Discount on bonds and miscellaneous	23,189
Total	$70,058,589

Liabilities.

Common stock	$31,000,000
1st preferred stock	8,500,000
2nd preferred stock	8,500,000
First mortgage bonds	18,803,000
Car trust and locomotive trust notes	1,243,379
Vouchers	370,938
Pay rolls	269,627
Foreign roads	89,857
Coupons	11,620
Accrued taxes	215,555
Interest accrued, not due	313,383
Equipment renewal fund	62,740
Rails released	1,887
Miscellaneous	12,445
Profit and loss	664,158
Total	$70,000,589

Income and profit and loss account for year ended and at June 30, 1903 :

Earnings :

Freight	$4,790,420
Passenger	1,083,390
Express, mail and miscellaneous	269,179
Gross earnings	$6,142,989

Expenses :

Maintenance of way, etc	$994,900
Maintenance of equipment	913,979
Conducting transportation	2,573,364
General expenses	192,238
Taxes	233,630
Total expenses and taxes	$4,908,111

Net earnings	$1,234,878
Income from investments	58,875
Total income	$1,293,753

Deduct—Interest	$772,568
Miscellaneous	24,232

Surplus for year	$496,953
Dividend on 1st preferred (4%)	340,000

Balance to profit and loss	$156,953
Profit and loss balance forward	507,205

Profit and loss balance June 30, 1903	$664,158

Stocks.—Both the 1st and 2nd preferred is 4% non-cumulative.

All classes of stocks are held in a voting trust until January 1, 1904, and then until the 1st preferred stock shall have paid 4% for three consecutive years. The arrangement, however, may be terminated at an earlier date.

Funded debt.—Bond issue authorized $20,000,000 1st gold 4%, 1929, the unissued being reserved for additions and improvement and for the acquisition of coal properties. Except those used for acquiring coal properties the bonds may be issued at a rate not to exceed $300,000 per annum.

Dividends.—1st preferred 1900, 2% ; 1901, 3½% ; 1902, 3½% ; 1903, 4% ; 1904, April, 2%.

Gross earnings for the year above reported on show an increase of 10.08% over the previous year, but a decrease in net earnings of 4.40%. The percentage of expenses to earnings increased from 76.34 to 79.89 in the same period.

The increase in expenses is partly attributed by President Trumbull to higher prices for labor and material, which, however, is thought to have reached maximum figures.

A further cause is shown in lack of equipment and trackage, resulting in congestion with resultant expense in handling traffic. The rate earned per ton per mile fell off, showing the large increase in traffic to be chiefly in low rate freight. An additional passenger train was put into service between Denver and Fort Worth to meet competition, but in spite of this fact passenger earnings show a slight reduction over the previous year. This is one of the roads affected adversely, owing to its shortage of equipment, by the new car service arrangement, which is now charged upon a per diem instead of mileage basis.

The track appears to have been kept up at a fair average rate, there having been re-laid with 75 pound steel 53.5 miles, and about 400,000 ties renewed.

Main office.—Denver, Colorado.

Annual meeting.—Third Thursday in November.

Directors.—Grenville M. Dodge, Henry Budge, Jos. P. Cotton, Fred'k P. Olcott, John J. Emery, Edward J. Berwind, Edward C. Henderson, Adolph Lewisohn, Edwin Hawley, Norman B. Ream, Henry Bronner, Harry Walters and Frank Trumbull.

DELAWARE, LACKAWANNA & WESTERN RAILROAD COMPANY.

Incorporated under the laws of Pennsylvania in 1832. The present system is the outgrowth of a consolidation in 1853 of the Ligett's Gap Railroad and the Delaware & Cobb's Gap Railroad. Operations were commenced in 1856.

Since this date the mileage has been extended by additions, extensions and leases.

The company is ranked amongst the largest producers of anthracite coal, which is mined from its own extensive properties.

The mileage operated, including main line from Hoboken, N. J., to Buffalo, and branches throughout the anthracite region, is 965 miles, of which 194 miles is owned and 771 miles leased.

General balance sheet, December 31, 1903:

Assets.

Cost of road	$17,401,195
Cost of equipment	8,019,201
Other permanent investments	6,671,504
Stocks in treasury	7,906,114
Bonds in treasury	4,390,206
Advance to leased and controlled roads	1,169,439
Coal on hand	2,159,219
Material, fuel, etc	1,444,781
Cash	1,453,108
Bills receivable	46,000
Agents, conductors, individuals, companies, etc	830,839
Coal bills and sundry accounts	2,901,878
Suspense account	73,438
	$54,466,921

Liabilities.

Capital stock	$26,200,000
Consolidated mortgage bonds	3,067,000
Rentals accrued, not due	1,529,573
Interest accrued, not due	71,377
Past due dividends, etc	125,328
Dividend payable in January	458,500
Audited vouchers	1,949,128
Audited pay rolls	1,151,183
Taxes, not due	490,113
Mortgage on real estate	62,074
Companies and individuals	572,432
Profit and loss, surplus	18,790,213
	$54,466,921

Income and profit and loss account for year ended and at December 31, 1903:

Earnings from—

Coal	$13,826,844
Miscellaneous freight	8,354,908
Passenger	5,083,142
Mail, express, etc	1,916,069
Total	$29,180,963

Expenses:

Maintenance of way, etc	$3,647,959
Maintenance of equipment	2,793,086
Conducting transportation	8,264,894
General	464,602
Taxes	872,862
Total	$16,043,403

Net earnings	$13,137,560

Additions to income:

Interest on investments	115,162
Dividends on stock	335,916
Coal department earnings*	3,036,194
Miscellaneous interest, etc	13,664
Total income	$16,638,496

Deductions from income:

Interest on bonds...	$214,409
Rentals leased lines..	5,071,249
Accounts charged off...	805,236
Rentals New York terminals..................................	143,198
Renewa's and betterments....................................	4,319,166
Total..	$10,553,258
Net income..	$6,085,238
Dividend (7%)	$1,834,000
Balance, surplus for year....................................	$4,251,238
Profit and loss June 30, 1902................................	14,538,974
Profit and loss June 30, 1903...............................	$18,790,212

* Results of coal department were:

Earnings..	$36,736,325
Expenses..	33,700,131
Profit...	$3,036,194

The gross earnings of the railroad show about 35% increase over the previous year, which in turn averaged those of 1900 and 1901. Gross coal earnings increased about 90%, and net earnings nearly 400%.

Comparing with a year not affected by the coal strike, say 1901, it is found that the net earnings for 1903 show an increase of some 80%.

President Truesdale in his report says that such phenomenally large earnings will probably not be equalled again for several years, attributing the cause of such heavy business to the stocking up process following the depletion due to the strike.

Stock authorized is fully issued.

Dividends.—7%, quarterly at 1¾% in January, April, July and October. This rate has been maintained since 1886, prior to which time the rate from 1880 ranged from 6¾ to 8%.

Annual meeting.—Tuesday before last Friday in February.

Main office.—New York.

Directors.—Samuel Sloan (chairman), Fredk. W. Vanderbilt, Wm. W. Astor, Eugene Higgins, Henry A. C. Taylor, J. Rogers Maxwell, Geo. F. Baker, Wm. Rockefeller, Hamilton McK. Twombly, James J. Stillman, M. Taylor Payne, Harris C. Fahnestock, Frank Work, John D. Rockefeller, Jr.

DELAWARE & HUDSON COMPANY.

A New York corporation dating from 1823, originally building and operating a canal from Rondout, N. Y., to Honesdale, Pa., a distance of 108 miles. In 1899 the title of the corporation as above was adopted and the sale of the canal was effected.

The company operates a line of railroad from Wilkesbarre, Pa., via Albany, to Rouses Point, N. Y., which with branches is 821 miles in length, of which there is owned 193 miles and leased 628.

In addition, the company owns about 200 miles of tramways at its vast coal properties.

The company is one of the largest miners and carriers of antracite coal, the average production being for several past years about 5,000,000 tons per annum. The tonnage carried however is much in excess of its own product, being 8,657,966 tons in 1903, 4,640,772 tons in 1902, and 7,571,298 tons in 1901.

The business of 1902 was naturally very seriously affected by the coal strike.

General balance sheet, December 31, 1903:

Assets.

Real estate	$5,146,357
Unmined coal	12,607,634
Railroad construction	10,830,950
Adirondack Railway	1,000,000
Chat. & Lake Placid Railway construction	286,299
Railroad equipment	8,374,292
Schenectady & Duane Railroad	500,000
Marine equipment	10,000
Coal department equipment	820,944
Mining plant, breakers, etc	2,300,000
Coal handling and storage plants	190,032
Supplies on hand	2,150,082
Shop machinery, tools, etc	544,610
Stocks and bonds owned	5,451,488
Advances on unmined coal	876,298
Cash	900,520
Due from paymasters, etc	1,772,205
Bills and accounts receivable	1,705,678
Total	$55,467,389

Liabilities.

Capital Stock	$34,407,100
Bonds	9,500,000
Interest, dividends, etc., due January 1	575,050
Interest, etc., unclaimed	125,461
Sinking fund to retire capital stock	313,585
Fire insurance fund	159,321
Audited pay rolls	1,134,681
Audtied vouchers	2,469,184
Other accounts payable	189,853
Profit and loss	6,593,154
Total	$55,467,389

Income account for year ended December 31, 1903 :

Income, coal department :
Coal sales	$19,529,034
Coal added to stock	654,197
Miscellaneous profits	12,979
Interest on investments	347,207
Total	$20,543,417

Expenses, coal department :
Mining and preparing coal	$11,528,821
Railroad transportation	4,703,997
General, taxes, handling, etc	399,788
Total	$16,632,606

Net income, coal department	$3,910,811

Income from railroads :
Earnings—
Lines in Pennsylvania	$4,045,206
Albany & Susquehanna Railroad	4,773,526
Rensselaer & Saratoga Railroad and Adirondack	3,303,148
New York & Canada Railroad	1,521,074
Total earnings	$13,642,954

Operating expenses—
Lines in Pennsylvania	$2,123,383
Albany & Susquehanna Railroad	2,565,541
Rensselaer & Saratoga Railroad and Adirondack	2,485,467
New York & Canada Railroad	994,805
Total operating expenses	$8,169,196

Net earnings, railroads	$5,473,758
Deduct interest, rentals, etc	2,994,860
Net income from railroads	$2,478,898
Total income	$6,389,709
Charged off	$2,290,363
5% sinking fund on coal mined	184,552
Net income for year	$3,914,794
Dividends (7%)	2,450,000
Surplus for year carried to profit and loss	$1,464,794

Note.—The surplus at December 31, 1902, is stated to have been $6,670,528, which added to the surplus for the year as above would make $8,135,322. This has been reduced to the figure shown at December 31, 1903, viz., $6,593,154, chiefly by charging off values shown in equipment, new railroad construction, mining plant, washeries, etc., aggregating $1,472,878.
Betterments charged against income for the year amounted to $1,831,000.

Stock.—Authorized $45,000,000, of which $10,000,000 was authorized March 7, 1904. The proceeds are to be used to retire $5,000,000 New York & Canada Railroad bonds maturing May 1, 1904, $344,000 for retirement of C. & Lake Placid bonds, and about

$1,600,000 for standard gauging that road. The balance will be held for similar purposes in the future.

$7,000,000 of this stock has been subscribed for at $135.

The balance sheet shows an asset of $12,607,634 for unmined coal, which has been increased in late years, probably by acquisition of additional property. Just what offset to the reduction of the value of such property from mining operations is not clear, but the plan adopted in 1899, to set aside every year as a sinking fund to retire stock and bonds and guaranteed securities, an amount equal to at least five cents per ton of coal sold, to be charged against income, may answer the question.

Since the resolution, about $150,000 of such stock has been purchased and cancelled each year.

The Delaware & Hudson Company is guarantor of interest and dividends on some $40,000,000 stock and bonds of its controlled roads, which however its rental payments to said companies is fully able to take care of.

Dividends.—1884, 7%; 1885, 6%; 1886, 5%; 1887, 5%; 1888, 6%; 1889 to 1896, 7% yearly; 1897 to 1900, 5% yearly; 1901 to March, 1904, 7% yearly, and fixed for the year at that rate payable quarterly.

Annual meeting, second Tuesday in May. Main office, New York.

Managers.—Robert M. Olyphant, Chauncey M. Depew, John Jacob Astor, E. H. Harriman and twelve others.

DENVER & RIO GRANDE RAILROAD COMPANY.

This company is the outgrowth of a reorganization in 1886, of the D. & R. G. R. R. It is understood to be jointly controlled by the Missouri Pacific Railway Company and the Rockefeller interests.

The road as operated comprises 2,460 miles of track, of which 921 miles is narrow gauge, and 62 miles operated under lease. It also owns the entire capital stock and has assumed the funded debt of the Rio Grande Western, a line extending from Grand Junction to Salt Lake City, Utah.

The line is a very important link in trans-continental traffic, operating a line through the Rocky Mountain range, besides which the local territory reached is the richest mineral country in the United States and productive of high rate traffic.

General balance sheet, June 30, 1903:

Assets.

Cost of road and structures	$114,968,863
Rio Grande Western stock	20,750,000
Equipment	10,343,420
Material and supplies	1,253,060
Agents and conductors	282,925
Individuals and companies	978,130
Securities in treasury and investments	3,218,044
Securities in trust company	9,568,064
Loans and bills receivable	2,800,900
Special renewal fund	451,797
Miscellaneous accounts	158,376
Cash	1,730,530
Total	$166,504,111

Liabilities.

Capital stock:	
Common	$38,000 000
Preferred	44,400,000
Bonds	75,896,100
Renewal fund	451,797
Vouchers	490,584
Pay rolls	763,496
Interest on bonds	1,321,717
Equipment renewal fund	171,761
Improvement fund	242,593
Insurance fund	123,606
Accrued taxes	300,341
Miscellaneous	74,688
Dividends	1,110,450
Profit and loss	3,156,975
Total	$166,504,111

Income account for year ended June 30, 1903:

Earnings:	
Freight	$12,281,492
Passenger	3,827,924
Miscellaneous	1,195,143
	$17,304,559
Expenses:	
Maintenance of way	$1,897,253
Maintenance of structures	396,211
Maintenance of equipment	1,942,914
Conducting transportation	5,770,018
Express expenses	465,604
General expenses	157,849
	$10,629,850
Net earnings	$6,674,709
Other income	209,717
Total income	$6,884,426

Deductions from income:

Interest on bonds	$3,083,404
Taxes and insurance	662,041
Renewal fund	120,000
Betterments, etc	436,797
Miscellaneous rentals	176,420
Total	$4,478,662
Ba'ance, net income for year	$2,405,764
Dividend on preferred stock (5%)	2,220,000
Surplus for year	$185 764

Profit and loss account:

Dr.

Discount on 1st consolidated mortgage bonds sold	$85,000
Discount on R. G. W. 1st consolidated mortgage 4% bonds sold	330,000
Balance June 30, 1903	3,156,975
	$3,571,975

Cr.

Balance June 30, 1902	$3,377,643
Surplus for year ended June 30, 1903	185,764
Old vouchers, etc., closed out	3,836
Sundry adjustments	4,732
	$3,571,975

Stock.—Issued as authorized (see balance sheet).

The preferred is 5% non cumulative.

Funded debt.—The amount of bonds per above balance sheet is made up as follows:

D. & R G. R. R. Co. 1st consolidated mortgage 4%	$33,517,000
D. & R. G. R. R. Co. 1st consolidated mortgage 4½%	6,382,500
D. & R. G. R. R. Co. Improvement mortgage 5%	8,120,000
R. G. W. Ry. Co. 1st trust mortgage 4%	15,200,000
R. G. W. Ry. Co. 1st consolidated mortgage 4%	12,676,600
Total	$75,896,100

Dividends since 1891 have been as follows: 1893, 2%; 1896 and 1897, 2%; 1898, 2½%; 1899 and 1900, 4%; 1901, 1902 and 1903, 5%; and January 1904, 2½%.

Whilst the net earnings for 1903 were slightly less than during the previous year, due entirely to increased expenses, both such years show a marked advance over earnings for 1900 and 1899, being about 60 and 70% respectively.

Percentage of expenses to earnings for past years has been as follows: 1903, 61.42; 1902, 60.64; 1901, 62.20; 1900, 63.30.

Annual meeting.—Third Tuesday in October.

Main office.—Denver, Colorado.

Directors.—George J. Gould, M. L. Scheff, E. H. Harriman, etc., etc.

DETROIT SOUTHERN RAILROAD COMPANY.

Formed under the laws of Michigan in 1891 and acquired the Detroit & Lima Northern and Ohio Southern Railroads through foreclosure.

The road operates from Detroit to Ironton, via Lima, and including 43 miles of trackage, comprises 432 miles of track, of which 362 miles are owned.

It has also about 120 miles of yard tracks, sidings and mine tracks. The line reaches into the bituminous fields of southern Ohio.

General balance sheet, June 30, 1903:

Assets.

Cost of road and equipment	$25,634,600
Cash in treasury	47,677
Agents, U. S. P. O., etc	140,992
Traffic balances	52,060
Individuals and companies	36,466
Material and supplies	45,824
Ohio Southern Division treasury bonds	28,000
Total	$25,985,620

Liabilities.

Common stock	$10,500,000
Preferred stock	6,500,000
Bonds and car trust notes	8,700,233
Accounts payable	102,920
Pay rolls	57,391
Interest and taxes accrued	91,597
Traffic balances	11,008
Miscellaneous accounts	1,624
Profit and loss	20,846
Total	$25,985,620

Income and profit and loss account for year ended and at June 30, 1903:

Earnings:

Freight	$1,116,231
Passenger	180,302
Mail	23,333
Express	15,402
Miscellaneous	109,631
Gross earnings	$1,444,899

Expenses:

Maintenance of way and structures	$204,588
Maintenance of equipment	231,339
Conducting transportation	611,386
General expenses	42,620
Total expenses	$1,089,934
Net earnings	$354,965

Deduct:

Taxes	$54,000
Interest on funded debt	288,673
Total	**$342,673**
Net income	$12,291
Profit and loss balance June 30. 1902	9,245
Total	**$21,536**
Ohio Southern claims prior July 1, 1901	690
Profit and loss June 30, 1903	**$20,846**

Capital stock.—In addition to that shown in above balance sheet, which was the full amount authorized at date thereof, there was authorized July 21, 1903, an increase of $16,000,000 common and $1,000,000 preferred.

Cost of road and equipment has been increased during the year in the sum of $2,273,573, for cost of Iron Railway and additions to equipment. The funds were provided by the sale of treasury stock, which realized from 20½ to 21⅞ for the common, and 39⅝ to 41⅜ for the preferred.

Earnings show substantial improvement over the previous year, although expenses due to the higher prices of labor and material have more than kept pace, but in spite of an increased percentage of expenses, the increased volume of business has resulted as shown above in a surplus of $12,292, against a deficit in the previous year of $73,204.

No dividends paid.

Bonded debt.—Authorized, $14,500,000; outstanding, $8,110,000; in addition to which there is $590,233.91 car trust notes payable at the rate of about $120,000 per annum.

Annual meeting.—Last Monday in October.

Main office.—Detroit.

Directors.—Otto T. Bannard, Simon Borg, John E. Borne, Evans R. Dick, Don M. Dickinson, Samuel Hunt, Cyrus J. Lawrence, Frederick J. Lisman, Wm. C. McMillan, T. D. Rhodes, A. B. Voorhees, Leopold Wallach, Benjamin S. Warren.

DULUTH, SOUTH SHORE & ATLANTIC RAILWAY COMPANY.

CONTROLLED BY THE CANADIAN PACIFIC RAILWAY COMPANY.

This company purchased the Detroit, Mackinac & Marquette Road, which was sold under foreclosure proceedings in 1886, and in the same year acquired the stock of the Marquette, Houghton & Ontonagon Company, which it first leased, but subsequently purchased in 1890.

The road operates 573 miles between Duluth and Sault Ste. Marie, all of which, with the exception of about 10 miles, it owns.

General balance sheet, June 30, 1903:

Assets.

Road and equipment	$45,424,115
Mackinac Transportation Company	237,372
Lake Superior T. & T. Ry.	22,242
Lake Mich. & L. S. Ry.	7,662
Mineral Range Railway	474,795
Ste. Marie Union Depot Company	56,018
Western Express Company	25,000
Current accounts and miscellaneous	435,409
Materials	225,197
Profit and loss	1,970,417
Total	$48,878,227

Liabilities.

Common stock	$12,000,000
Preferred stock	10,000,000
Bonds	23,000,000
Contracts	295,111
Canadian Pacific Railway, guaranteed interest advance	2,383,555
Canadian Pacific Railway, general account	198,013
South Shore Land Company	115,994
M., H. & O. lands	13,374
Bills payable	16,000
Current accounts	432,682
Accrued interest and taxes	423,497
Total	$48,878,227

Income and profit and loss account for year ended and at June 30, 1903:

Earnings:

Merchandise freight	$1,339,560
Iron ore freight	259,549
Passenger	993,879
Mail, express, etc.	179,146
Gross earnings	$2,772,135

Expenses:

Maintenance of way and structures.............................	$433.516
Maintenance of equipment	236,446
Conducting transportation	1,001,693
General expenses...	86,435
Total expenses...	$1,758,090
Net earnings...	$1,014,045
Other income..........................	14,665
Total income......................	$1,028,710
Interest on bonds...	$859,700
Taxes..	200,214
Total....................	$1,059,914
Deficit..	31,204
Balance forward..	1,939,213
Profit and loss deficit June 30, 1903..............................	$1,970,417

Stock.—Fully issued as authorized. The preferred is 6% non-cumulative.

Bonds.—All owned by the Canadian Pacific Railway, which company guarantees interest.

With a slight increase in passenger business the gross returns for the year are about the same as the year 1902. The net results, however, are about $10,000 short of the showing for that year. This is more than accounted for from the fact that $36,717 was spent on bridge improvements for the year 1903, as compared with only $16,073 in 1902.

Fifty per cent. of the freight traffic consists of ores.

Annual meeting.—Third Thursday in September.

Main office.—Marquette, Mich.

President.—W. F. Fitch, Marquette, Mich.

ERIE RAILROAD COMPANY.

A New York corporation of 1895, formed to succeed the New York, Lake Erie & Western.

The company operates 2,152 miles of railroad, and controls, but does not operate, 165 miles additional.

With numerous branches, especially into the coal regions of Pennsylvania, the line extends from Hoboken, opposite New York City, to Cleveland, Chicago and Dayton, Ohio.

Of the mileage operated the company owns either outright or through ownership of the entire capital stock, 1,644 miles, controls a majority of the stock in 157 miles, and leases 351 miles.

The company also controls by stock ownership the New York, Susquehanna & Western R. R., is owner of the Union Steamboat Co., and controls large coal properties, including the entire capital stock of the Pennsylvania Coal Co. and controlling interests in the Hillsdale Coal & Iron Co., Blossburg Coal Co., etc.

General balance sheet, June 30, 1903 :

Assets.

Cost of road and equipment	$350,548,002
Miscellaneous securities owned	7,630,710
New York, Susquehanna & Western capital stock :	
Preferred	6,262,400
Common	5,748,900
Materials and supplies	2,724,080
Securities in trust for insurance fund	500,000
Chicago & Western Ind. sinking fund	13,034
Cash with trustees of sinking fund	1,005
Pennsylvania collateral trust bonds, redeemed	378,789
Line traffic association and agency	53,968
Due from subsidiary companies	1,271,554
Insurance and expenses paid in advance	35,745
Cash on hand and in transit	8,305,643
Due from agents	805,583
Due from U. S. Government	119,348
Due from individuals and companies	1,252,156
Total	$385,650,920

Liabilities.

Capital stock:	
1st preferred	$47,892,400
2nd preferred	16,000,000
Common	112,378,900
Bonded debt:	
Erie Railroad Co	145,470,600
Leased lines	23,960,500
Chicago & Erie	12,300,000
Construction obligations	566,701
Mortgage on real estate	770,850
Equipment trusts	5,959,224
Interest and rentals accrued, not due	1,654,347
Dividend on 1st preferred payable August 31	957,848
Reserve funds	1,829,668
Accrued Pennsylvania Coal Co. sinking fund	550,336
Interest and rentals due	1,962,121
Pay roll	1,750,399
Audited vouchers	1,451,233
Due connecting lines	550,650
Profit and loss	9,645,143
Total	$385,650,920

Income and profit and loss account for year ended and at June 30, 1903:

Earnings :

Freight	$21,690,503
Coal	11,384,421
Passenger	8,021,892
Mail	472,479
Express	811,035
Rents	130,178
Miscellaneous	998,630

Earnings R. R.	$43,509,139
Other operations	2,321,274

Gross earnings	$45,830,413

Expenses:

Maintenance of way and structures	$3,652,914
Maintenance of equipment	5,728,761
Conducting transportation	16,291,666
General expenses	952,397
Taxes	971,770

Expenses R. R.	$27,597,508
Other operations	2,328,250

Total	$29,925,758

Net earnings	$15,904,654
Income from securities owned	1,430,230

Total income	17,334,885
Deduct—Interest and rentals	8,901,618

Net income	$8,433,266

Deduct :

Addition and improvements	$808,451
Dividends on preferred stock	1,676,234

Total	$2,484,685

Surplus	$5,948,580
Deduct for amount credited to fund for additions, etc	1,569,404

Balance to credit of profit and loss	$4,379,176
Profit and loss balance forward	5,265,966

Profit and loss June 30, 1903	$9,645,142

Increase in gross earnings for the year is shown to be 12.07% over the year ended June 30, 1902, and the net earnings 22.65% increase. The percentage of expenses to earnings decreased in the same period 2.99%.

Notwithstanding the fact that anthracite coal represents about 25% of the freight transported, and that by reason of the coal strike, this industry was closed during the first four months of the operating year, only 1.59% less was transported.

This commodity therefore netted a much increased tonnage during the remaining eight months than for a similar previous period.

Thus the increased traffic is seen to have been entirely with other business than hard coal, indicating a very heavy development along other lines. This is found to have been chiefly in bituminous coal.

Passenger earnings increased 5.01% over the same period.

Capital stock.—1st preferred, authorized, $48,000,000 ; outstanding, $47,892,400, is 4% non-cumulative.

2nd preferred, $16,000,000, issued as authorized, is 4% non-cumulative.

Common, $113,000,000, authorized ; issued, $112,378,900.

Prior to May 1st, 1904, the stock was lodged with a voting trust, the members of which were associated with the firm of Messrs. J. P. Morgan & Co. This voting trust expired under the terms of its limitations, which were contingent upon payment of dividends for a specified time on the first preferred stock. The property consequently is now in the hands of its stockholders and it is not believed that any individual interest has sufficient of the stock for control. It has been reported that Mr. E. H. Harriman and his associates are large holders.

Dividends.—1st preferred, 1½%, August 30, 1901 ; in 1902, 3%, (F. and A); in 1903, February, 1½%; August, 2% ; in 1904, February, 2%.

Annual meeting.—Second Tuesday in October.

Main office.—New York.

Directors.—Chas. Steele, J. J. Goodwin, John G. McCullough, D. O. Mills, Alexander E. Orr, F. D. Underwood, Samuel Spencer, Francis Lynde Stetson, J. Lowber Welsh, J. J. Hill, Norman B. Ream, H. McK Twombly, E. H. Harriman, William B. Lane and Louis L. Stanton.

GENERAL ELECTRIC COMPANY.

Incorporated under the laws of New York April 15, 1892 under a special charter, for the purpose of combining the interests of the Edison, the Thomson-Houston, and other electrical manufacturing plants.

It owns the Edison and other patents for electric lighting in the United States and abroad; also United States rights to manufacture Curtis steam turbines.

The business consists of granting rights, under its patents, for lighting and heating to local companies, and manufacturing electrical supplies, the Schenectady plant being one of the largest of its kind in the world.

The Westinghouse Electric Manufacting Company uses a number of its patents; in fact, it is understood that the patents of the two companies are pooled for joint use.

A controlling interest in the British Thomson-Houston Company, Ltd., of London, England, was acquired in 1901, and in February, 1903, all but a small amount of the capital stock of the Stanley Electric Manufacturing Company was secured.

General balance sheet, January 31, 1903:

Assets.

Factory plants	$5,000,000
Patents. franchises. and good will	2,000,000
Merchandise inventories:	
Factories	10,297,595
General and local offices	1,165,921
Consignments	97,700
Cash	3,632,556
Stocks and bonds	12,682,214
Real estate	431,456
Notes and accounts receivable	12,816,607
Work in progress	1,769,456
Total	$49,893,507

Liabilities.

Capital stock	$41,880,733
5% gold coupon debentures	99,000
3½% gold coupon debentures	2,049,400
Accrued interest on debentures	825
Accounts payable	1,378,960
Unclaimed dividends	1,886
Surplus	4,482,702
Total	$49,893,507

Income and profit and loss account for year ended and at
January 31, 1903:

Sales		$26,685,598
Royalties		814,959
Gross income		$37,500,557
Cost of sales		28,844,881
Net earnings		$8,655,676
Additions to income:		
Dividends and interest on securities owned		393,961
Interest and discount		253,883
Profit on sale of stocks and bonds		973,650
Total income		$10,277,170
Interest on debentures		44,531
Net income for year		$10,232,639
Deduct:		
Dividends		$2,677,264
Deduction from patent account, chiefly account Sprague patents.		1,613,880
Total		$4,291,144
Surplus for year		$5,941,495
Surplus January 31, 1902		15,287,141
Total		$21,228,636
Stock issued in restoring percentage of reduction made in 1898		16,746,134
Surplus January 31, 1903, per balance sheet		$4,482,502

Stock.--Authorized January 31, 1903, $42,031,600 ; outstanding,
$41,880,733. At January 31, 1902, the stock outstanding was $24,-
910,900. During the year $223,900 was issued in exchange for
debentures, and $16,745,933.33 was issued to restore the 40%
reduction made in 1898.

Orders received and net earnings for past years :

Year ended January 31.	Orders.	Net earnings.
1897	$11,170,319	$2,120,441
1898	14,382,342	2,148,520
1899	17,431,327	4,166,325
1900	26,323,626	5,832,464
1901	27,969,541	6,244,439
1902	34,350,840	8,598,241
1903	39,944,454	8,655,676

During the past year the orders received included generators
and rotary convertors, railway motors, transformers, stationery
motors and arc lamps.

A marked increase in the displacement by electric motors of
steam and hydraulic auxiliaries in mills, mines and steamships is

reported, and after the fullest tests the Interborough Rapid Transit Company of New York City placed with the General Electric Company contract for all control equipment for their cars. Thirty-one other electric lines located in the principal cities of the United States and England are equipped or have contracted for this company's controller devices for their cars.

Dividends.—July 15, 1899, to July, 1900, 6% per annum; October, 1900, to April, 1904, inclusive, 8% in quarterly payments, excepting 1901, when 1% extra was paid in the January quarter.

Annual report.—Second Tuesday in May.

Main office.—Schenectady, N. Y.

Directors.— J. Pierpont Morgan, Eugene Griffin, George Foster Peabody, J. P. Ord, Charles Steele, C. A. Coffin, T. Jefferson Coolidge, Jr.; H. L Higginson, Oliver Ames, R. T. Paine, Gordon Abbott, George P. Gardner, Frederick P. Fish.

THE HOCKING VALLEY RAILWAY COMPANY.

A corporation formed in 1899 under the laws of Ohio to take over the property of the Columbus, Hocking Valley & Toledo Railway.

The company owns a line from Pomeroy, O., to Walbridge, O., has trackage rights from Walbridge to Toledo, and with branches operates a total mileage of 347 miles, all but 6 miles of which is owned by the company. It also controls, through stock ownership, the Toledo & Ohio Central, which road is operated separately. The road owns about 24,000 acres of coal lands. About 60% of the company's business is from the bituminous coal trade.

General balance sheet, June 30, 1903 :

Assets.

Road and equipment	$32,325,229
Kan & M. equipment notes	1,331,229
Securities owned	14,575,201
Cash for construction and equipment	479,258
Materials and supplies	242,143
Cash (including in transit and for coupons)	770,945
Bills receivable	1,590,000
Roads, individuals and companies	887,071
Other accounts	337,136
	$52,538,212

Liabilities.

Common stock	$11,000,000
Preferred stock	15,000,000
Mortgage bonds	17,642,000
Car Trust obligations	2,931.162
Deferred payments for securities	876,404
Roads, individuals and companies	401,480
Interest and dividends due	737,109
Bills receivable, discounted	270,000
Accrued interest	116,207
Miscellaneous	333,549
Profit and loss	3,230,300
	$52,538,212

Income and profit and loss account for year ended and at June 30, 1903 :

Earnings:

Coal	$2,778,248
Freight	1,973,343
Passenger	786,300
Mail	40,653
Express	41,836
Miscellaneous	429,317
Gross earnings	$6,049,699

Expenses :

Maintenance of way, etc.	606,364
Maintenance of equipment	1,120,778
Conducting transportation	1,812,514
General	117,709
Taxes	181,161
Operating expenses and taxes	$3,838,526

Net earnings	$2,211,172

Additions to income:

Income from securities	$207,614
Net income sub. companies	420,530
Miscellaneous income	58,717
Total	$686,861

Total income	$2,898,033

Deductions from income:

Interest on funded debt	$872,576
Interest on unfunded debt	103,763
Lease rentals	24.699
Net deficit sub. companies	72,797
Miscellaneous	20,100
Total	$1,093,935

Surplus for year	1,804,098
Dividends on common stock (3%)	$321,324
Dividends on preferred stock (4%)	560,000
Balance to profit and loss	$922,774
Profit and loss balance forward	2,307,526
Profit and loss June 30, 1903	$3,230,300

Capital stock.—Issued as authorized (see balance sheet).

The preferred is 4% non-cumulative, but after both classes of stock receive 4% in any year they share alike.

The company may retire the preferred at par.

Dividends (J. & J.).—Preferred—1900, 3½%; 1901 to January, 1904, 4% yearly.

Common—July, 1901, to January, 1904, 3% yearly.

The controlling interest in the common stock, which had been deposited with J. P. Morgan with authority to sell for some time past, was sold in June, 1903, to five important railroad companies at $103 per share above all expenses.

There was issued by J. P. Morgan & Co. $7,270,410 three-year 5% gold participation certificates, due June 28, 1906, interest payable J. & D., secured by the stock acquired.

Net earnings show a steady increase during the past few years, those of 1903 being 10% increase over 1902, in spite of the fact that large expenditures were made and charged to operating expenses for maintenance of equipment, and average charges made for maintenance of way.

Annual meeting.—First Tuesday in October.

Main office.—Columbus, O.

Directors.—Charles B. Alexander, Robert Bacon, R. M. Gallaway, Thomas F. Ryan, Charles Steele, and seven others.

ILLINOIS CENTRAL RAILROAD COMPANY.

This line was chartered in 1851, and pays the State of Illinois 7% of the gross earnings of the 706 miles of line owned.

The system operated reaches from Chicago to New Orleans, Chicago to Council Bluffs, Iowa, and Memphis to Louisville, Ky., which together with numerous branches make up a total mileage of 4,301 miles. Of this mileage 706 miles are owned, 1,322 miles are consolidated with the Illinois Central by authorization of the stockholders, and 2,273 miles are leased lines.

General balance sheet, June 30, 1903 :

Assets.

Road and equipment..	$175,320,981
Real estate...	312,136
Material and supplies...	2,208,097
Stocks owned...	6,601,388
Bonds owned..	42,624,300
Net assets, (excess of cash and accounts receivable over accounts etc. payable)..	6,563,602
Advances..	6,786,514
Insurance fund...	1,480,540
Surplus dividend fund...	1,178,187
Pension fund	250,000
Total...	$243,325,744

Liabilities.

Capital stock..	$95,040,000
Leased line stock..	10,000,000
Bonds (I. C. R. R.)..	112,969,525
Bonds (C. S & L. & N. O. R. R.)	16,234,000
Betterment fund...	161,332
Insurance fund..	1,480,540
Set apart for dividend...	2,851,200
Surplus dividend fund..	1,178,187
Pension fund..	250,000
Profit and loss..	3,160,960
Total...	$243,325,744

Income and profit and loss account for year ended and at June 30, 1903 :

Earnings :

Passenger...	$8,977,228
Freight...	30,592,094
Mail, express, etc...	5,616,754
Gross earnings..	$45,186,077

Expenses:

Maintenance of way and structures......................................	$5,909,196
Maintenance of equipment	6,274,587
Conducting transportation	16,676,332
General expenses	975,769
Taxes	1,862,072
Total expenses and taxes.....	$31,697,956

Net earnings..	$13,488,121

Additions to income :

Interest, etc..	$3,445,318
Land office...	15,830
	$16,949,269

Deductions from income :

Interest and rentals	$6,319,877
Betterments	4,881,253
Total	$11,201,130
Surplus for year	$5,748,139
Dividends	5,702,400
Balance to profit and loss	$45,739
Profit and loss balance forward	3,115,221
Profit and loss June 30, 1903	$3,160,960

Stocks.—Issued as authorized.

The special or " Leased Line Stock " is entitled to 4%.

Dividends.—Common stock, 1886, 7½%; 1887, 7%; 1888, 7%; 1889, 5½%; 1890, 6%; 1891 to 1899, 5% yearly; 1900, 5½%; 1901 to March, 1904, 6% yearly. Payable semi-annually March and September.

Statistics:

Year.	Net earnings.	Surplus for year.	Betterments charged against income.	Dividends.
1899-00	$9,742,571	$40,600	$2,416,674	$3,300,000
1900-01	11,058,668	42,260	2,895,400	3,780,000
1901-02	12,806 690	43,961	4,340,172	4,752,000
1902-03	13,488,121	45,739	4,881,253	5,702,400

The change in amounts paid for dividends is due to increase in capital stock during the years above reviewed. It will be noted that after providing for dividends, every dollar available was expended for betterments, a policy which should strengthen the value of the property and greatly increase its earning capacity.

Annual meeting.—Third Wednesday in October.

Main office.—Chicago.

Directors.—Walter Luttgen, John W. Auchincloss, J. T. Harahan, Charles M. Beach, Cornelius Vanderbilt, Stuyvesant Fish, E. H. Harriman, John Jacob Astor, Charles A. Peabody, John C. Welling, W. Morton Grinnell, R. W. Goelet and Hon. Richard Yates.

INTERNATIONAL MERCANTILE MARINE COMPANY.

A New Jersey corporation formed in the year 1893, under the name of the International Navigation Company. The present title was adopted in 1902.

The old company owned the American and Red Star Lines of ocean steamships, and in 1902, under the new name and with increased capital absorbed the principal lines engaged in the transatlantic traffic.

It also has an agreement with the German lines and with the Harland & Wolff Shipbuilding Company of Belfast, Ireland, practically controlling the output of their works in the interest of the combine on a basis of cost, plus 5%, on new ships; 10% on new machinery in old ships, and 15% on repairs, thus insuring maintenance at a minimum cost.

Lines owned:

White Star,	Leyland,
American,	Atlantic Transport,
Red Star,	Dominion,

besides which a large interest is understood to be held in the Holland-American Line.

Capitalization.—The capital stock authorized is $60,000,000 6% cumulative preferred and $60,000,000 common, limited to 10% dividends as long as there are outstanding any debentures.

Bonded debt.—Authorized, $75,000,000 4½% collateral trust debenture bonds, due October 1, 1922; amount outstanding, $50,-000,000; interest, A. & O.; subject to call after 1907 at 105% and interest.

Of the capital stock $12,000,000 common and $5,400,000 preferred are in the treasury.

Dividends.—None have been paid. The stock is dealt in on the New York Curb Market.

Main office.—New York.

Executive committee.—C. A. Griscom, P. A. B. Widener, E. J. Berwind, Chas. Steele, George W. Perkins.

INTERNATIONAL PAPER COMPANY.

A New York corporation formed in 1898, and took over 28 mills in New York and the New England States, having a combined capacity of about 80% of the wood pulp production of the country. It also owns about 1,000,000 acres of woodland contiguous to the mills.

The product is chiefly consumed by the newspapers, although bags and wrapping paper are also largely manufactured.

General balance sheet, June 30, 1903:

Assets.

Mills and plants	$41,925,446
Woodlands	4,015,044
Securities of sundry companies	5,621,487
Land rights and water powers	104,727
Patents	12,000
Furniture and fixtures	37,003
Cash	848,605
Accounts and notes receivable	4,492,611
Inventory merchandise on hand, etc	3,696,955
Total	$60,753,878

Liabilities.

Common stock	$17,442,800
Preferred stock	22,406,700
First mortgage bonds	9,866,000
Divisional mortgage bonds	3,023,000
Notes and accounts payable	2,405,637
Accrued interest, taxes, etc	350,568
Surplus	5,259,173
Total	$60,753,878

Income and profit and loss account for year ended and at June 30, 1903:

Gross income	$20,142,771
Cost of raw materials, manufacturing, etc	16,529 310
Net earnings	$3,613,461
Taxes, insurance, etc	1,082,927
Net income	$2.530,534
Dividends on preferred (6%)	1,344,402
Surplus for year	$1,186,132
Previous balance	4,073,041
Profit and loss surplus June 30, 1903	$5,259,173

Surplus from operations of the past four years are as under :

1899–00..	$939.172
1900–01.	1,709,988
1901–02.	553,053
1902–03.	1,186,152

Over $1,000,000 is said to have been expended in repairs and improvements and charged against income during the past year.

Stock.	Authorized.	Issued.
Common.	$20,000,000	$17,442,800
Preferred	25,000,000	22,406,700

The preferred is 6% cumulative (quarterly, J., A., J. & O.), and may be increased $10,000,000 to retire the company's bonds.

Bonds.—First consolidated 6% mortgage, $10,000,000, which are convertible into preferred stock.

Dividends.—Preferred—July, 1898, to April, 1904, inclusive, 6% yearly.

Common—1% in December, 1898 ; 2% in 1899 ; none since.

Dividends on common were passed to create a larger working capital.

Annual meeting.—Fourth Wednesday in August.

Main office.—Corinth, N. Y.

Officers.—President, Hugh J. Chisholm ; 1st Vice-President, F. H. Parks ; 2d Vice-President, T. T. Waller ; Treasurer, A. N. Burbank ; Secretary, E. W. Hyde.

LOUISVILLE & NASHVILLE RAILROAD COMPANY.

This line was chartered in 1850, and the line between Louisville and Nashville opened for business in 1859. The road has been extended from time to time until it now consists of 5,530 miles, extending from Cincinnati to Louisville and St. Louis to New Orleans, thence eastward to the Florida line, together with branches throughout the more populous sections along its main lines.

Of this total the L. & N. owns 3,335 miles. 1,920 miles are operated separately, and 275 miles are leased to other companies. The lines operated separately include the Nashville,

Chattanooga & St. Louis, the Georgia Railroad and the Atlanta, Knoxville & Northern.

Control of the property was acquired in November, 1902, by the Atlantic Coast Line.

General balance sheet, June 30, 1903 :

Assets.

Road and equipment	$123,355.252
Timber lands, etc	1,079,566
Stocks owned	7,800,269
Bonds owned	5,023,426
Stocks and bonds in trust	25,012,612
Bills and accounts receivable, individuals and companies and agents	2.830,473
Material, fuel, etc	4,311,065
Cash	1,911.724
Advances to sub companies	4.728.816
Improvements and betterments	2,638.665
Miscellaneous	2,515,406
Total	**$181,207,274**

Liabilities.

Stock	$60,000,000
Bonded debt	104,287.321
Interest and rents	1.954.577
Dividends	1.563,582
Individuals and companies	529.296
Pay rolls, vouchers, etc	3,613.741
Reserve fund	39,304
Miscellaneous	926.743
Profit and loss	8.292,710
Total	**$181,207,274**

Income and profit and loss account for year ended and at June 30, 1903 :

Earnings :

Freight	$26.578,620
Passenger	7.044,087
Mail	791,991
Express	703.596
Miscellaneous	331,084
Gross earnings	$35,449,378

Expenses :

Transportation	$12,449.169
Maintenance of way, etc	5,344,161
Maintenance of equipment	5,320,072
General	857,410
Total expenses	$23.970,812

Net earnings	$11,478.565
Income from investments	1,122,493
Total income	$12,601,058

Deductions :

Taxes	$844,474
Interest on bonds	4,845,033
Other interest	73,112
Rents	265,931
Sinking fund	144,400
To S. & N. A.	89,905
Miscellaneous	127,155
Total	$6,390,010
Net income	$6,211,048
Dividends (5%)	3,000,000
Surplus for year	$3,211,048
Profit and loss balance forward*	5,081,662
Profit and loss June 30, 1903	$8,292,710

*The profit and loss balance at June 30, 1902, was $7,723,682, against which has been charged for discount on various bond issues accumulated since 1894, $2,701,472.60, and sundry adjustments reducing same as above.

Stock.—Issued as authorized, (see balance sheet above).

Dividends (F. & A.)—Dividends were suspended from August, 1893, until February, 1899, when same were resumed at the rate of 3% yearly. In August, however, 2% was paid, making 3½% for the year. In 1900 4% was paid, and from 1901 to the first half year in 1904, the rate of 5% yearly has been maintained.

Statistics :

Year.	Miles operated.	Surplus for year after dividend.	Per cent. of expenses to earnings.	Average train load. Tons.	Rate per ton per mile.
1899-00	3,007	$1,507,237	67.06	239	0758 cts.
1900-01	3,169	1,586,114	65.07	222	0769
1901-02	3,327	1,850,309	68.06	231	0741
1902-03	3,439	3,211,048	67.62	231	0779

Annual meeting.—First Wednesday in October.

Main office.—Louisville, Ky.

Officers.—Chairman, Henry Walters ; President, M. H. Smith ; 2d Vice-President, A. W. Morris.

Directors.—August Belmont, W. G. Raoul, Walter G. Oakman, John J. Waterbury, R. G. Erwin, etc., etc.

MANHATTAN RAILWAY COMPANY.

(LEASED TO INTERBOROUGH RAPID TRANSIT COMPANY.)

Incorporated under the laws of New York in 1875. Owns and operates all the elevated railways in the Boroughs of Manhattan and The Bronx, New York City, having a total mileage of 37 miles.

In January, 1903, the road was leased for 999 years to the Interborough Rapid Transit Company upon the terms of a guaranteed dividend of 6%, and 1% extra if earned, until January 1, 1906, after which 7% is guaranteed.

The capital stock authorized is $60,000,000, of which $55,200,000 has been issued.

The Interborough Rapid Transit Company was organized principally to maintain and operate the Rapid Transit Railroad, a subway now being constructed by the City of New York the entire length of the Island of Manhattan, which has been leased for a term of 50 years, with the privilege of a renewal for a further term of 25 years, and which it will shortly commence to operate.

The income for the past three years ended June 30 was as follows:

	1902-3.	1901-2.	1900-1.
Gross earnings	$12,208,337	$10,665,911	$9,416,888
Operating expenses	5,460,794	5,518,585	5,253,230
Net earnings	$6,747,543	$5,147,326	$4,163,658
Other income	346,859	625,800	836,384
Total income	$7,094,402	$5,773,126	$5,000,042
Fixed charges	2,820,859	2,699,671	2,677,706
Balance	$4,273,544	$3,073,455	$2,322,335
Dividends	(6¾) 3,546,000	(4) 1,920,000	(4) 1,920,000
Surplus for year	$727,544	$1,153,455	$402,335

Bonds.—The consolidated mortgage is limited on the present mileage to $40,000,000.

Dividends.—Payable quarterly, January—5½%, 1889; 1890 to 1896, 6% yearly; 1897, 4½%; 1898 to 1902, 4%; 1903 to date, 7%.

Annual meeting.—Second Wednesday in November.

Main office.—New York.

Directors.—Russell Sage, R. M. Gallaway, Edwin Gould
George J. Gould, Samuel Sloan, G. P. Morosini, Donald MacKay
Howard Gould, Thomas T. Eckert, James H. Hyde, John T. Terry
Alfred Skitt, Eugene Foss.

METROPOLITAN SECURITIES COMPANY.

Incorporated under the Business Corporation Law of New York
in February, 1902, which enables the company to acquire securi
ties of all classes of transportation corporations, including surface
elevated and underground, and of those furnishing electrica
power.

It has acquired all the stock of the New York City Railway—
the successor to the Interurban Street Railway Company—so far
issued, which company in turn leases the Metropolitan Stree
Railway. This latter company is made the subject of a specia
report herein.

The stock of Metropolitan Securities Company is authorized
and issued, $30,000,000.

The Metropolitan Street Railway is leased to the Interurban
which guarantees dividends of 7% on the entire capital stock, and
has assumed its fixed charges.

The Securities Company has also acquired all the stock of the
People's Traction Company and the New York, Westchester &
Connecticut Company, and its combined holdings give it contro
of practically all the surface lines on the Island of Manhattan.

Main office.—New York.

Directors.—Herbert H. Vreeland, William H. Baldwin, Jr.; Ed
ward J. Berwind, Paul D. Cravath, Thomas P. Fowler, George G
Haven, James H. Hyde, August D. Juilliard, Richard W. Meade
Thomas F. Ryan, Edward W. Sayre, Mortimer L. Schiff.

METROPOLITAN STREET RAILWAY COMPANY.

A New York corporation of 1903. The franchise is perpetual. The company operates practically all the surface car lines in the borough of Manhattan, New York City, amounting to a total of 435 miles of track.

It is considered that under certain conditions the Metropolitan Street Railway Company might become bidders for any new subway line that the Commission might decide to build.

The property is leased to the New York City Railway, the successor to the Interurban Street Railway Company, for 999 years, which company guarantees 7% dividends annually on its stock and has assumed its fixed charges.

The stock of the New York City is all held by the Metropolitan Securities Company.

Stocks.—Authorized and issued $52,000,000.

Dividends.—From 1894 to 1898 inclusive. 5%, and 7% since.

From the Interurban balance sheet below, the resources of the company guaranteeing to continue such rate on the Metropolitan stock may be seen, and its capacity to do so may be judged from the 1903 income account also shown.

Consolidated general balance sheet June 30, 1903, of Interurban Street Railway Company, lessee of the Metropolitan Street Railway Company :

Assets.

Construction, equipment, leases and franchises...................	$141,239,201
Additions and betterments, leased lines...........................	21,376,239
Investments............................	4,125,369
Materials and supplies..	1,034. 144
Current assets..	3,873.755
Metropolitan Securities Co. subscription to Interurban Street Railway Company's securities....................................	10,202.000
Dividends accrued on stocks owned	13,894
Prepaid insurance, rentals, etc..................................	286,153
Total assets..	$182,150,754

Liabilities.

Capital stock...	$67,582,100
Funded debt...	88,097,000
Interurban Street Railway Company, 10 year notes................	3,465,000
Real estate mortgages..	950,000
Metropolitan Securities Company, securities due under subscription	12,132,500
Current liabilities...	3,519,490
Accrued interest, taxes, etc.....................................	1,981,161
Profit and loss..	4,423,503
Total liabilities..	$182,150,754

Income account for year ended June 30, 1903, Interurban Street Railway Company:

Gross earnings :

Metropolitan lines...	$16,178,563
Third Avenue lines	5,370,982
	$21,549,545

Operating expenses :

Metropolitan lines	$7,806,318
Third Avenue lines	3,582,791
	$11,389,109

Net earnings	$10,160,436

Income from other sources :

Metropolitan lines	$248,599
Third Avenue lines	324,809
Total	$573,408

Total income	$10,733,844

Deductions from income Metropolitan lines :

Rentals of leased lines, etc	$3,715,964
Interest on $11,000,000 Metropolitan 4% bonds	431,444
Cross-town earnings due minority, etc	11,305
Taxes	952,791

Third Avenue lines :

Interest on funded debt	$2,027,000
Taxes	227 684
Total deductions	$7,366,188

Balance	$3,367,656
Guaranteed dividend 7% on Metropolitan stock, (net)	3,639,791
Deficit for year ended June 30, 1903	$272,135

The fixed charges for the year increased $431,444 for interest upon $11,000,000 increase in Metropolitan Street Railway bonds issued, which will more than account for the deficit above. The improvements made possible by this additional fund should be productive of increased earning capacity in the future.

Annual meeting.—First Monday in December.

Main office.—New York.

Directors.—H. H. Vreeland, P. A. B. Widener, W. L. Elkins, Thomas Dolan, D. B. Hasbrouck, Milton G. Starrett, Richard W. Mead, Henry A. Robinson, D. C. Moorehead.

MEXICAN CENTRAL RAILWAY COMPANY, LIMITED.

This is the principal railroad in Mexico, but is a Massachusetts corporation, formed under the laws of that State in 1880.

The line extends from Ciudad Juarez, opposite El Paso, Texas, to the City of Mexico, through the centre of the State, with two lines extending eastward to Tampico, on the Gulf of Mexico, besides numerous branches.

A subsidy was acquired from the Mexican Government of some $15,000 per mile.

The mileage owned and operated at January 1, 1903, was 2,898 miles.

The company operates under some disadvantage in the matter of its funded obligations, which, being largely held in the United States, are payable in gold, whereas the company receives its remuneration for services in Mexican money.

General balance sheet, December 31, 1902 (U. S. Currency):

Assets.

Construction and equipment	$164,612,747
Equipment and collateral trusts	2,014,529
Materials, fuel and supplies	714,018
Mexican Government bonds deposited as a guarantee	31,115
Tampico Harbor Company 1st mortgage bonds	1,991,285
Accounts receivable	780,429
Cash in banks and on hand	1,609,489
Subsidy trust fund assets in hands of trustee	8,041,146
Total	$179,794,761

Liabilities.

Capital stock	$47,962,100
Priority bonds, 5%	5,597,000
Consolidated mortgage 4% bonds	66,678,000
1st mortgage bonds not converted	275,000
1st mortgage scrip exchangeable	11,052
Coupon notes and scrip (interest ceased)	700
1st consolidated income bonds	20,527,000
1st consolidated income bond scrip	36,400
2d consolidated income bonds	11,282,000
Registered income bonds scrip	367,200
5% equipment and collateral gold bonds:	
1st series	750,000
2d series	850,000
Collateral trust 4½% bonds, 1st series	10,000,000
Equipment and collateral bonds called	9,000
Tampico Harbor Company, rent accrued	28,030
Interest due and accrued	1,568,219
Notes payable	2,215,000
Accounts payable	3,504,632
Mexican Government subsidy proceeds	8,041,146
Equipment renewal fund	88,683
Income account, surplus	3,597
Total	$179,794,761

Income account for year ended December 31, 1902 (Mexican Currency):

Earnings:

Passenger	$3 854,995
Freight	16,151,912
Express, etc	1,125,320
Gross earnings	$21,132,227

Expenses:

Maintenance of way, etc	$2,800,329
Maintenance of equipment	3,171,159
Transportation of traffic	7,888,983
General	1,310,150
Total expenses	$15,170 621

Net earnings	$5,961,606
Equivalent in U. S. Currency	$2,513,384

Income account for year ended December 31, 1902 (U. S. Currency):

Net earnings	$2,513,384
Miscellaneous income	279,234
Total income	$2,792.618

Deductions:

Interest on bonds	$3,125,382
Rentals, etc	163,639
Total	$3.289,021

Balance deficit	$496,403
Add—drawn from subsidy	500,000
Balance	$3,597

The gross earnings for the year show an increase of 12.31% over those of 1901. The low average price of the Mexican dollar (42.16, as against 47.82 in 1901) added to the cost of supplies purchased for operating expenses. With a better price for silver the road should be able to meet its fixed charges.

Stock.—Authorized at the rate of $25,600 per mile.

Bonds.—Priority bonds—Of the $7,000,000 authorized $1,403,000 have been redeemed and cancelled, and the balance now outstanding have been purchased for the subsidy trust fund.

Consolidated mortgage are 4%, due July 1, 1911. Authorized at the rate of $32,000 per mile.

1st consolidated income are 3%, due January 1, 1939. Interest non-cumulative.

2d consolidated income 3% non-cumulative, due July 10, 1939. These bonds stand next to the 1st incomes and ahead of the stock.

A proposition was put forward to exchange the income bonds for debentures on the basis of $230 and $140 respectively for each $1,000 of the 1st and 2d, but appears to have been abandoned. Some new plan to better the condition of the finances of the company is looked for at any moment.

Dividends.—None on stock, and no interest on 2d income bonds, but on the 1st incomes the regular rate was paid in 1890, 1891 and 1892, but none since.

Annual meeting.—First Wednesday in May.

Main office.—St. Louis.

Executive committee.—H. Clay Pierce (Chairman of the Board), Breckenridge Jones, A. A. Robinson (President), Gabriel Morton, F. H. Prince, C. D. Simpson, Eben Richards, E. N. Foss, and J. C. Van Blarcom.

MINNEAPOLIS, ST. PAUL & SAULT STE. MARIE RAILWAY.

A consolidation in May, 1888, of the Minneapolis, Sault Ste. Marie & Atlantic, Minneapolis & Pacific, Aberdeen, Bismark & Northwestern, and Minneapolis & St. Croix, since which time extensions and additions have been made.

The main line extends from Sault Ste. Marie, Mich., to Portal, N. D., a distance of 1,039 miles, where it connects with the Canadian Pacific.

Total line operated July 1, 1902, 1,453 miles, of which all but about 20 miles is owned outright.

The Canadian Pacific owns a controlling interest.

General balance sheet, June 30, 1903:

Assets.

Road, equipment, etc	$57,190,961
Advances pending issue of bonds	1,388,369
Real estate	308,191
Stocks and bonds	423,432
Material and supplies	1,222,377
Foreign roads	384,265
Agents and conductors	388,618
Post office department	50,138
Bills and accounts	776,037
Cash	1,964,199
Other accounts	7,502
Total	$64,104,089

Liabilities.

Common stock	$14,000,000
Preferred stock	7,000,000
Funded debt	37,103,000
Car trust notes	175,059
West. Express Company	14,000
Interest due July 1	670,800
Taxes, not due	286,918
Vouchers	589,052
Pay rolls	314,530
Addition and improvement fund	210,978
Profit and loss	3,739,752
Total	$64,104,089

Income and profit and loss account for year ended and at June 30, 1903:

Earnings:	
Freight	$5,254,735
Passenger	1,524,378
Mails	206,928
Express and miscellaneous	251,223
Gross earnings	$7,237,264
Expenses:	
Maintenance of way	$800,792
Maintenance of equipment	661,058
Transportation	2,098,027
General expenses	160,045
Total	$3,719,922
Net earnings	$3,517,342
Other income	56,479
Total income	$3,573,821
Deductions from income:	
Interest on bonds	$1,428,115
Rental	84,066
Taxes	394,939
Miscellaneous	2,203
Additions, improvements, etc	200,000
Total	$2,109,323
Surplus for year	$1,464,498
Profit and loss, June 30, 1902	2,275,256
Profit and loss, June 30, 1903	$3,739,752

The above shows an increase over the previous year in gross earnings of 16.5%, and in net earnings of 7.8%. Operating expenses show an increase of 26.4%, being 51.4% as against 47.3% to earnings. This percentage is unusually low in either case, the percentage of operating expenses to earnings for roads in the same group being nearer 65%.

A large factor in this road's future will be settlement of the tributary territory, a great deal of which is fertile prairie in the wheat belt.

Stock.—Issued as authorized (see balance sheet.)

Bonds.—The Canadian Pacific guarantees by endorsement 4% interest on all bonds assenting to reduction of interest to that rate. Over half of the bonds are assented.

Dividends.—From the earnings of the calendar year 1902 there was declared and paid 7% on the preferred and 2% on the common. On April 15, 1904, semi-annual dividends of 2% on the common and 3½% on preferred were paid.

Annual meeting, third Tuesday in September.

Main office, Minneapolis.

Directors.—W. D. Washburn, E. Penington, John Martin, Thomas Lowry, C. H. Pettit, G. R. Newell, Sir William C. Van Horne, Sir Thomas G. Shaughnessy, R. B. Angus and E. A. Young.

MISSOURI, KANSAS & TEXAS RAILWAY COMPANY.

A consolidation in 1896 of the Missouri, Kansas & Texas Railway Company, the Missouri, Kansas & Eastern Railway Company, the Southwestern Mineral Railway Company, and the St. Louis & Kansas City Railway Company, since which several small branches have been acquired.

The line extends from St. Louis, Kansas City and Hannibal, Mo., to Denison and Galveston, Texas, and Shreveport, La., and the total mileage operated at April 1, 1904, was 2,991 miles, of which 2,329 mlies was owned, 392 miles controlled and leased.

General balance sheet, June 30, 1903 :

Assets.

Road and equipment	$156,920,632
Bonds and stocks	489,231
Cash	1,114,090
Due from agents, individuals and companies	703,472
Material and supplies	1,316,488
Advance account of construction	857,824
Total	$161,401,737

Liabilities.

Common stock, M. K. & T. Ry.. $56 100,300
Preferred stock, M. K. & T. Ry....................................... 13,000,000
Capital stock, M. K. & T. of Texas.................................. 2,623,900
Capital stock, Boon R. R. Br. Co.................................... 1,000.000
Funded debt outstanding... 79,269,000
Improvement fund.. 871,815
Deferred payments.. 3,798,220
Accrued interest and taxes.. 878,483
Sundry accounts... 16,038
Current liabilities.. 2,644,563
Surplus income.. 1,199,417

Total.. $161,401,737

Income and profit and loss account for year ended and at June 30, 1903 :

Earnings :
    Passenger.... .... $3,160,455
    Freight......................... 13,256,900
    Mail, express, etc.. 790,838

Gross earnings.. $17,208,193
Expenses :
    Conducting transportation..................................... $6,913,309
    Maintenance of way... 2,779,995
    Maintenance of equipment...................................... 1,651,077
    General expenses... 778,750
    Taxes...... 325,952

    Operating expenses and taxes......... .... $12,449,083

Net earnings... $4,759,110
Other income... 99,565

Total income... $4,858,675
Deductions :
    Interest on bonds.. $3,291,396
    Rentals....................................... 467,363

Total... $3,758,759

Balance surplus for year... $1,099,916
Balance June 30, 1902.. $1,260,348
Equipment payments during year....................... 1,160,847

Balance forward.. $99,501

Balance surplus June 30, 1903.. $1,199,417

The net earnings for the year show an increase of above 5% over 1902, and business outlook for the future is most encouraging, due chiefly to the settling up of the rich country in Oklahoma and lands adjacent to the company's line.

The company has a land grant in the Indian Territory of 3,110,-400 acres subject to Indian title.

The road is rated a Gould-Rockefeller property.

Stock.—Issued as authorized.

Dividends.—None paid on either class of stock.

Annual meeting.—Third Wednesday in May.

Main office.—Parsons, Kansas.

Directors.—John D. Rockefeller, Wm. Rockefeller, Henry C. Rouse, Colgate Hoyt, Henry W. Poor, Joel F. Freeman, Chas. G. Hedge, James Brown Potter, Herbert L. Satterlee, Myron T. Herrick, A. A. Allen, James Hagerman, B. P. McDonald, Alfred J. Poor, T. N. Sedgwick and H. J. DeMarez Oyens.

MISSOURI PACIFIC RAILWAY COMPANY.

This company was incorporated in 1876 and took over the property of the Pacific Railroad Company of Missouri which had been sold under foreclosure proceedings. A consolidation was effected in 1880 with the St. Louis & Lexington Railroad, Kansas City & Eastern Railroad, Lexington & Southern Railroad, St. Louis, Kansas & Arizona, Missouri River Railroad, and Leavenworth, Atchison & Northwestern Railroad, to which has been since added sundry acquisitions and extensions.

The company acquired in 1881 all but a few shares of the stock of the St. Louis, Iron Mountain & Southern Railway Company, and is a large holder of Denver & Rio Grande Railroad and Texas & Pacific Railway stock, the balance of control being with friendly interests.

The Missouri Pacific Railway has a total mileage of 3,507 miles, of which 3,055 miles is owned or controlled and the balance leased. In addition it draws revenues from 2,200 miles in the shape of almost the entire dividend from the St. Louis, Iron Mountain & Southern road.

Missouri Pacific Railway Company's general balance sheet, December 31, 1903 :

Assets.

Road and equipment	$67,612,350
Stocks and bonds	72,005,620
Materials and supplies	2,429,153
Cash	1,872,402
Sundry accounts receivable	3,967,954
Due from St. Louis, Iron Mountain & Southern Railway	8,092,073
Miscellaneous accounts	1,674,873
Equipment not delivered	459,208
Total	$158,113,633

Liabilities.

Capital stock	$77,802,875
Bonds	54,012,000
Equipment obligations	5,776,800
Interest due and accrued	956,005
Notes payable	1,121,733
Accounts payable	4,716,981
Loans payable	5,111,209
Dividend	1,945,057
Special fund	1,557,621
Improvement fund	21,389
Miscellaneous	340,003
Income account surplus	4,751,960
Total	$158,113,633

Missouri Pacific Railway Company's income and profit and loss account for year ended and at December 31, 1903:

Earnings:

Passenger	$4,019,097
Freight	14,788,907
Mail, express, etc	3,142,740
Gross earnings	$21,950,744

Expenses:

Transportation	$5,651,540
Motive power	5,084,704
Maintenance of way	3,057,074
Maintenance of cars	1,397,180
General	456,532
Total expenses	$15,647,030
Net earnings	$6,303,716

Additions:

Dividends, interest and rents	2,340,927
Dividends on St. Louis, Iron Mountain & Southern stock	2,573,379
Total income	$11,218,021

Deductions:

Interest on bonds	$2,854,637
Taxes	778,382
Rentals	174,736
Equipment association	321,128
Interest and exchange	680,339
Other charges	29,325
Total	$4,838,547
Net income	$6,379,474
Dividend (5%)	3,890,115
Surplus for year	$2,489,359
Balance, December 31, 1902, less charged for betterments, etc.	2,262,601
Balance, December 31, 1903	$4,751,960

The Missouri Pacific Railway annual report shows both individual and combined figures with the St. Louis, Iron Mountain &

Southern, and since the revenues of the latter so materially affect the former the following figures are given.

St. Louis, Iron Mountain & Southern Railway Company's general balance sheet, December 31, 1903 :

Assets.

Road and equipment.	$87,704,245
United States land grants.	933,876
Stocks and bonds	35,813,612
Cash on hand.	307,124
Land grant accounts.	276,260
Projected lines expenses.	3,598,264
Little Rock & Ft. Scott Railway	3,306,919
Equipment not delivered	1,065,297
Discount on bonds sold	2,052,156
Miscellaneous.	30,045
Total.	$135,087,798

Liabilities.

Capital stock.	$25,795,710
Bonds.	84,601,675
Car trusts.	5,983,000
Interest due and accrued.	1,216,760
Due Missouri Pacific Railway.	8,092,073
Loans payable.	2,904,500
Rentals guaranteed, accrued.	94,627
Accounts payable.	483,258
Income account surplus.	5,916,194
Total.	$135,087,798

St. Louis, Iron Mountain & Southern Railway Company's income and profit and loss account for year ended and at December 31, 1903 :

Earnings :	
Passenger.	$2,857,883
Freight.	15,310,673
Mail, express, etc.	1,406,794
Gross earnings.	$19,575,350
Expenses :	
Transportation.	$5,289,615
Motive power.	3,899,879
Maintenance of way.	2,292,961
Maintenance of cars.	876,233
General.	496,377
Total.	$12,855,065
Net earnings.	$6,720,285
Additions, dividends, etc	1,428,572
Total income.	$8,148,857
Deductions :	
Interest on bonds.	$3,624,601
Taxes	339,657
Rentals	215,017
Premium, adjustment interest, etc.	501,831
Total.	$4,681,106

Net income... $3,467,751
Dividends.............. .... $2,578,831

Surplus for year.. $888,920
Balance December 31, 1902, less charges for betterments, etc........ 5,027,274

Surplus at December 31, 1903... $5,916,194

From the combined surplus of the two companies a total of $1,249,672 was appropriated for improvements.

Net earnings for the year 1902 were over 14% in the case of the Missouri Pacific and 1.11% in the case of the Iron Mountain over the previous year.

Stock.—Missouri Pacific Railway, authorized $100,000,000 ; issued $77,802,875.

Dividends.—Missouri Pacific Railway (J & J): 1882, 6¼%; 1883 to 1887, 7% yearly; 1888, 5¼%; 1889 and 1890, 4% yearly; 1891, 3%; 1892 to 1900, none; 1901, 2½%; 1902 to January, 1904, 5% yearly.

Annual meeting, second Tuesday in March.

Main office, St. Louis, Mo.

Directors.—George J. Gould, Russell Sage, Fred T. Gates, Edwin Gould, E. Parmalee Prentice, Samuel Sloan, John D. Rockefeller, Jr., James H. Hyde, Howard Gould, Frank J. Gould, W. K. Bixby, Charles G. Warner, Russell Harding.

NATIONAL LEAD COMPANY.

This is a New Jersey corporation organized in 1901 to succeed the Lead Trust.

The company owns extensive white lead works and smelters in New York, Pennsylvania, Missouri, Ohio and several other States, comprising in all 26 plants, also owns lead mines in Missouri.

At one time a plan was on foot to combine with the Union Lead & Oil Company, a plant controlling patents for improved methods of manufacture ; the scheme was said also to contemplate taking in the linseed oil interests.

General balance sheet, December 31, 1903 :

Assets.

Plant investment	$24,143,299
Other investments	618,150
Stock on hand	5,910,486
Treasury stocks	190,600
Cash in banks	150,105
Notes receivable	174,088
Accounts receivable	1.519,423
Total	$32,706,151

Liabilities.

Common stock	$15,000,000
Preferred stock	15,000,000
Mortgages	12,603
Accounts payable	130,717
Notes payable	600,000
Surplus	1,962,831
Total	$32,706,151

Income account for years ended December 31:

	1903.	1902.	1901.
Net earnings	$1,569,069	$1,202,514	$1,112,140
Dividend 7% preferred	1,043,280	1,043,280	1,043,280
Surplus for year	$525,789	$159,234	$68,860
Previous surplus	1,437,042	1,277,808	1,208,948
Surplus to date	$1,962,831	$1,437,042	$1,277,808

Stock.—The preferred is 7% cumulative, and both classes are fully issued as authorized.

Bonds.—The company has no bonded debt, although at the reorganization as above $3,000,000 was authorized, but so far none has been issued.

Dividends (Q. M.).—Preferred, 7% yearly to March 1904, inclusive.

Common, 1892, nothing ; 1893, 2% ; 1894, 3% ; 1895, 1% ; 1896 and 1897 none ; 1898 to 1900, 1% yearly ; none since.

Annual meeting.—Third Thursday in February.

Main office,—New York.

Directors —W. H. Thompson, E. C. Gorham, F. W. Rockwell, L. A. Cole, R. R. Colgate, A. P. Thompson and seven others.

NATIONAL RAILROAD OF MEXICO.

A corporation formed under the laws of Utah in 1902 to take over the property of the Mexican National Railroad Company, which company was reorganized without foreclosure.

The line operated extends from Corpus Christi, Texas, to the City of Mexico, with branches to Uruapan and elsewhere, and has a total mileage of 1,577 miles, of which 992 miles is standard gauge and the balance narrow gauge. The company owns all but 57 miles, which is leased.

The company controls through stock ownership the Mexican International Railroad, a road extending from Eagle Pass, Texas, to Durango, Mexico, and the National Railroad of Mexico, the combined mileage of which is 1,460 miles. Also has acquired a large interest in the Interoceanic Railway.

The Government of Mexico recently purchased about 47% of the stock of this company, and has consented to the consolidation of the National, the International and Interoceanic Railways, with a 20 years' concession to construct a road in a zone 50 kilometers wide extending from the Gulf of Mexico, along the Rio Grande, to a point 100 kilometers northwest of Ciudad Porfirio Diaz.

General balance sheet, June 30, 1903 (U. S. currency):

Assets.

Cost of road, etc.	$75,342,434
Bonds and stocks owned	20,700,622
Mexican International consolidated 4s (per contra)	5,839,000
Securities pledged	8,764,740
Advances to purchase railroads	323,544
Advances to Texas Mexican Railway.	251,382
Construction of El Salto extension	3,294,090
Change of gauge	7,061,936
Cash deposited for coupons	461,775
Individuals and companies	88,983
Cash	370,335
Assets in Mexico (gold values)	1,796,731
	$124,295,572

Liabilities.

Common stock	$796,400
Deferred stock	10,851,200
Preferred stock	32,000 000
2d preferred stock	21,702,400
Bonds and notes	50,500,000
Accrued interest	326,250
Coupons accrued, not due	450,000

Liabilities (continued).

Coupons past due, not presented	11,775
Loan from bankers	349,265
Individuals and companies	33,190
Mexican International consolidated 4s (per contra)	5,835,000
Due on purchase securities pledged	258,775
Reserve for readjustment expenses	170,782
Liabilities in Mexico (gold value)	864,860
Net revenue surplus	141,675
	$124,295,572

Earnings and expenses for year ended June 30, 1903 (Mexican currency):

Earnings:

Freight	$8,713,540
Passenger	1,677,307
Express	493,300
Telegraph and miscellaneous	459,872
Gross earnings	$11,344,019

Expenses:

Maintenance of way and structures	$930,788
Maintenance of equipment	1,157,096
Conducting transportation	5,054,369
General	492,336
Total expenses	$7,634,589
Net earnings	$3,709,430
Net earnings (U. S. currency)	$1,563,086

Income account for year ended June 30, 1903 (U. S. currency):

Net earnings	$1,563,086
Interest, discount and exchange	23,358
Interest on balances, bonds, etc	335,236
Gain on Mexican money assets	155,998
Total income	$2,077,678

Deduct:

Taxes	$21,237
Rentals	7,587
Interest on bonds and notes	1,867,861
Texas Mexican Railway, net earnings	72,262
Total deduction	$1,968,947
Surplus for year	$108,731
Net revenue surplus, June 30, 1902	32,944
Net revenue surplus, June 30, 1903	$141,675

Stock.—Authorized and issued--Preferred, $32,000,000 4% non-cumulative; common, $33,350,000.

The common stock has recently been converted one-third into deferred stock and two-thirds into second preferred stock, on the basis of one share of deferred and two shares of second preferred for each three shares of common. The second preferred is entitled to receive dividends when earned, at not exceeding 5% per annum, before any dividend shall be paid on the deferred stock, after which the second preferred and deferred share alike in any further dividends.

Dividends.—None paid.

Annual meeting.—First Monday in April.

Main office.—New York.

Directors.—C. H. Dodge, E. C. Henderson, Adrian H. Iselin Jr.; Juan N. Navarro, J. N. Wallace, Geo. W. Wickersham, Chas. H. Tweed, Wm. G. Raoul, L. F. Loree, Ernesto Madero, etc., etc.

NEW YORK CENTRAL & HUDSON RIVER RAILROAD COMPANY.

This line of road originated with consolidation in 1869 of the New York Central Railroad Company and the Hudson River Railroad.

The total mileage operated is 3,422 miles, of which 810 miles are owned, 2,374 leased, and the balance being operated under trackage rights, etc.

The line extends from New York via Albany to Buffalo; also from Boston to Albany and northward by two lines to Ogdensburg and St. Lawrence River points

Amongst the leased lines are included the Boston & Albany, the West Shore, and the Rome, Watertown & Ogdensburg lines.

Through stock ownership the company controls the Lake Shore & Michigan Southern, the Michigan Central, which lines, having a mileage of over 3,000 miles, are operated separately. Lake Shore in turn controls the New York, Chicago & St. Louis; the Lake Erie & Western, and the Big Four, a further mileage of about 3,800 miles, which, together with sundry small properties, makes up a system either operated and controlled by the New York Central of over 11,000 miles.

Jointly with the Pennsylvania, the New York Central controls
also the C. & O. and the Reading.

The system is known as a Vanderbilt property.

Condensed general balance sheet, June 30, 1903:

As·ets.

Cost of road.	$143,405,427
Leased lines construction.	3,671,109
Equipment.	48,808,739
Railroad stocks owned, proprietary interest.	115,267,134
Railroad bonds owned.	4,314,495
Miscellaneous stocks owned	8,587,700
Real estate not used in operating road	3,081,069
Bridges at Albany	2,256,363
Advances to New York & Harlem Railroad	5,891,155
Advances to other companies.	2,672,358
Cash.	9,382,557
Traffic balances.	4,641,880
Sundry collectible accounts.	7,312,038
Fuel and supplies.	5,592,763
Sinking fund for debentures.	1,919,521
Securities acquired from lessor companies.	3,036,813
Total.	$369,841,143

Liabilities.

Capital stock.	$132,245,100
Consolidation certificates.	4,900
Bonded debt	194,780,546
Bonds and mortgages payable.	150,000
Wages and supplies.	6,702,619
Traffic balances payable.	3,822,887
Interest and rentals accrued	5,544,451
Dividends payable July.	1,653,125
Dividends and interest unclaimed.	77.517
Sundry accounts payable.	1,590,197
Special improvement fund.	1,967,920
Securities in trust for lessor companies	3,036,813
Accounts with lessor companies.	2,374,486
Profit and loss.	15,890,580
Total.	$369,841,143

Income and profit and loss account for year ended and at June
30, 1903:

Earnings:

Freight.	$46,858,713
Passenger.	23,581,576
Express.	2,387,939
Mail.	2,398,285
Rentals.	2,175,077
Miscellaneous	204,189
Gross earnings.	$77,605,778

Gross earnings..	$77,605,778
Expenses :	
Maintenance of way, etc...	$10,469,570
Maintenance of equipment......................................	10,882,375
Transportation..	30,317,130
General	1,790,239
Total expenses..	$53,459,314
Net earnings	$24,146,464
Additions to income:	
Dividend on L S. & M. So. stock................................	$3,170,244
Dividend on Mich. Cent. stock..................................	672,572
Dividend and interest on other stocks, etc......................	1,069,387
Interest on loans, etc.....	327,946
Sundry..	32,595
Total income..	$29,419,208
Deductions from income:	
Interest on funded debt...	$7,299,968
Rentals leased lines...	9,421,474
Taxes on real estate	2,687,737
Tax on capital stock..	794,292
Miscellaneous	191,433
Total..	$20,394,908
Net income...	$9,024,304
Deduct:	
Reserve to redeem bonds.........	$300,000
Special improvement fund..	1,750,000
Dividends (5)...	6,604 158
Surplus for year..	$370,146
Miscellaneous profits and expenses (net)............................	314,233
Balance carried to profit and loss	$55,913
Profit and loss balance June 30, 1902......................	15,834,667
Profit and loss June 30, 1903..............................	$15,890,580

Capital Stock.—Authorized, $150,000,000 ; issued, $132,245,100, at June 30, 1903, per above balance sheet.

Bonds.—Total outstanding June 30, 1903, $194,780,546.

On January 1, 1903, the outstanding first mortgage 7% bonds, amounting to $18,327,000, and $5,724,094 6% sterling bonds matured and were exchanged for 3½% gold mortgage bonds.

This will result in an annual saving in interest of $784,000.

Out of the surplus for the year $1,750,000 was added to the special improvement fund, following the practice and keeping up the average charge of the past three years. The net income shows an increase of 8.5 over the year ended June 30, 1902, this in spite of the fact that the percentage of expenses to earnings increased 2.80%, due to higher cost of materials and labor.

The percentage of expenses to earnings was in 1902-03, 68.89; 1901-02, 66.09; 1900-01, 64.20; 1899-1900, 62.41.

Dividends (Q. J.).—1892, 5¼%; 1893 and 1894, 5% yearly; 1895, 4¼%; 1896-98, 4% yearly; 1899, 4%; 1900 to April, 1904, 5% yearly.

Annual meeting.—Third Wednesday in April.

Main office.—New York.

Directors.—W. K. Vanderbilt, F. W. Vanderbilt, Chauncey M. Depew, Samuel F. Barger, J. Pierpont Morgan, William Rockefeller, Hamilton McK. Twombly, William H. Newman, Charles C. Clarke, D. O. Mills, William Bliss, Geo. L. Bowdoin and Jas. Stillman.

NEW YORK, ONTARIO & WESTERN RAILWAY COMPANY.

Incorporated under the laws of New York in 1879, being a reorganization of the New York and Oswego Midland.

The line operated, including branches, is 549 miles in length, extending from Oswego, N. Y., to Weehawken, N. J., of which 319 miles is owned and the balance leased line.

This is a large coal carrying road, having access to the Lackawanna region. It owns considerable coal properties and colleries in the Scranton district.

General balance sheet, June 30, 1903 :

Assets.

Franchises and property	$72,121,272
Investments in other companies	13,180,344
Cash at bankers	317,254
Stores, fuel, etc	505,920
Sundry accounts receivable	1,025,248
Traffic accounts	553,141
Loans and bills receivable	116,589
Accrued interest	256,790
Miscellaneous	4,000
Cars under lease (car trusts)	858,000
Total	$88,938,558

Liabilities.

Common stock...	$58,113,983
Preferred stock..	4,000
Refunding 4% bonds..	16,937,000
Interest due and accrued...................................	229,407
Sundry accounts payable........	886,368
Traffic accounts payable.................................	122,305
Loans and gold notes......................................	5,644,560
Rolling stock under lease..................................	858,000
Profit and loss..	6,142,935
Total..	$88,938,558

Income and profit and loss account for year ended and at June 30, 1903:

Earnings:

Passenger...	$981,288
Freight...	4,964,601
Mail, express, etc....................................	133,213
Miscellaneous..	97,415
Gross earnings.......................................	$6,176,517

Expenses:

Conducting transportation............................	$2,493,682
Maintenance of equipment.............................	831,358
Maintenance of way...................................	925,699
General expenses.....................................	156,761
Taxes..	149,587
Total expenses.......................................	$4,557,087

Net earnings...	$1,619,430
Interest, etc..	401,937
Total income..	$2,021,367

Deductions:

Interest on bonds....................................	$677,480
Interest and discount................................	280,047
Rentals..	202,870
Total..	$1,160,397
Surplus for year.....................................	$860,970
Less—Appropriated for cost of second track between Cadosia and Cornwall....................................	423,214
Balance..	$437,756
Profit and loss balance, forward.....................	5,705,179
Profit and loss, June 30, 1903.......................	$6,142,935

Statistics:

	1902-03.	1901-02.	1900-01.	1899-00.
Net earnings.....	$1,619,430	$1,298,942	$1,545,747	$1,548,566
Percentage of expenses and taxes to earnings........	73.78	76.19	70.96	68.80
Surplus	$860,970	$658,959	$879,233	$859,024
Tons of freight carried......	3,972,561	3,612,487	3,508,508	3,416,606

Stock.—Common: Issued as authorized (see balance sheet); preferred to the amount of $2,000,000 was issued in the reorganization, but all but $4,000 has been exchanged at par for 1st mortgage bonds.

The exchanged preferred is held alive under a voting trust and elects eight of the thirteen directors until a dividend shall have been paid on the common stock.

Dividends.—None paid. The surplus for the past two years has been appropriated for double tracking improvements.

Annual meeting, last Wednesday in September.

Main office, New York.

Directors.—C. Ledyard Blair, Henry W. Cannon, Francis R. Culbert, Thomas P. Fowler, Gerald L. Hoyt, Grant B. Schley, John B. Kerr, Chauncey M. Depew, Albert S. Roe, O. D. Ashley, Chas. S. Whelen, Joseph Price, H. Pearson.

NORFOLK & WESTERN RAILWAY COMPANY.

This company dates its origin from the reorganization in 1896 of the Norfolk & Western Railroad Company through foreclosure.

The line extends from Norfolk, Va., to Columbus, Ohio, and northward to Hagerstown, Md., with branches to the coalfields of West Virginia.

The mileage operated is 1,722 miles of which all but four miles is owned.

The company owns the entire capital stock of the Pocahontas Coal & Coke Co. Through stock ownership the property is controlled by the Pennsylvania Railroad interests.

General balance sheet, June 30, 1903:

Assets.

Cost of road, franchises, etc.	$130,816,100
Rolling stock	12,363,521
Cost of Cinti P. & V. R. R	2,292,782
Iager & Southern Railroad	52,655
Kenova & Big Sandy Railroad	1,349,340
Equipment trust certificates	482,000
Companies' securities	1,560,450
Investments in other companies	1,143,390
Due from agents, U. S. Gov't and other railroads and companies	1,662,819
Insurance paid in advance	26,432
Material and supplies	1,618,860
Pocahontas Coal & Coke Co., advances	249,000
Cash	1,451,224
Total	$155,068,577

Liabilities.

Capital stock :	
Adjustment preferred....................................	$23,000,000
Common...	66,000,000
Funded debt..	56,099,500
Equipment mortgage bond, 1888.....................................	1,000
Interest on funded debt accrued.....................................	705,869
Due for vouchers, pay rolls, traffic balances, etc....................	2,378,225
Taxes accrued..	249,687
Betterment fund................................,...................	2,697,996
Reserve funds, equipment, etc....................,.................	935,710
Profit and loss.............................	3,000,587
	$155,068,577

Income and profit and loss account for year ended and at June 30, 1903 :

Earnings :	
Freight..	$17,676,348
Passenger...	2,841,491
Express...	247,026
Mails...	217,694
Miscellaneous...	178,116
Gross earnings..	$21,160,675
Expenses and taxes :	
General...	887,348
Maintenance of way, etc...............................	2,754,199
Maintenance of equipment..............................	3,041,415
Conducting transportation.............................	6,014,468
Total...	$12,697,430
Net earnings..	$8,463,245
Other income..	148,259
Total income..	$8,611,504
Deductions :	
Interest on bonds.....................................	$2,435,690
Interest on car trusts................................	625
Deferred interest on P. C. & C. bonds.................	159,176
Discount on bonds, etc................................	347,078
Rent of equipment....................	135,000
Total...	$3,077,569
Surplus for year......................................	$5,533,935
Deduct :	
Betterment fund.......................................	$2,500,000
Dividend on preferred (4%)...........................	914,818
Dividend on common (3%)..............................	1,934,076
Total...	$5,348,894
Balance to profit and loss............................	$185,041
Profit and loss June 30, 1902.........................	2,815,546
Profit and loss June 30, 1903.........................	$3,000,587

Stock.—Issued as authorized (see balance sheet).

The preferred is 4% non-cumulative.

Bonds.—Besides the funded debt as shown above, the Railway Company is joint endorser with the Coal Company of the Pocahontas Coal & Coke Co. 4% bonds.

Dividends.—Preferred (F. & A.)—1897, 1%; 1898, 3%; 1899 to February, 4% yearly.

Common (J. & D.)—1901, 2%; 1902, 2½%; 1903, 3%.

Of the freight traffic for 1902-03, 56% was bituminous coal and coke. Net earnings for the year showed an increase of 14.1% over that of 1901-02, resulting from large increase in all branches of the service.

The percentage of expenses to earnings increased from 57.75% to 60%, but is still less than the average of the two preceding years.

Annual meeting.—Second Thursday in October.

Main office.—Roanoke, Va.

Directors.—Henry Fink, Victor Morawetz, L. E. Johnson, S. M. Prevost, Samuel Rea, N. Parker Shortridge, W. H. Barnes, Joseph I. Doran, John P. Green, James McCrea and Walter H. Taylor.

NORTHERN PACIFIC RAILWAY COMPANY.

This is one of the roads whose stocks are affected by the famous "Merger Decision," the outcome of the purchase of control by the Northern Securities Company, now in the process of dissolution, after the exciting times on May 9, 1901, upon which date the stock sold at $1,000 per share.

The company succeeded the Northern Pacific Railroad, sold under foreclosure in 1896. The original company operated under a charter from Congress, July 6, 1864.

The mileage owned and controlled at July 1, 1903, was 5,976 miles, of which 5,587 was operated directly, and of the total mileage all but about 470 miles is owned or controlled absolutely. There was leased to other companies 389 miles.

Reaching from St. Paul, Minn., and Duluth, Wis., to Manitoba and to Tacoma, Seattle and Portland, Oregon, with numerous branches, the line is one of the leading lines to the Pacific.

Jointly with the Great Northern this company controls the Burlington property.

A land grant was made by Congress to the "railroad" company of about 43,000,000 acres, of which at the sale the "railway" company acquired all remaining west of the Missouri River. At June 30, 1902, over 15,500,000 acres remained unsold.

General balance sheet, June 30, 1903 :

Assets.

Northern Pacific estate.	$279,041,836
Equipment.	28,496,038
Collateral with trustee for Nor. Pac.-Gt. Nor. joint bonds issued to acquire Burlington stock.	109,091,310
Sinking fund	2,665,912
Cash	8,023,620
Accounts receivable.	5,509,887
Bills receivable.	33,347
Material on hand.	3,460,461
Treasury securities.	13,828,047
Betterments, etc., fund.	1,403,629
Leased to government of Manitoba	7,000,000
Collateral with trustee, St. Paul-D. division bonds.	2,047,140
Insurance fund.	596,804
Land department.	5,531,554
	$466,729,585

Liabilities.

Common stock.	$155,000,000
Mortgage debt.	277,738,500
Bonds of other companies assumed.	13,540,678
Pay rolls, vouchers, etc.	4,147,200
Taxes accrued.	652,036
Interest on bonds.	1,655,616
Dividends.	2,327,014
Reserve funds.	1,232,119
Insurance fund.	596,804
Liquidation fund.	113,963
Profit and loss.	9,725,656
	$466,729,585

Income and profit and loss account for year ended and at June 30, 1903 :

Earnings:

Freight.	$33,301,958
Passenger.	10,595,447
Mail, express and miscellaneous.	2,244,700
Gross earnings.	$46,142,105

Expenses:

Maintenance of way.	$7,117,335
Maintenance of equipment.	3,887,807
Transportation.	11,384,780
General.	1,642,171
Total expenses.	$24,032,093

Net earnings...	$22,110,012
Miscellaneous income, not including land sales....................	1,112,550
Total income...	$23,222,562
Deductions:	
Taxes..	$1,421,434
Rentals, etc..	150,543
Interest..	6,904,697
Additions and improvements...........	3,000,000
Total..	$11,476,674
Surplus for year..	$11,745,888
Dividend, 6½%...	10,074,942
Balance to profit and loss...................................	$1,670,946
Profit and loss, June 30, 1902...........................	8,054,710
Profit and loss, June 30, 1903...........................	$9,725,656

Stock.—Issued as authorized, viz.: $155,000,000. Under the reorganization there was $80,000,000 common and $75,000,000 preferred, but on November 13, 1901, the directors gave notice that the preferred would be retired at par, common stock for the same amount being authorized to provide the necessary funds.

In November, 1901, the Northern Securities Company announced that their stock would be exchanged at the rate of 115 for each share of Northern Pacific, and under this plan acquired nearly all the stock.

Bonds.—Prior lien 4%; $130,000,000 authorized; outstanding, $101,892,500. General lien bonds issued for the present $60,000,-000, with $130,000,000 to be issued to retire the prior lien bonds at maturity.

Besides other bonds secured by divisions of the line and its lands amounting to about $10,000,000, there is shown in the balance sheet this company's proportion of liability amounting to $107,590,000 for its one-half interest in $215,180,000 bonds issued jointly with the Great Northern for the purpose of acquiring the stock of the Burlington line.

This issue is secured by deposit of the stock with trustees, and in event of default of either, the other company becomes owner of all the shares and must assume full liability for the bonds.

Besides maintaining the property and charging sundry betterments against income, following the practice of past years, an amount, viz., $3,000,000, being somewhat in excess of the average annual amounts previously provided, has been charged out to provide for extraordinary improvements.

The net earnings show an increase of over 10% above the previous year, which in turn was 26% above the year 1900-1901, on a slightly decreased mileage.

Dividends.—Preferred (now retired): 1898, 5%; 1899, 4%; 1900, (Q M) 4%; 1901, 4%.

Common: 1898, none; 1899, 2%; 1900, 4%; 1901, 4%; 1902, 5½%; 1903, 7%; 1904, February, 1½%; payable quarterly, February, May, August and November.

Annual meeting, third Thursday in October.

Main office.—Executive office, St. Paul; administration office, New York.

Officers.—President, Howard Elliott; Vice-President, Dan. S. Lamont; Secretary, Geo. H. Earl; Treasurer, C. A. Clark.

NORTHERN SECURITIES COMPANY.

Now in process of dissolution under decision of the U. S. Supreme Court in March, 1904, that the company was a combination in violation of the " Anti-Trust Law " of 1892.

The company was incorporated in November, 1901, under the laws of the State of New Jersey, with an authorized capital of $400,000,000, with power to invest in and hold the securities of other companies.

Its object was considered to be the harmonizing of interests in the northwestern roads.

Large interests in the stocks of the Great Northern & Northern Pacific Railways were acquired by exchange, on the basis of 100 for 180 and 115 respectively in Northern Securities stock.

The financial condition after over 13½ months' existence is shown below.

General balance sheet, December 31, 1902:

Assets.

Charter account	$85,048
Investments, railroad stocks	360,343,333
Other investments	5,214,951
Accounts receivable	811
Cash	32,797
Total	$365,676,940

Liabilities.

Capital stock...	$364,867,849
Vouchers...	50,461
Accrued rental...	523
Profit and loss..	758,107
Total..	$365,676,940

Income account for 13½ months ended December 31, 1902 :

Dividends from stocks owned..	$15,364,262
Less :	
Expenses of administration.......................................	93,578
Interest and exchange..	258,418
Taxes...	190,514
Total..	$542,510
Net income...	$14,821,752
Dividends paid (4%)..	14,063,645
Balance carried to profit and loss..................................	$758,107

Since the 1902 dividend above there has been paid for 1903, 4½%, and February, 1904, 1⅛%. The plan of dissolution was first the reduction of the capital stock to $3,954,000, and in return for each 100 shares of Northern Securities stock owned the holders will receive 99 times $39.27 stock of Northern Pacific, and 99 times $30.17 stock of the Great Northern, and a stub for 1% of the original Northern Securities stock owned to represent the interest in the assets still remaining, pending completion of dissolution.

THE PACIFIC COAST COMPANY.

Organized in November, 1897, under the laws of New Jersey, to purchase the Oregon Improvement Company, which was sold under foreclosure.

The franchises acquired are extremely liberal, vesting in the company the right to operate railroads, steamships and conduct mining operations, in all of which business the company is actively engaged.

The mining property of the company comprises about 5,000 acres along its line in the State of Washington, and it owns about

10,000 acres of agricultural and timber land in the States of Oregon and Washington.

The company owns all the securities and stock of the Pacific Coast Railway and the Columbia & Puget Sound Railroad, also all the stock of the Pacific Coast Steamship Company, besides owning a large interest in the stocks of the Alaska Southern Wharf Company, the Cumberland Coal Association, Sacramento Coal Company, Anthracite Coal Company, Alaska Railway & Transportation Company, and Franklin Coal Company.

Revenues are chiefly derived from the shipping interests, its lines operating between San Francisco, Portland, Victoria, Sitka, etc. Sales of coal are next in importance, while the two railroads having a mileage of 57 miles broad gauge and 80 miles narrow gauge combined, are third in importance.

General balance sheet, June 30, 1903:

Assets.

Property (including stocks and bonds of proprietary companies)....	$16.476.106
Bonds and stock in treasury....	389,200
Cash....	1.550,720
Accounts receivable....	247,339
Agency accounts....	204,293
Materials and supplies....	177,886
Miscellaneous accounts....	20,761
Depreciation and renewal fund....	264,720
Total....	$19,421,025

Liabilities.

Stock:

Common....	$7,000,000
1st preferred....	1,525,000
2d preferred....	4,000,000
1st mortgage bonds....	4,446,000
Accounts payable....	37,898
Unpaid vouchers....	137,411
Unpaid pay rolls....	109,828
Interest on bonds....	18,525
Taxes accrued....	18,443
S. S. improvement and exhaustion fund....	264,720
Miscellaneous....	16,410
Surplus fund of proprietary companies deposited with Pacific Coast Company....	482,638
Profit and loss....	1,364,153
Total....	$19,421,025

Income and profit and loss account for year ended and at June 30, 1903 :

Earnings :

Pacific Coast Steamship Company	$3,598,959
Pacific Coast Railway Company	116,307
Columbia & Puget S. R. R Co	521,251
Port Townsend & So. R. R Co	12,389
Coal department	1,251,060
Lumber, grain, rentals, etc	106,787
Gross earnings	$5,606,753
Operating expenses and taxes	$4,394,775
Net earnings	$1,211,978
Interest, discount and miscellaneous	44,378
Total income	$1,256,356
Deductions from income :	
Interest on bonds	$222,300
Improvement, equipment, etc	18,115
Exhaustion fund	21,504
Total	$261,919
Surplus for year	$994,437
Dividends :	
1st preferred	$76,250
2nd preferred	200,000
Common	350,000
Total dividends	$626,250
Balance to profit and loss	$368,187
Balance forward	1,478,604
Balance June 30, 1903	$1,846,791
Divides :	
Surplus proprietory companies	$482,638
Profit and loss	1,364,153
Total	$1,846,791

Net earnings for the year show an increase of 11.3% over the year ended June 30, 1902. The coal department net earnings increased $62 440.54, in spite of the fact that competition from British Columbia had to be met from January 7, 1903, owing to suspension for one year from that date of the duty of 67 cents per ton.

Stock.—Issued as authorized (see balance sheet). The 1st preferred has first preference to the amount of 5%, then the 2d preferred to the amount of 4%, after which the common is entitled to 4%. Further dividends divide between the 2d preferred and common.

Dividends.—1st preferred—1898, 5%; 1899, 4⅛%; 1900 to August, 1902, 5% yearly; August, 1902, to May, 1904, 1¼% quarterly.

2d preferred—1898, 2%; 1899, 3⅓%; 1900 to August, 1902, 4% yearly; August, 1902, to May, 1904, 1¼% quarterly.

Common—1898, 2%; 1899, 2%; 1900 to August, 1902, 4% yearly; August, 1902, to May, 1904, 1¼% quarterly.

Annual meeting.—Second Wednesday in October.

Corporate office, Jersey City; New York office, 10 Wall Street; Main office, Seattle, Wash.

Executive Committee.—Henry W. Cannon, E. H. Harriman, Daniel S. Lamont, T. Jefferson Coolidge, Jr., and Grant B. Schley.

PACIFIC MAIL STEAMSHIP COMPANY.

(CONTROLLED BY SOUTHERN PACIFIC COMPANY.)

Incorporated under the laws of New York in 1848. The company operates lines of steamships between San Francisco, Panama and Mexican and Central American west coast ports, also between San Francisco and Hong Kong, Honolulu and Yokohama.

By arrangement with the Panama Railroad Company the company withdrew its east coast trade in consideration of the Panama Company withdrawing from the west coast.

The line is operated in connection with the Southern Pacific Railroad, which company controls the steamship company through a slight majority in stock ownership, acquired in November, 1900.

General balance sheet, April 30, 1903:

Assets.

Steamers	$9,950,874
Other floating equipment	311,985
Real estate, etc.	673,525
Cash	73,970
Agents and pursers	23,709
Traffic balances.	120,756
Individuals and companies.	48,087
Material, fuel, etc.	228,817
Capital stock terminal companies.	111,597
Mexican and Guatemala bonds.	43,549
Deferred assets.	5,461
Contingent assets.	79,905
Profit and loss	11,091,533
Total	$22,763,773

Liabilities.

Capital stock..	$20,000,000
Advanced by Southern Pacific Railway account cost of new steamers.	1,728,408
Accounts payable...	104,317
Unclaimed dividends..	8,910
Unadjusted accounts..	159
Fund for depreciation, repairs, etc.	921,979
Total..	$22,763,773

Profit and loss account at April 30, 1903 :

Debit balance. April 30, 1902..	$11,046,83
Add:	
Adjustment in accounts..	39,014
Uncollectible accounts charged off..................................	13,965
Total...	$11,099,813
Deduct:	
Surplus income for year ended April 30, 1903.......................	8,280
Profit and loss balance, debit, April 30, 1903......................	$11,091,533

Stock.—Issued as authorized.

There is no preferred stock or funded debt.

Dividends.—After a lapse of nine years without dividends the company paid 1% in 1896, 2% in 1897, 2½% in 1898, 3% in 1899, but none since.

Annual meeting, last Wednesday in May.

Main office, New York.

Directors.—George J. Gould, E. H. Harriman, E. Hawley, etc.

PENNSYLVANIA RAILROAD COMPANY.

Operated under a charter from the State of Pennsylvania dated April 13, 1846.

The entire Pennsylvania System has a mileage of 10,914 miles, but lines west of Pittsburg are operated by the Pennsylvania Company, chartered in 1870 for that purpose. The entire stock of the " Company " is owned by the " Railroad."

The mileage operated by the "Railroad" is 3,723 miles, and lines under direct control with a mileage of 2,129 report separately. These latter include the Philadelphia, Baltimore & Washington, the Northern Central and the Long Island Railroads.

Lines west of Pittsburg are operated as follows : Operated directly: Pennsylvania Company, 1,651 miles, and Pittsburg, Cincinnati

& St. Louis, 1,339 miles; reported separately, 2,072 miles, including Grand Rapids & Indianapolis and the Terre Haute & Indianapolis lines.

The system extends from New York via Philadelphia to Pittsburg, Erie, Cleveland, Toledo, Chicago and Burlington, and to Washington, Cincinnati and St. Louis.

In 1901 large interests in the Baltimore & Ohio, the Chesapeake & Ohio and the Norfolk & Western were acquired, and the same year control of the Pennsylvania & Cambria Steel Company was obtained. In turn the Baltimore & Ohio, jointly with the Vanderbilt interests, has virtual control of the Reading.

Tunnels under the East and North Rivers are under process of construction, the estimated cost at completion being $40,000,000. This will afford through service via New York City between the South and the New England States.

A vast terminal passenger station at New York City is also projected.

General balance sheet, December 31, 1903 :

Assets.

Construction, equipment, etc.	$181,248,013
Cost of bonds owned	32,486,698
Cost of stocks owned	192,330,396
Trust of October 9, 1878	5,275,748
Penn. R. R. consolidated mortgage sinking fund	6,360,630
Sun., Haz. & W. sinking fund	125,000
Insurance fund	10,000
Mortgages and ground rents	108,038
Securities of U. N. J. Cos	3,283,462
Materials on hand	10,492,416
Advances to other companies for construction, etc	44,577,363
Bills receivable	1,299,811
Due from agents	5,986,817
Cash	17,191,156
Miscellaneous assets	4,103,927
Total	$504,879,475

Liabilities.

Capital stock	$299,991,812
Funded debt	110,315,340
Mortgages and ground rents	6,400,945
H., P., Mt. J. & Lancaster stock guarantee	1,182,550
H., P., Mt. J. & Lancaster bond guarantee	700,000
Net traffic balances due other roads	1,818,876
Payments for leased equipment	1,127,000
Pay rolls and vouchers	15,486,413

Liabilities (continued).

Matured dividends and interest....	130,597
Due controlled companies other than traffic balances................	13,500 458
Due employee's savings fund..	196,708
Due relief fund...	359,230
Due insurance fund...	92,582
Securities of Un. N. J. Cos. transferred with lease...................	3,283,462
Fund for purchase of securities guaranteed (trust, October 9, 1878)..	5,425,172
Trustee of consolidated mortgage....................................	59,506
Consolidated mortgage bonds sinking fund...........................	8,307,610
Sun., Haz. & W. sinking fund.......................................	125,000
Interest accrued on Penn. R. R. bonds..............................	1,779,852
Miscellaneous..	9,854,138
Balance to profit and loss	24,742,225
Total...	$504,879,475

Income and profit and loss account for year ended and at December 31, 1903:

Earnings:

Freight	$89,895,723
Passenger...	26,391,382
Express..	2,581,946
Mails..	2,044,424
Miscellaneous...	1,712,944
Gross earnings...	$122,626,419

Expenses:

Maintenance of way, etc...	$14,586,420
Maintenance of equipment...	19,803,161
Transportation..	47,633,384
General	2,343,815
D. & R. Canal.. ...	406,276
Total..............................	$84,773,056
Net earnings...	$37,853,363

Additions to income:

Interest on investments	$9,462,569
Interest on N. J. R. R. and Canal securities.......................	221,482
Interest for use of equipment......................................	421,537
General interest and miscellaneous................................	637,373
Total income...	$48,596,324

Deductions from income:

Rentals on per cent. basis..........................	$7,381,462
Fixed rentals	4,715,771
Interest on funded debt	5,570,974
Interest on stock allotment..	100,210
Interest on mortgage and ground rents............................	197,059
Interest on car trusts..	896,434
Equipment trust loan and sinking fund	136,400
Taxes on Penn. R. R. Co...	1,931,033
Miscellaneous	160,473
Total..	$21,089,816
Net income...	$27,506,508

Net income...	$27,506,508
Deductions:	
Payment to trust funds................................	149,424
Consolidated mortgage sinking fund...............	401,810
Extraordinary expenses...............................	9,472,728
Principal of car trusts paid...........................	2,684,615
Miscellaneous...	5,000
Total...	$12,713,577
Balance surplus for year	$14,792,931
Dividends (6%)	14,792,931
Balance	......
Profit and loss December 31, 1902	$24,742,225
Add profit from securities..............................	$17,362,551
Deduct extraordinary expenditure account..........	17,362,551
Profit and loss balance December 31, 1903...........	$24,742,225

Consolidated income account (entire system) for year ended December 31, 1903 :

Gross earnings...	$242,517,758
Expenses..	175,379,438
Net earnings...	$67,138,320
Other income..	18,795,337
Total income...	$85,933,657
Deduct :	
Interest, rent, dividends and extraordinary.........	82,866,409
Surplus for year...	$3,067,248

This surplus, all shown by the lines west of Pittsburg, accrues to the Pennsylvania Railroad in proportion to its interests in said lines.

The entire surplus of the "Railroad" has been appropriated to the several reserves for improvement, etc., such accounts during the year having been charged with $21,835,279 out of $44,006,385, expended for real estate, shop facilities, right of way and equipment.

The premium on sale of securities amounting to $17,362,551 contributed largely to this liberal appropriation.

Expenditures for maintenance indicate that the property was maintained up to as high a standard as in previous years, the increase of 2.51 in the percentage of expenses to earnings of the "Railroad" being probably sufficient to cover higher wages and cost of material. The same is true in general of the western lines.

The largest increase in cost of operating is felt in the transportation department, and where not entirely due to increased cost of labor and material, a decrease may be looked for when the many plans for additional facilities now under consideration shall have been perfected.

Earnings show improvement in every line, the gross earnings being over $22,000,000 in excess of the figures of the previous years. This is about evenly distributed between the lines east and west of Pittsburg, and is evenly distributed between both branches of the service, which shows largely increased tonnage, number of passengers carried, and better returns per ton per mile and per passenger train mile.

Stock.—Capital stock : authorized, $400,000,000 ; issued, $299,-991,812. During the year the stock outstanding has been increased over $75,000,000 to provide for the important improvements now in progress, $20,980,350, however, having been used to exchange for $29,302,500 of the convertible gold bonds.

Funded debt.—This was increased during the year 1902 by an issue of $50,000,000 3½% ten year convertible bonds to provide funds for the tunnel under the City of New York and the new passenger station, but was reduced during the year 1903 by the above mentioned conversion.

Other smaller changes leave the amount outstanding at January 1, 1904, $110,315,340. (See balance sheet.)

Dividends.—1883, 8½%; 1884, 7%; 1885, 1886, 5% yearly; 1887, 5½%; 1888, 1889, 5% yearly; 1890, 5½%; 1891, 1892, 6% yearly; 1893 to 1899, 5% yearly; 1900 to 1903, 6% yearly. In 1893 paid also 2% in scrip, payable May 31 and November 30.

Annual meeting, second Tuesday in March.

Main office, Philadelphia.

Directors.—Alexander M. Fox, N. Parker Shortridge, Rudulph Ellis, Alexander J. Cassatt, Clement A. Griscom, Amos R. Little, William H. Barnes, Geo. Wood, C. Stuart Patterson, Effingham B. Morris, Thomas DeWitt Cuyler, Jas. McCrea, Lincoln Godfrey, John P. Green, Chas. B. Pugh, Sutherland M. Prevost, Samuel Rea.

PEOPLE'S GAS LIGHT & COKE COMPANY OF CHICAGO.

An Illinois corporation formed under a special charter in 1855, and amended in 1865. In July, 1897, an act was passed by the Illinois Legislature allowing the consolidation of all the Chicago gas companies, and this company by consolidation or subsequent acquisition, virtually controls the gas supply of that city.

At the end of the year 1903, the company had 1,872 miles of mains, 347,750 meters and 25,000 public lamps.

Differences with the city were settled on the basis of acceptance by the city of gas for 25,000 street lamps, with Welsbach burners, free, on account of its percentage of gross earnings. Such service to be credited as at $375,000, and any balance to be paid in cash.

The city agrees not to attack the company's franchise, but reserves the right to continue the Ogden 75 cent gas suits, which, however, has already been declared by the Court of first instance to be illegal.

General balance sheet, December 31, 1903 :

Assets.

Real estate, franchises, tunnels, mains, etc.	$71,145,318
Materials	1,000.476
Securities	2,243,682
Accounts receivable	444,505
Bond coupon deposits	346,630
Gas bills receivable	899,306
City of Chicago	99,227
Cash	686,915
Total	$76,866,059

Liabilities.

Capital stock	$35,000,000
Mortgage bonds	34,496,000
Gas bill deposits	102,238
Accounts payable	351,635
Coupons past due	348,540
Bond interest accrued	217,858
Surplus	6,349,788
Total	$76,866,059

Income and profit and loss account for year ended and at December 31, 1903:

Gross receipts........	$11,854,800
Operating expenses......................,..................	6,440,362
Net earnings..	$5,414,438
Interest on bonds..	1,857,300
Depreciation..	656,431
Total..	$2,513,731
Net income...	$2,900,707
Dividends (6½).............	1,978,146
Surplus for year..	$922,561
Surplus December 31, 1902..	5,427,227
Surplus December 31, 1903..	$6,349,788

Gross earnings for 1900 were $9,090,337, and have shown a steady increase up to 1903. During the same period the relative increase in expenses has been larger, with result that the percentage of net earnings, although increased 16%, is not so large as that of gross earnings. Fixed charges have not changed in the four years, and the amount written off for depreciation has been rateable throughout the years.

Stock.—Authorized, $35,000,000 ; issued, $32,969,100. The full amount authorized is shown in the balance sheet, and $2,030,900 included in the asset " securities."

Bonds.—The People's Gas Light & Coke Co. refunding mortgage for $40,000,000, was issued in 1897, and $29,046,000 is reserved to retire underlying bonds. The balance may be issued for additional property.

Dividends.—In 1895 and 1896 owing to pending litigation, since satisfactorily closed, the rate was materially reduced. 1889, 4% ; 1890, 3% ; 1891, 3% ; 1892, 5¼% ; 1893, 6% ; 1894, 6% ; 1895, 2½%;1896, 1½%; 1897, to February, 1904, 6% yearly, (1½% Q F).

Annual meeting.—February 10.

Main office.—Chicago.

Directors—Anthony N. Brady, Walton Ferguson, Anson R. Flower, C. K. G. Billings, George O. Knapp.

PRESSED STEEL CAR COMPANY.

Incorporated January 12, 1899, under the laws of New Jersey. The company was organized for the purpose of combining the interests of the Schoen Pressed Steel Company and the Fox Pressed Steel Equipment Company, and for the manufacture of passenger, freight and street cars of pressed steel, and pressed steel parts for cars. It has three active plants—at Allegheny, Pa., McKee's Rocks, Pa., and Joliet, Ill. A large forging plant has recently been constructed at Allegheny, and a commodious fire-proof general office building with vaults for the housing of clerks and safekeeping of valuable records and drawings, has been erected at McKee's Rocks.

The capacity is indicated by the production for the year ended December 31, 1903, which was 20,683 all steel and composite cars, and 4,481 underframes.

General balance sheet, December 31, 1903 :

Assets.

Properties and franchises	$26,063,190
Securities—stocks owned	2,110,646
Taxes and insurance not accrued	16,620
Accounts receivable	857,670
Stock of materials on hand	1,536,407
Cash in banks	3,527,165
Collateral bills receivable	477,200
Total	$34,588,898

Liabilities.

Capital stock:	
Common	$12,500,000
Preferred	12,500,000
Five per cent. first mortgage gold notes, payable $500,000 annually	3,500,000
Purchase money mortgages (4%)	310,000
Accounts payable	797,570
Accrued salaries and wages	120,606
Accrued interest	72,988
Accrued preferred dividends	218,750
Surplus	4,568,984
Total	$34,588,898

Profit and loss account, December 31, 1903:

Dr.

Dividends on preferred stock (7%)	$875,000
Dividends paid on common stock (4%)	500,000
Extra dividend on common (1%)	125,000
Charges pertaining to previous years	121,392
Inventory adjustments	650,000
Depreciation and renewals	260,000
Balance	4,568,984
Total	$7,100,376

Cr.

Balance, January 1, 1903	$4,331,479
Profits for year 1903	2,768,897
Total	$7,100,376

The gross sales for the year 1903 are reported as $26,273,910, a decrease of over $7,000,000 compared with the previous year, but an increase of $3,250,000 over the sales of 1901. The falling off in the last year was entirely in the second half, the first six months showing a very substantial increase over previous comparative periods.

The expenses include $529,000 for repairs, and renewals and as may be seen above, $260,000 has been charged out for depreciation, besides readjustment of inventory to current values, involving a charge to profit and loss of $650,000.

In view of the amount carried for inventory, viz.: $1,536,407, this latter adjustment would appear to be very conservative.

The interest on securities owned exceeded fixed charges for the year by $31,366.

Stock.—The preferred stock is 7% non-cumulative.

Dividends.—On preferred: $1\frac{3}{4}$% quarterly (Q F) to February, 1904.

Common, (Q F): 1900, 6%; 1901, 4%; 1903, 5%; 1904, February, 1%.

Main office, Pittsburg.

Annual meeting, third Wednesday in February.

Directors.—James A. Blair, James H. Reed, F. N. Hoffstot, A. S. Matheson, T. H. Given, J. W. Friend, F. G. Ely, G. E. Macklin, Adrian H. Larkin.

READING COMPANY.

A Pennsylvania corporation chartered in 1871. Assumed present name in 1896 for the purpose of carrying out the reorganization of the Philadelphia & Reading Railroad Company, the
securities of which company, with its coal companies and other
properties, it has power to hold.

The Philadelphia & Reading Railway Company was organized
in 1896 to take over the properties of the Philadelphia & Reading
Railroad, sold under foreclosure.

The Reading Company owns all the stock of the "Railway"
Company ; also all the stock of the Philadelphia & Reading Coal
& Iron Company. The property of the coal and iron company
consists of extensive anthracite coal property, mines and collieries.

A majority of the stock of the Reading Iron Company is also
owned, and a controlling interest in the Central Railroad of New
Jersey.

The Reading Company in turn is controlled jointly by the
Baltimore & Ohio, representing the Pennsylvania interests, and
the Lake Shore & Michigan Southern, representing Vanderbilt
interests.

The railroad system, including lines owned, leased and controlled, has a total mileage of 2,145 miles, and centering at Philadelphia extends to Jersey City and other points on New York
harbor, to Atlantic City and Cape May, and westward throughout
the Pennsylvania coal regions to Williamsport, Harrisburg and
Gettysburg.

The mileage operated is 1,010 miles, embracing 365 miles owned
and 645 miles leased line.

General balance sheet, June 30, 1903 :

Assets.

Railroad equipment	$19,792,119
Floating equipment	2,107,650
Equipment accounts	9,424,265
Real estate	17,351,936
Philadelphia & Reading Railway purchase money mortgage	400,000
Philadelphia & Reading Railway bonds owned	20,000,000
Bonds of sundry companies	18,745,318
Philadelphia & Reading stock owned	20,000,000
Philadelphia & Reading Coal and Iron stock owned	8,000,000
Stocks of sundry companies	51,269,338

Assets (*continued*).

Philadelphia & Reading Coal & Iron Company	79,116,721
Sundry railroads, etc.	1,009,985
Philadelphia & Reading Railway, account new Reading shops	1,200,000
Cash	592,089
Accrued income	320,623
Miscellaneous	731,729
Total	$250,061,774

Liabilities.

Capital stock:

1st preferred	$28,000,000
2d preferred	42,000.000
Common	70,000,000

Bonds:

General mortgage loan, 1897–1997	69,020,000
Reading Company, Jersey Central collateral gold bonds	23,000,000
Other bonds and equipment trust certificates	11,284.040
Contingent account	1,050,663

Current liabilities:

Current business	929,865
Accrued interest, taxes, etc. (est.)	922,982
General mortgage bonds purchased and cancelled	1,520,000
Sinking fund general mortgage loan	752
New equipment to be purchased account equipment dismantled	70,311
Surplus	2,263,159
Total	$250,061,774

Income and profit and loss account for year ended and at June 30, 1903:

Income:

Interest on purchase money mortgage	1,200,000
Interest account leased lines, wharves and equipment	2,178,844
Real estate rented	126,145
Interest on debt of P. & R. C. & I. Co	1,582,334
Interest and dividend receipts	1,344,388
Total income	$6,431,711
Expenses	90,950
Net earnings	$6,340,761
Fixed charges and taxes	4,230,739
Surplus for year	$2,110,022

Surplus June 30, 1902		$1,239,912	
Less dividend on 1st preferred, October 1, 1902	$280,000		
Less dividend on 1st preferred, March 9, 1903	560,000		
Less general mortgage sinking fund	246,775		
		1,086,775	
			153,137
Surplus June 30, 1903			$2,263,159

The surplus of the three companies for the year ended and at June 30, 1903, was as under:

	For Year.	At June 30, 1902
Reading Company	$2,110,022	$153,137
Philadelphia & Reading Railway Company	2,317,515	2,794,587
Philadelphia & Reading Coal & Iron Company	770,245	652,116
Total	$5,197,782	$3,599,840

Surplus for three companies June 30, 1903 .... $8,797,622

which, whilst carried on the books of the subsidiary companies, all accrues to the Reading Company's surplus through ownership of the entire stock. Condition of the railway and coal company at June 30, 1903, and results of the year's operations are shown below.

Philadelphia & Reading Railway Company, general balance sheet, June 30, 1903:

Assets.

Railroad	$79,851,857
Philadelphia terminal	8,500,000
Philadelphia subway	2,741,000
Real estate	28,087
Leased equipment W. & N. R. R. Co	346,640
Chestnut Hill R. R. Stock	75,000
Reading Company P. M. mortgage bonds	1,200,000
Cash	2,276,147
Bills receivable	700,890
Freight and toll bills	1,940,251
Materials on hand	2,468,650
Railroad companies	1,787,707
Philadelphia & Reading Coal & Iron Company	1,120,953
Individuals and firms	490,595
Deposit, account insurance fund	75,459
Insurance fund securities	828,298
Deposit, subway loan	93,151
Subway loan securities	268,406
New locomotive and machine shops	1,600,000
Total	$106,393,092

Liabilities.

Capital stock	$20,000,000
Prior mortgage loans	5,241,700
Consolidated mortgage loan, 1871-1911	18,811,000
Improvement mortgage loan, 1873-1897-1947	9,363,000
Consolidated mortgage loan, 1882-1922-1937	5,766,717
Consolidated mortgage loan, 2d series	1,535
Debenture loan, 1891-1941	8,500,000
Purchase money mortgage	20,000,000
Philadelphia subway loan	2,741,000
Bonds and mortgages on real estate	1,027,405
Unpaid vouchers	2,887,809
Railroad companies	946,811
Individuals and companies	453,703
Rents matured	274,547

Liabilities (*continued*).

Interest matured	$108,717
Rent, interest, taxes, etc., accrued	1,513,678
Reading Company	64,094
Sundry funds	1,985,132
W. & N. R. R. equipment lease	346,640
Reading Company bonds and mortgages retired	47,500
Reading Company, account new locomotive and machine shops	1,200,000
Surplus	5,112,103
Total	$106,393,092

Philadelphia & Reading Railway Company, income and profit and loss account for year ended and at June 30, 1903 :

Earnings :

Freight—coal	$13,134,624
Freight—mdse	12,564,293
Passenger	5,235,897
Miscellaneous	773,709
Gross earnings	$31,708,523

Operating expenses :

Maintenance of way and structures	3,019,881
Maintenance of equipment	4,901,011
Conducting transportation	10,526,643
General expenses	644,549
Total expenses	$19,092,084
Net earnings	$12,616,439
Other earnings	721,267
Total earnings	$13,337,706
Fixed charges	9,519,011
Improvements and insurance funds	1,501,180
Surplus for year	$2,317,515
Surplus June 30, 1902	2,794,587
Surplus June 30, 1903	$5,112,102

The Philadelphia & Reading Coal & Iron Company, general balance sheet, June, 30, 1903 :

Assets.

Coal lands	$60,014,897
Timber lands	659,965
New York and Eastern depots	707,002
Western yards and depots	618,012
Miners' and other houses	548,038
Pottsville shops, real estate, and improvements	369,667
Storage yards and washeries	389,124
Other real estate	121,288
Improvements at collieries	7,078,690
Equipment at collieries	2,302,468
Deadwork at collieries	3,711,477
Stocks and bonds of companies controlled	9,746,073
Cash	961,944

Assets (continued)

Bills receivable and loans..	$1,000,000
Coal accounts...	2,829,194
Rent accounts..	39,477
Companies and individuals...	423,296
Coal on hand...	1,014,943
Supplies and materials on hand..	676,186
Depletion of coal lands fund :	
Securities..	2,018,472
Cash deposited...	12,285
Stocks, bonds and mortgages...	2,033,556
Total..	$97,276,054

Liabilities.

Capital stock...	$8,000,000
Bonds..	5,186,000
Reading Company..	79,116,721
Pay rolls and vouchers...	1,182,307
Due for coal land purchased...	290,457
Due for royalty on coal mined...	129,746
Freight and tolls due foreign roads.......................................	31,428
Companies and individuals...	65,205
Interest due and uncollected..	22,842
Interest and taxes accrued...	507,404
Income from investments :	
Account depletion of coal lands fund...................................	153,450
Improvement fund account new collieries..................................	300,000
Philadelphia & Reading Railway Company current account................	1,118,133
Profit and loss..	1,422,361
Total..	$97,276,054

The Philadelphia & Reading Coal & Iron Company, income and profit and loss account for year ended and at June 30, 1903 :

Receipts:

Coal sales (anthracite)...	$22,088,146
Coal sales (bituminous)...	705,666
Coal rents	241,460
House and land rents..	91,426
Interest and dividends..	46,430
Miscellaneous...	106,111
Total..	$23,279,240

Expenses:

Expenses of production and repairs.....................................	19,341,138
Colliery improvements, etc..	867,330
Depletion of coal lands fund..	340,446
Total..	$20,548,914

Profit from operating, etc..	$2,730,326
Fixed charges and taxes..	377,748
Total income..	$2,352,578
2% interest on Reading Company loans.....................................	1,582,334
Surplus for year..	$770,244
Profit and loss, June 30, 1902...	652,116
Profit and loss, June 30, 1903...	$1,422,360

Earnings and expenses.—The Reading Company's net earnings show an increase for 1902-03, over the previous fiscal year of $1,110,980, chiefly due to increased rate of interest paid by the Coal Company on the Reading Company loan and higher rates of dividends received from the Central Railroad of New Jersey and other companies whose stocks are owned. Expenses increased only $8,000 in the same period.

The gross earnings of the Philadelphia & Reading Railway Company show an increase of $3,088,152 rateably distributed over the several sources. Operating expenses increased in the same period $2,548,310, and net earnings increased $922,187.

The revenues from coal traffic were much affected by the coal strike, but such loss, as will be seen from the above results, was more than compensated by increased tonnage in other commodities.

In part, the increased expenses may be accounted for by a charge of $1,228,760, charged thereto for real estate, extensions of tracks, sidings, yards, improvements to bridges, additional buildings, etc. Increased wage scale probably accounts for the balance.

Coal Company earnings were to be expected to show a reduction. The production and purchases, however, was only 9.5% less than the year 1901-02, and sales 11.1% less. Gross earnings fell off rather more, being about 14% less than the previous year, chiefly explained in the higher cost of purchases.

Expenses during the year decreased 20%, but the amount charged for colliery improvement and depletion of coal lands was, based upon production, quite equal to the charge for 1901-02.

Capital stock.—Reading Company—Issued as authorized.

The 1st and 2d preferred are both 4% non-cumulative. After 4% has been paid on the 1st preferred for two consecutive years, the company may convert the 2d preferred into one-half common and one-half 1st preferred.

Pending such a consummation, the stock is held in a voting trust.

Dividends.—On 1st preferred, 1900, 3% ; 1901, 4% ; 1902, 3% ; 1903, 4% ; March 10, 1904, 2%.

2d preferred, 1½%, November 10, 1903 ; 2% May 10, 1904.

Annual meeting.—Reading Company, first Tuesday in June.
P. & R. Ry. Co. and P. & R. C. & I. Co., second Monday in
October.

Main office.—Philadelphia.

Directors.—Joseph S. Harris, George F. Baer, John Lowber
Welsh, E. T. Stotesbury, Henry A. Dupont, Henry P. McKean,
Samuel Dickson, Charles Steele and H. McK. Twombly.

REPUBLIC IRON & STEEL COMPANY.

Organized May 3, 1899, under the laws of the State of New
Jersey, and is a consolidation of numerous properties in the iron
and steel business in Michigan, Minnesota, Pennsylvania, Ohio,
Kentucky, Indiana, Illinois and Alabama.

The properties include valuable iron, coal and limestone lands,
iron and coal mines, coke furnaces, blast furnaces, steel plants
and rolling mills.

The annual capacity of the combined plants exceeds 1,300,000
tons of finished iron and steel and 600,000 tons of pig iron, besides
which it mines and cokes its own blast furnaces and smelter requirements.

General balance sheet, June 30, 1903:

Assets.

Plants, etc.	$40,708,481
New construction	6,066,603
Stock in sundry companies	486,318
Producing oil properties	144,360
Prepaid royalties, etc.	301,957
Inventories of raw and finished materials	4,614,739
Accounts and bills receivable	3,379,616
Cash	857,495
Total	$56,559,569

Liabilities.

Capital stock issued:	
Preferred	$20,416,900
Common	27,191,000
Accounts and bills payable	4,931,556
Preference dividend (paid July 1, 1903)	357,296
Reserve for depreciation of ore and coal mines	201,331
Reserve for taxes and insurance	144,379
Reserve for doubtful collections	68,901
Profit and loss, surplus	3,248,206
Total	$56,559,569

Income and profit and loss account for year and at June 30, 1903:

Profits	$4,123,500
Depreciation, etc.	1,382,600
Net profits	$2,740,900
Dividend 7% on preferred	1,427,082
Surplus for year	$1,313,818
Profit and loss, June 30, 1902	1,934,388
Profit and loss, June 30, 1903	$3,248,206

The net profits and surplus after dividends for past years, is shown below:

	Net Profits.	Surplus after Dividends.
1899-1900 (14 months)	$3,643,729	$2,222,050
1900-1901	309,099	(deficit) 1,112,384
1901-1902	2,248,832	824,725
1902-1903	2,740,900	1,313,818

Stock.—Common : Authorized, $30,000,000; issued, $27,191,000. Preferred : Authorized, $25,000,000 ; issued, $20,416,900.

The preferred is 7% cumulative.

The company has no funded debt.

Dividends.—On preferred : October, 1899, to October, 1903, 7% yearly in quarterly payments of 1¾% (Q-J).

The January, 1904, dividend was deferred.

Annual meeting, third Wednesday in October.

Corporate office, Jersey City; main office, Chicago.

Directors.—August Belmont, Grant B. Schley, George R. Sheldon, G. Watson French, Harry Rubens, John F. Taylor, Alexis W. Thompson, Edward N. Ohl, L. C. Hanna, Charles H. Wacker, George A. Baird, John Crevar, William H. Hassinger, Peter L. Kimberly, Archibald W. Houston.

THE ROCK ISLAND COMPANY.

Incorporated under the laws of New Jersey on July 30, 1902, and acquired all the stock of the Chicago, Rock Island & Pacific Railroad Company, which company owned nearly all of the stock of the Chicago, Rock Island & Pacific Railway Company. Subsequently about 90% of the issue of common stock of the St.

Louis & San Francisco Railway was acquired. Early in the present year the stock of the Rock Island Company was exchanged for one-half the stock of the St. Louis, Kansas City & Colorado Railroad Company and sundry small lines in Texas and Indian Territory.

The system, including the roads controlled and leased by the old Rock Island road and those controlled directly, was at July 1, 1903, 7,123 miles. The lines more recently acquired, viz., the St. Louis & San Francisco, etc., as above, have a total mileage of 5,843. It is proposed also to acquire one-half interest in the Houston & Texas Central; the Houston, East & West Texas, and Houston & Shreveport lines, with a combined mileage of 922 miles.

Total over all, 13,888 miles.

The lines of the company on the above basis will reach northward from Chicago, to Minneapolis, Sioux Falls and Watertown; westward from Chicago via Kansas or Omaha to Denver and Pueblo; southwest from Kansas City to El Paso; south to Houston and Galveston, and a line from Memphis westward to Amarillo, Texas, where it joins the Colorado Southern and becomes a part of a system reaching from the lower Mississippi River to Denver and the Northwest.

Balance sheet, The Rock Island Company, June 30, 1903:

Assets.

Stocks owned	$118,250,707
Cash	90,594
Due from companies and individuals	1,018,840
Total	$119,360,141

Liabilities.

Capital stock:	
Common	$69,558,775
Preferred	48,690,232
Unpaid vouchers and accounts	121,096
Dividends (payable August 1)	486,902
Balance, surplus	503,136
Total	$119,360,141

Income and profit and loss account, The Rock Island Company, for year ended and at June 30, 1903:

Income from dividends and stock owned	$2,166,000
Other income	8,290
Gross income	$2,174,290
Expenses and taxes	216,299
Net income for year	$1,957,991
Less dividends on preferred	1,454,856
Surplus for year and to date	$503,135

*General balance sheet, Rock Island System, operated lines, June 30, 1903:

Assets.

Property and franchises	$150,262,988
Stocks and bonds of constituent companies	32,322,270
Advances for construction and equipment	34,911,054
Stocks and bonds auxiliary companies	580,038
Cash	14,677,542
Agents and conductors	1,641,361
Companies and individuals	2,388,598
Loans and bills receivable	663,425
U. S. Government	367,934
Express companies	57,025
Treasury securities	2,522,258
Material, fuel and supplies	4,235,855
Unadjusted accounts	195,552
Total	$244,825,900

Liabilities.

Capital stock	$90,796,345
Funded debt	112,098,000
Collateral trust notes	4,500,000
Unpaid vouchers and accounts	4,589,138
Unpaid wages	1,912,748
Traffic mileage balances	264,320
Matured interest and rentals	1,901,935
Dividends payable August 1, 1903	935,156
Unclaimed coupons and dividends	20,012
Interest, taxes and rentals accrued (not due)	1,137,723
Stockholders' improvement loan	1,222,941
Insurance fund	350,000
Hospital fund	23,659
Replacement fund	46,871
Improvement fund	1,104,545
Contingent account	5,255,357
Profit and loss	18,667,150
Total	$244,825,900

*Not including Burlington & Cedar Rapids or Rock Island & Peoria, operated during the year under lease.

Income account, Rock Island System operated lines, year ended
June 30, 1903:

Earnings:
```
      Freight ........................................................  $30,917,231
      Passenger......................................................   11,490,544
      Mail and express...............................................    1,815,777
      Miscellaneous..................................................      123,018
```

```
Gross earnings.......................................................  $44,376,620
```
Operating expenses:
```
      Maintenance of way and structures. ............................   $6,822,552
      Maintenance of equipment......... ..... .......................    4,176,321
      Conducting transportation......................................   14,293,284
      General and traffic expenses ..................................    2,767,008
      Other expenses.................................................      244,152
```

```
Total...............................................................  $28,303,317
```

```
Net earnings........................................................  $16,073,303
Additions to income.................................................    1,690,873
```

```
Total income........................................................  $17,764,176
```

```
Taxes...............................................................   $1,319,300
Rentals ..... .....................................................    1,040,544
Interest............................................................    7,909,740
```

```
Total deductions....................................................  $10,269,584
```

```
Net income .........................................................   $7,494,592
Dividends...........................................................    3,050,200
```

```
Surplus for year....................................................   $4,444,392
```

The above surplus accrues to the holding company in proportion to its holdings, which at June 30, 1903, was about two-thirds.

Earnings reported are for an average mileage operated of 6,978
miles, of which 5,579 represented the Chicago, Rock Island &
Pacific Railway, the balance being for the Choctaw, Oklahoma &
Gulf Railroad (1,080 miles) and sundry small lines.

The financial results of the Chicago, Rock Island & Pacific are
shown for 15 months to June 30, 1903, due to a change in fiscal
year. During this period the gross earnings are reported to have
been $42,752,566. Statistics have been reduced to an annual basis,
and the following are noteworthy:

Year.	Mileage.	Percentage of Expenses.	No of Passengers Carried.	Earnings per Passenger per Mile.	Tons of Freight Carried.	Average rate per Ton per Mile.
1899-1900..	3,617	66.15	6,420,623	2.062 cents.	7,538,366	.99 cents.
1900-1901..	3,819	67.67	7,406,909	2.081 cents.	7,706,535	.99 cents.
1901-1902..	3,910	64.31	8,228.579	2.115 cents.	8,245,978	1.04 cents.
1902-1903..	5,579	66.02	9,548,940	2 2 cents.	10,597,541	1. cent.

Stock, Rock Island Company.—Common : Authorized, $75,000,-
000 ; issued, $69,558,775.

Preferred : Authorized, $52,500,000 ; issued, $48,690,232.

The preferred stock is preferred as to capital and also as to non-
cumulative dividends at the rate of 4% to 1909, then 5% to 1916,
and thereafter 6%.

The preferred stockholders are entitled to elect a majority of
the directors.

Bonds.—None issued by holding company. Total Rock Island
System, including Burlington & Cedar Rapids and Rock Island &
Peoria Companies, was at June 30, 1903, $137,925,000. A new
plan proposes an issue of $163,000,000 to take care of maturing
obligations and to provide funds for new acquisitions from time
to time.

Dividends.—1% quarterly (Q F).

Annual meeting, first Wednesday in June.

Main office, Chicago.

Directors.—W. B. Leeds, Wm. H. Moore, D. G. Reid, F. L.
Hine, Geo. G. McMurty, A. R. Flower, Geo. S. Brewster, D. G.
Boissevain, Ogden Mills, R. R. Cable, James H. Moore, Marshall
Field, B. F. Yoakum, H. C. Frick, Geo. T. Boggs.

RUBBER GOODS MANUFACTURING COMPANY.

A holding company incorporated under the laws of New Jersey
January 26, 1899, to bring about the consolidation of concerns
engaged in the manufacture of rubber goods, excepting boots and
shoes.

The company with slight exception owns the entire capital stock
of the following concerns : Mechanical Rubber Company, owner of
Chicago Rubber Works ; Cleveland Rubber Company; New York
Belting & Packing Company; Fabric Fire Hose Company; Stough-
ton Rubber Company; Morgan & Wright ; Peerless Rubber Manu-
facturing Company; India Rubber Company, Akron, O.; Sawyer
Belting Company; Hartford Rubber Works ; Indianapolis Rubber
Company; and American Dunlop Tire Company.

In 1902 the company acquired the rubber manufacturing interests of the American Bicycle Company.

General balance sheet, March 31, 1903 :

Assets.

Investments, stocks of allied companies	$24,808,280
Plants owned	120,000
Office furniture and fixtures	1,027
Cash	56,619
Mortgage notes (for property sold)	31,000
Accounts and bills receivable	205,537
Total	$25,222,463

Liabilities.

Preferred stock	$8,051,400
Common stock	16,941,700
Surplus	229,363
Total	$25,222,463

Income and profit and loss account for 15 months and at March 31, 1903:

Income :		
Dividends received from subsidiary companies		$1,570,403
Expenses :		
Interest	$47,483	
Expenses	142,675	
Loss and depreciation	650,426	
Total		$840,584
Net income		$729,819
Dividends paid		704,497
Surplus for period		$25,322
Surplus, January 1, 1902		204,041
Surplus, March 31, 1903		$229,363

The net earnings of the constituent companies for the year ended December 31, 1903, were $1,449,749. Dividends for the year were paid, and in addition the dividend for the three months to March 31, 1903, was charged out, the total being $1,678,724.

Including the surplus brought forward at January 1, 1902, and without considering the result of three months operations to March 31, 1903, the unapplied surplus of the combined companies was at March 31, 1903, $492,208, of which $22,606 accrues to outside holdings and the balance belongs to the Rubber Goods Company.

Stock.—Common : Authorized, $25,000,000; issued, $16,941,700. Preferred : Authorized, $25,000,000; issued, $8,051,400.

The preferred is 7% cumulative.

No bonded debt can be incurred without the consent of two-thirds of the preferred and a majority of the common stock-holders.

In 1902 the directors were empowered to borrow $5,000,000 on the securities owned. This however does not yet appear to have been done. Funded debt of constituent companies amounts to $1,145,225.

Dividends.—Preferred : 1¾% quarterly (Q M) paid regularly to date.

Common : 1% July, 1900, to July, 1901, inclusive ; none since.

Directors.—Charles H. Dale, Ernest Hopkinson, Harry Keene, Talbot J. Taylor, James B. Taylor, Henry Steers, Charles A. Hunter, Wm. T. Cole, M. S. Burrill, Edward Lauterbach, H. C. Winchester, C. J. Butler, Lewis D. Parker, Frank W. Eddy and A. L. Kelley.

ST. LOUIS SOUTHWESTERN RAILWAY COMPANY.

This property is a reorganization of the St. Louis, Arkansas & Texas Railway Company, whose property was sold under fore-closure in October, 1890. Three distinct companies were formed in January, 1891, viz.: The St. Louis Southwestern Railway Company; The St. Louis Southwestern Railway Company of Texas, and the Tyler Southwestern Railway Company. Later the last mentioned company was absorbed by the Texas Company.

The company has since purchased the Stuttgart & Arkansas River, 35 miles ; the Dallas, Fort Worth & Gulf, a belt line now known as the Dallas Terminal & Union Depot Company ; also owns 50% of the capital stock of the Pine Bluff, Arkansas River Railway, 24 miles, and a controlling interest in the Paragould Southeastern Railway Company, 25 miles, and all of the stock of the Texas & Louisiana Railroad, 22 miles in length.

The lines in the State of Texas are operated separately, but the operations are included in the statements which follow.

The total mileage of the system, including 652 miles of the Texas Company, is 1,280 miles.

The system extends from Cairo, Ill., and Gray's Point, Mo., to Texarkana, Tex., and Texarkana, Tex., to Gatesville, Tex., with branches from the main line to Little Rock, Ark., Memphis, Tenn., and Sherman, Fort Worth and Lufkin, Tex. It is known as the Cotton Belt Route.

Condensed general balance sheet, June 30, 1903:

Assets.

Road and equipment	$67,346,050
Gray's Point Terminal Railway	380,000
Investments in stocks and bonds	11,862,883
Advances	1,255,386
Cash	716,430
Accounts collectible	631,280
Supplies and materials	1,397,494
Trust equipment	3,519,731
Miscellaneous	51,365
Total	$87,160,619

Liabilities.

Preferred stock	$20,000,000
Common stock	16,500,000
Funded debt:	
1st gold 4s certificates	20,000,000
2d income gold 4s ($6,727,500 owned by company)	10,000,000
1st consolidated gold 4s	13,205,750
Reserve funds	68,434
Equipment trust notes ($3,271,696 owned by company)	3,519,731
Interest on bonds	455,046
Sundry accounts payable	1,720,373
Miscellaneous accounts	14,187
Surplus	1,677,098
Total	$87,160,619

Income and profit and loss account for year ended and at June 30, 1903:

Earnings:	
Passenger	$1,337,732
Freight	5,538,014
Mail, express, etc	402,828
Gross earnings	$7,278,575
Expenses:	
Transportation	$2,560,940
Maintenance of equipment	828,015
Maintenance of way, etc	1,424,686
General	442,523
Total expenses	$5,256,164

Net earnings...	$2,022,411
Other income...	182,602
Total income...	$2,205,013
Deductions from income:	
Taxes...	$161,751
Interest..	1,297,200
Rentals and miscellaneous...........................	51,228
Total...	$1,510,179
Surplus for year...	$694,835
Interest on 2d mortgage income bonds.................	130,460
Surplus after providing full interest on 2d income......	$564,375
Profit on securities acquired............................	199,472
Total...	$763,847
Appropriated for additional property and improvements...	544,765
Surplus over all charges..............................	$219,081
Surplus from June 30, 1902...........................	1,458,017
Surplus June 30, 1903.................................	$1,677,098

Gross earnings per mile in 1898–9 were $4,690 per mile, and in 1902–3, $5,636. During the same period the percentage of oper ating expenses to gross earnings has increased from 71.80 to 72.21 During 1896–1898 this figure averaged about 80%.

Compared with the previous year, it is found that the net earn ings for 1902–3 show an increase of $21,800. The recent increase in operating expenses is attributed generally by President Gould, to heavy rains during the year, labor replacing 272 miles of light with heavier steel, and higher prevailing wages.

After all deductions, including full interest on the income bonds and an appropriation of $544,765 for additional property, the sur plus for the year above reported on is seen to be $219,081. This would amount to a little above 1% on the preferred stock.

Stock.—Preferred—Authorized, $30,000,000; issued, $20,000,000. Common—Authorized, $35,000,000; issued, $16,500,000.

The preferred is 5% non-cumulative.

Funded debt.—The $20,000,000 1st gold certificates are issued for securities of constituent companies deposited with trustees.

The income bonds are 4% non-cumulative, and the company has taken up at 90% in 1st consolidated mortgage bonds, $6,727,500, which are deposited as security for the new mortgage.

The 1st consolidated mortgage is authorized at $25,000,000, of which $13,205,750 has been issued, the unissued being reserved for retirement of the balance of the income bonds. This will leave about $10,000,000 for branches, betterments and new equipment.

Dividends —None paid on either class of stock.

Annual meeting.—First Tuesday in October.

Main office, St. Louis, Mo.; New York office, 195 Broadway.

Directors.—Edwin Gould, R. M. Gallaway, Howard Gould, Winslow S. Pierce, William H. Taylor, E. T. Jeffery, Murray Carleton, F. H. Britton, and Charles Parsons.

SEABOARD AIR LINE RAILWAY.

Organized in April, 1900, as successor to the Richmond, Petersburg & Carolina Railroad Company, and later assumed the operation of several lines which subsequently were merged.

The system has a mileage of 2,617 miles, extending from Richmond, Va., to Tampa, Fla.; Wilmington, N. C., to Atlanta, Ga.; Savannah, Ga., to Montgomery, Ala., and branches.

The company owns a one-sixth interest in the Richmond-Washington Company, controlling the road between Richmond and Washington, and under traffic agreement with the Pennsylvania Railroad, maintains through car service between New York and its northern terminal.

An extension from Atlanta to Birmingham is to be completed in the present year.

A large interest is held in the Baltimore Steam Packet Company and in the Old Dominion Steamship Company.

Condensed balance sheet, June 30, 1903 :

Assets.

Cost of road, equipment and property	$105,039,287
Securities owned	631,803
Securities owned by proprietary companies	2,369,272
Preferred stock in treasury	5,600,000
Common stock in treasury	8,500,000
Leasehold interest in Wilmington Railway Bridge (per contra)	108,500
Cash with treasurer, etc.	866,775
Due from agents and conductors	274,745
Due from individuals and companies	877,650

Assets (continued).

Due from U. S. Government..	$75,005
Due from other railroads (claims)............................	33,814
Notes receivable...	85,827
Unearned interest, equipment trust notes...........................	13,640
Unearned insurance premiums....................................	16,970
Material and supplies on hand.......................................	752,628
Freight claims in suspense...................................	141,285
Sundry accounts...	217,172
Due from proprietary companies...................................	54,004
Sundry accounts...	95,357
Total..	$125,753,734

Liabilities.

Preferred capital stock...	$25,000,000
Common capital stock..	37,500,000
1st mortgage bonds...	12,775,000
Refunding collateral trust bonds....................................	10,000,000
Mortgage bonds proprietary companies...........................	29,720,000
Wilmington Railway Bridge bonds (per contra)...................	108,500
Equipment trust obligations..	2,652,701
Traffic balances...	35,356
Claims authorized...........................	27,143
Agents' drafts in transit......	65,307
Audited vouchers...	1,347,318
Pay rolls..	462,904
Accrued taxes, not due..	145,183
Accrued interest, dividends and rentals, not due.................	268,166
Coupons matured, not presented....................................	700,328
Sundry accounts...	645,594
Due to proprietary companies.....................................	2,147,318
Reserve for outstanding stock of proprietary companies...........	306,188
Other reserves...	199,239
Profit and loss, surplus...	1,647,487
Total..	$125,753,734

Income and profit and loss account for year ended and at June 30, 1903 :

Earnings :		
	Passenger...	$2,354,561
	Freight...	8,599,280
	Mail and express................................	559,797
	Miscellaneous....................................	643,290
	Gross earnings....................................	$12,156,928
Expenses:		
	Maintenance of way and structures...............	$1,483,017
	Maintenance of equipment........................	1,449,297
	Conducting transportation.......................	5,014,801
	General expenses................................	493,980
	Total expenses...................................	$8,441,095
Net earnings...		$3,715,833
Other income..		110,031
Total income..		$3,825,864

Total income	$3,825,864
Deductions from income:	
Interest on funded debt	$2,481,400
Other interest	104,668
Taxes	434,133
Rentals	43,600
Dividends on guaranteed stock of proprietary companies	6,307
Other deductions	5,324
Total	$3,075,432
Surplus for year	$750,432
Surplus forward	897,055
Profit and loss, June 30, 1903	$1,647,487

The year above reported on seems to have been a banner year for the company—the gross earnings having reached the highest figure in its history.

The annual report includes a table showing that the gross earnings per mile were in 1895 $2,556, and showing a somewhat regular increase up to the past year, at which time the figure reached $4,663.

The statistics for the year compared with the year ended June 30, 1902, show that the increase in the average rate received from freight per ton per mile was .46 mills.

Freight earnings show an increase of 8.8%, the increase in tonnage being 4.3%. Not only has the volume of business been advanced, but the grade of commodities transported are such as will stand higher rates, a fairly good sign of local development.

Passenger earnings increased 15.4%, but the average rate per passenger per mile declined from 2.357 cents to 2.286 cents. The number of passengers carried one mile increased 17.6%.

Stocks.—Preferred: Authorized, $25,000,000; issued, $19,400,000. Common: Authorized, $37,500,000; issued, $29,000,000.

The preferred is 4% non-cumulative.

Both classes of stock are held under a voting trust, until or before 1910.

Bonds.—1st mortgage bonds, authorized in no case to exceed $75,000,000; outstanding, $12,775,000; deposited to secure $10,000,000 collateral trust bonds, $20,000,000; reserved to retire underlying bonds, $29,725.000, and the balance for additional property at not exceeding, $1,500,000 per year.

Dividends.—None paid; The amount carried to surplus from the past year's operations was nearly equivalent to 4% on the outstanding preferred stock.

Annual meeting.—Friday after second Thursday in November.

Main office.—Richmond, Va. New York office, 15 Wall St.

Directors.—John Skelton Williams, Jos. M. Barr, H. Clay Pierce, J. W. Middendorf, S. Davies Warfield, James H. Dooley, B. F. Yoakum, Ernst Thalmann, Oakleigh Thorne, Thomas F. Ryan, James A. Blair, C. Sidney Shepard, T. Jefferson Coolidge, Nathaniel Thayer, Norman B. Ream and Geo. W. Watts.

SOUTHERN PACIFIC COMPANY.

A holding company organized under the laws of the State of Kentucky in 1884 for the purpose of consolidating lines extending from New Orleans to San Francisco, Cal., Portland, Ore., and Ogden, Utah.

A strong working control of the capital stock is owned by the Union Pacific Railway.

The total mileage at June 30, 1903, was 9,176 miles, of which 351 miles are leased and the balance controlled through ownership of all but a very small amount of the capital stock.

The lines controlled, operated by the Southern Pacific Company under leases to it, are as under:

Southern Pacific Railroad (less 242 leased to A., T. & S. F.)	3,047
South Pacific Coast Railway	101
Central Pacific Railway	1,363
Oregon & California	672

Lines controlled, operated by companies owning the lines:

Morgan's Louisana & Texas Railroad & S.S. Line.	324
Louisana Western Railroad	164
Texas & New Orleans Railroad.	433
Galveston, Harrisburg & San Antonio Railway	917
Galveston, Houston & Northern Railway	54
Houston, East & West Texas Railway	191
Houston & Shreveport Railroad	39
New York, Texas & Mexican Railway	151

Houston & Texas Central Railroad 690
Carson & Colorado Railway (narrow gauge) 300
Southern Pacific Company................... ... 10
Iberia & Vermillion Railroad..................... 16
Direct Navigation Company...................... —
Gulf, Western Texas & Pacific Railway........ ... 111

Lines not controlled, operated by Southern Pacific
Company under lease :

New Mexico & Arizona Railroad.................... 88
Sonora Railway................................. 263

Total....................................... 8,934
Track of Southern Pacific Railway leased to A., T.
& S. F 242

Total as above................................. 9,176

The Southern Pacific Company during the past year purchased
all the steamships and other property of the Cromwell Steamship
Company, which is now operated as part of the New York & New
Orleans Line. Also owns a controlling interest in the Pacific
Mail Steamship Company.

General balance sheet, Southern Pacific Company, June 30, 1903:

Capital assets :   *Assets.*
  Stocks and bonds owned, deposited $254,946,349
  Steamships.. 3,659,762
  Sinking funds... 1,044
Current assets :
  Bonds and stocks owned, not deposited........................... 2,321,886
  Agents and conductors... 1,774,721
  Loans and bills receivable............. 493,691
  Cash....... 3,917,588
  Individuals and companies....................................... 437,905
  Material, fuel, etc.......... 7,500,913
  United States Government transportation. 1,791,765
Deferred assets :
  Construction advances. 5,213,119
  Pacific Mail Steamship Company............................... 1,620,353
  Individuals and companies 239,489
  Lands. 219,345
  Other property... 799,135
  Real estate... 4,033,686
  Steamships and tugs... 3,513,224
  Rolling stock 9,936,814
  Wood preserving plant... 135,954
  Due from proprietary companies 15,773,604
Contingent assets :
  San Antonio & Aransas Pass Railway Company................. 2,280,000

Total... $320,610,347

Liabilities.

Capital liabilities :	
Capital stock..	$197,849,259
First mortgage 6% " S. S " bonds............................	2,144,000
4% gold bonds (C. P. stock collateral)......................	29,418,500
Two-five year 4½% gold bonds...............................	20,000,000
Current liabilities :	
Unpaid dividends..	10,099
Interest coupons due but not presented.....................	175,839
Interest coupons due July 1, 1903...........................	1,403,763
Interest accrued but not due.................................	2,570,590
Loans and bills payable	23,409,721
Traffic balances...	764,759
Vouchers and pay rolls.......................................	6,090,953
Deferred liabilities :	
Taxes, estimated to June 30..................................	226,000
Wells Fargo & Company's express contract...................	368,000
Due to proprietary companies................................	22,589,412
Contingent liabilities :	
Individuals and companies....................................	385,541
Marine insurance fund	1,149,925
Rolling stock replacement fund..............................	81,419
Rolling stock depreciation fund..............................	318,880
Floating equipment replacement fund.........................	585,702
Structures replacement fund..................................	121,842
Steamship insurance fund.....................................	1,603,686
Unadjusted accounts..	69,909
Profit and loss...	9,272,548
Total..	$320,610,347

Income account, Southern Pacific Company, for year ended June 30, 1903 :

Gross receipts properties operated under lease :	
Central Pacific...	$21,121,672
Oregon & California Railroad.................................	3,991,347
South Pacific Coast Railway..................................	972,550
Southern Pacific Railroad.....................................	30,974,266
New Mexico & Arizona Railroad..............................	242,309
Sonora Railway..	479,195
Total...	$57,781,339
Other receipts :	
Gross receipts from steamship lines operated................	$4,900,604
Interest, dividends, rentals, etc.............................	1,692,582
Total...	$6,593,186
Gross income..	$64,374,525
Disbursements.—Operating expenses :	
Central Pacific Railway.......................................	$21,121,671
Oregon & California Railroad.................................	3,991,347
South Pacific Coast Railway..................................	1,763,512
New Mexico & Arizona Railroad..............................	263,694
Sonora Railway..	629,786
Operating expenses, taxes and proportion of net profits payable, etc., under lease of Southern Pacific Railroad.......................	30,398,897
Deficit—Oregon & California Railroad Company after all expenses, betterments, etc...	320,090
Total...	$58,488,997

Total..	$58,488,997

Other expenses:

Expenses, steamship lines operated..............................	$3,831,724
Interest and rentals...	3,056,157
Insurance, taxes, etc...	508,806
Annual payment, redemption of steamship bonds...............	75,000
Advances to S. A. & A. P. Railway for account of operations, betterments and additions	352,888
Depreciation Southern Pacific Company's rolling stock.........	318,880

Total..	$8,143,455
Total disbursements..	$66,632,452
Deficit for year..................................	$2,257,925

General balance sheet, proprietary companies, June 30, 1903 :

Assets.

Capital assets:

Cost of road and franchises	$648,256,893
Expenditures for new lines..................	6,716,466
Sinking funds..	15,486,436
Land grant account..	5,057,774
Trust funds..	237,704

Current assets:

Agents and conductors	416,465
Loans and bills receivable....................,.................	44,498
Cash	416,980
Individuals and companies	1,059,575
Material, fuel, etc..	3,752,945
Traffic balances...	215,988
U. S. Government...	162,718
Bonds owned..	1,309,736
Cash and bonds deposited against bonds satisfied of mortgage...	808,504

Deferred assets:

Individuals and companies	95,438
Land and other property...	633,049
Stocks owned	798,462
Unadjusted accounts	104,143
Due from proprietary companies.............................	7,471,188
Due from Southern Pacific Company	22,589,412

Contingent assets:

Individuals and companies	415,972
Replacement funds..	6,468
Unadjusted accounts	143,762

Total..	$716,200,576

Liabilities.

Capital liabilities:

Capital stock..	$278,408,572
Preferred stock......	24,600 000
Funded and other fixed interest-bearing debt....................	268,834,636
Equipment trust obligations.....................................	2,863,654
3% notes favor U. S. A..	35,287,629

Current liabilities:

Individuals and companies......................................	225,365
Traffic balances..................	417,070
Coupons matured, not presented................................	263,613
Coupons due July 1..	422,445
Interest accrued, but not due...................................	656,062

Liabilities (continued).

Loans and bills payable...	$573,000
Vouchers and pay rolls	2,657,161
Unpaid dividends	7,159
Bonds satisfied of mortgage, but not presented	645,000
Deferred liabilities:	
Individuals and companies...	77,034
Taxes assessed, but not due	215,284
Sinking funds uninvested...	86,492
Due to proprietary companies...........................	7,198,337
Due to Southern Pacific Company................................	15,773,607
Contingent liabilities:	
Individuals and companies...	76,385
Unadjusted accounts	331,892
Principal of deferred payments on land contracts	5,057,774
Replacement funds...	439,511
Profit and loss...$82,435,755	
Less roads showing deficit.................................. 11,352,862	
	71,082,893
Total	$716,200,576

Income account, proprietary companies, for year ended June 30, 1903:

Receipts:	
Gross transportation receipts.....................................	$82,698,228
Rentals, trackage...	251,413
Rentals, other property and facilities	30,829
Income from investments...	93,458
Income from lands and securities not pledged for redemption of	
bonds..	678,612
Income from securities owned by sinking funds....................	280,465
Interest on open accounts..	1,133,226
Miscellaneous receipts...	44,885
Total receipts...	$85,211,116
Expenditures:	
Operating expenses..	$55,888,608
Taxes...	2,094,721
Rentals, trackage...	11,678
Rentals, other property and facilities............................	781,644
Interest on funded debt...	12,841,989
Interest on C. P. R. R. 3% notes to U. S. A........................	1,112,387
Interest on open accounts...	596,629
Land department expenses..	135,248
Taxes on granted lands..	102,902
Miscellaneous expenses..	55,356
Sinking fund contributions and income from sinking fund investments	720,465
Construction, improvements and real estate......................	107,145
Surveys	75,668
Total expenditures.	$74,524,440
Balance surplus..	$10,686,675
Payments to Southern Pacific Company under lease..................	$790,960
Payments by Southern Pacific Company under lease	575,368
Balance to profit and loss...	$10,902,267

Combined profit and loss account, Southern Pacific Company and proprietary companies, for year ended June 30, 1903 :

Dr.

Adjustment of unsettled accounts......	$232,187
Adjustment in land department accounts...........................	163,818
Difference between cost and proceeds from sale of steamships and other property....	401,215
Miscellaneous expenses...	35,929
Balance of unfunded discount on bonds sold, charged off.............	829,471
Loss in sale of bonds and securities exchanged......................	2,741
Premium on bonds purchased and cancelled	75,595
Dividends (proprietary companies).................................	1.059,200
Adjustment of interest claims......................................	173,333
Balance, June 30, 1903. viz.:	
Southern Pacific Company..	9,272,548
Proprietary companies	71,082,893
Total..	$83,328,930

Cr.

Balance June 30, 1902, viz.:		
Southern Pacific Company...		$10.176,309
Proprietary companies		58,707,857
Income account for year:		
Proprietary companies, credit..........................$10,902,267		
Southern Pacific Company, debit........................ 2,257,925		
Advances to Oregon & Cal. R. R. charged to income, now charged to Oregon & Cal. R. R................. 320,090		
		8,964,432
Annual contribution to sinking funds........................		515,000
Income from sinking fund investments...............................		280,465
Proceeds from sale of lands pledged for redemption of bonds........		1,381,641
Profits from sale of bonds, etc......................................		15,601
Adjustment of unsettled claims.....................................		175,220
Adjustment of interest claims......................................		200,000
Difference between cost and proceeds from sale of property		27,385
Miscellaneous receipts		173,214
Advances to reorganization committee collected.....		301,000
Dividends on stocks owned		1,057,920
Capital stock written off...		1,000,000
Advances to S. A. & A. P. Ry. charged to income account now charged to S. A. & A. P. Ry......................................		352,886
Total........................		$83,328,930

Gross receipts from transportation for all properties increased over the year 1901–02, 5.72%. The operating expenses, however, increased 9.85%, the per cent. to earnings being for railways 67.29, against 64.63.

This is rateably accounted for by increased train mileage and further, by liberal charges for maintenance of roadway and equipment. Increased cost of labor and material also entered into the situation.

Stock.—Southern Pacific Company—Authorized, $200,000,000 ; issued, $197,849,259.

Proprietary companies—Outstanding common, $278,408,572 ; preferred, $24,600,coo.

Funded debt.—Southern Pacific Company—Outstarding, 4½% bonds, $20,000,000, out of an issue limited to $30,000,000 ; outstanding, 4% Central Pacific collateral go'd bonds, $29,418,500 ; authorized, $36,819,000, the balance to be issued to take up additional Central Pacific preferred stock for improvements on the Central Pacific, at not exceeding $200,000 per annum ; 6% steamship bonds outstanding, $2,144,000; outstanding fixed interest bearing debt of proprietary companies, $306,985,919.

Dividends.—None paid by Southern Pacific Company. Of the proprietary lines, dividends aggregating $1,059,200 were paid by Houston, E. & W. Texas, the Houston & Shreveport and the Houston & Texas Central R. R. Co., the returns on all but a few shares accruing to the parent company.

Annual meeting.—Wednesday following first Monday in April. Main office, San Francisco ; New York office, 120 Broadway.

Directors.—T. Jefferson Coolidge, Jr., William D. Cornish, George J. Gould, Edward H. Harriman, Edwin Hawley, H. E. Huntington, James H. Hyde, Otto H. Kahn, D. O. Mills, Winslow S. Pierce, Jacob H. Schiff, James Speyer, James Stillman.

Southern Pacific Company and proprietary companies—Consolidated income account for the year ended June 30, 1903 :

Receipts :

Proprietary lines and miscellaneous income of proprietary companies...	$85,211,116
Non-proprietary lines	721,504
Southern Pacific Company from steamship lines—dividends on stocks owned, rentals, etc	6,593,186
Total receipts	$92,525,806

Disbursements :

Operating expenses and taxes proprietary lines, interest on funded debt and all other expenses of proprietary companies..	$74,524,440
Operating expenses, taxes and all other expenses incurred in connection with operation of non-proprietary lines.	893 480
Expenses of steamship lines operated	3,831,723
Net interest due proprietary companies on advances and on loans and open accounts	969,948
Charter of steamers, insurance, taxes, and miscellaneous and general expenses	528,138

Sinking fund contribution	$75,000
Fixed rentals	25,000
Depreciation on Southern Pacific Company rolling stock	318,879
Interest on S. A. & A. P. bonds	27,120
Advances to S. A. & A. P. Ry	352,888
Miscellaneous	11,499
Total	$81,558,115

Balance	$10,967,691

Deduct :

Interest on Southern Pacific Company 6% steamship bonds	$130,770
Interest on Southern Pacific Company 4% (Central Pacific stock collateral)	1,178,740
Interest on Southern Pacific Company 4½% 2-5 year bonds	693,750
Total	$2,003,260
Surplus for year	$8,964,431

The profit and loss account during the period shows adjustments evidently applicable to prior periods, amounting to net credit of $2,155,236, which would not enter into the year's returns—also there is a net debit on account of dividends on stocks amounting to $1,280 and the amount shown above as advances to S. A. & A. P. Ry., $352,888 is credited and charged to that company within the period..... 351,608

Surplus for year applicable to dividends	$9,316,039

This does not include surplus from sale of lands pledged for redemption of bonds, amounting to $1,381,640 for the year, and contained in the profit and loss credits above referred to.

SOUTHERN RAILWAY COMPANY.

Chartered by the Legislature of Virginia in 1894, to reorganize the Richmond and Westpoint Terminal, since when numerous other lines have been acquired by purchase or lease.

The total mileage operated at June 30, 1903, was 7,137 miles. In addition there was controlled but operated separately 956 miles, including the Mobile & Ohio and Augusta Southern. The company jointly with the L. & N. controls the Monon Route, the Alabama Great Southern, and has large working interests with the C., N. O. & T. P., the North Alabama and Ga. So. & Fla. lines; also has one-sixth interest in the Richmond-Washington Company, owning a line between Richmond and Washington.

The line operated extends, with numerous important branches, from Washington, D. C., to Jacksonville, Fla., via Charleston,

S. C., and Savannah, Ga., and from Washington via Charlotte, N. C., and Atlanta, Ga., to Greenville, Miss., and Mobile, Ala. Controlled and affiliated lines extend from Chicago, Cincinnati and St. Louis, to Mobile, Ala.

General balance sheet, June 30, 1903 :

Assets.

Cost of road	$265,694,928
Leasehold estates	29,627,562
Cost of equipment	24,840,049
Cost of securities pledged or held for control	54,339,339
Materials and supplies	2,496,144
Rails and fixtures leased	175,704
Miscellaneous securities	3,448,862
Bills receivable, deferred	434,979
Bills receivable, current	183,108
Insurance prepaid	5,235
Sinking funds	66,178
Insurance fund	275,000
Sundry accounts	133,099
Advance to sub. companies	349,258
Income accrued, not due	106,613
Cash on hand	2,994,818
Cash in transit	937,705
Due from agents	988,893
Due from U. S. Government	419,103
Due from other transportation companies	776,222
Due from individuals and companies	542,017
Total	$388,834,816

Liabilities.

Capital stock :	
Common	$120,000,000
Preferred	60,000,000
M. & O. stock trust certificates	4,932,600
Funded debt	138,870,321
Securities of leasehold estates	31,149,500
Equipment obligations	7,021,810
Certificates of indebtedness	8,800,000
Balance purchase, N. E. R. R., Ga.	107,000
Balance on real estate	75,000
Balance on Hartwell branch	14,021
Reserve funds	1,458,088
Sundry accounts	129,330
Interest and rentals accrued	847,617
Taxes accrued	493,141
Dividends payable, October 1, 1903	1,500,000
Interest and rental due and unpaid	2,299,999
Vouchers, wages and claims	4,040,068
Due other transportation companies	722,089
Due individuals and companies	411,670
Profit and loss	5,962,562
Total	$388,834,816

Income and profit and loss account for year ended and at June 30, 1903 :

Earnings:

Freight.................................	$28,081,034
Passenger..	10,804,542
Mail..	1,688,118
Express..........................	990,576
Miscellaneous....................................	789,791
Gross earnings.....................................	**$42,354,061**

Expenses:

Conducting transportation.......................................	$15,759,973
Maintenance of way and structures............................	5,733,997
Maintenance of equipment.......................................	6,916,823
General expenses...	1,391,088
Taxes...............................	1,187,259
Total expenses and taxes..	**$30,989,140**

Net earnings...	$11,364,921
Income from investments............................	1,164,011
Miscellaneous......................................	47,250
Total income...	**$12,576,182**

Deductions from income :

Fixed charges and rentals.........	$8,446,041
Miscellaneous....................................	422,663
Total...	**$8,868,704**

Surplus for year..	$3,707,478
Dividend on preferred (5%)...........................	3,000,000
Balance to profit and loss...	$707,478
Profit and loss, forward..	5,255,084
Profit and loss, June 30, 1903..........	**$5,962,562**

Comparing the above figures with those published for the year immediately preceding, it is found that the gross earnings increased 12.3%, operating expenses increased 15.5%, and net earnings increased 4.6%. The percentage of operating expenses to earnings increased from 71.19 to 73.16 during the same period; during the two preceding years this averaged about 70%.

The increased revenues were about evenly distributed. The largest increase in expenses is found to be in maintenance of equipment and conducting transportation. President Spencer in his annual report calls attention to the marked industrial growth throughout the territory reached by the lines, and states that "the number of new industrial plants of various classes completed during the year was 735, **and** the number under construction at close of the year was 146. Previously existing plants to the number of 208 were materially enlarged during the year.

"There were 29 cotton mills under construction at June 30 of this year ; an increase in number of 8 mills over corresponding date of the previous year. These new mills when completed will place in operation 12,537 looms and 443,002 spindles, an increase over similar equipment in new mills under construction at June 30 last year of 4,937 looms, and 100,802 spindles."

Local development in mineral and timber industries are also reported.

Freight tonnage is widely diversified, 30% being coal; 12% from mining industries other than coal ; 13% agricultural ; 4% cotton ; 26% product of manufacturers.

Stock.—Issued as authorized (see balance sheet).

Dividends on preferred : 1897 and 1898, 1% yearly ; 1899, 2% ; 1900, 3% ; 1902 and 1903, 5% yearly ; April, 1904, 2½% for the half year. None paid on common.

Annual meeting.—Second Monday in October.

Main office, Richmond, Va.; New York office, 80 Broadway.

Directors.—A. B. Andrews, Joseph Bryan, W. W. Finley, S. M. Inman, Adrian Iselin, Jr., Samuel Spencer, Charles Steele, James T. Woodward, Harris C. Fahnestock, Robert M. Gallaway, Charles Lanier and Edmund D. Randolph.

STANDARD ROPE & TWINE COMPANY.

Formed in 1896 under the laws of New Jersey to reorganize the United States Cordage Company, which company succeeded to the National Cordage Company.

The company is engaged in the manufacture of rope and twine, and has three mills in operation besides several idle mills. It owns the entire capital stock of the Canabis Manufacturing Company owning three mills, also the Chelsea & Boston mills and Wm. Wall & Sons.

General balance sheet, July 31, 1903:

Assets.

Real estate, buildings, machinery, good will, etc.	$20,308.948
Raw and manufactured goods, mill supplies, etc.	794,313
Stocks and bonds owned	211,957
Accounts and bills receivable	649,859
Cash	52,145
Profit and loss (deficit)	726,955
Total	**$22,744,177**

Liabilities.

Common stock	$12,000,000
Consolidated mortgage bonds	6,805,330
First mortgage bonds, less amount cancelled	2,740,000
Accounts and bills payable	1,198,847
Total	**$22,744,177**

Details of income account are not published in the report for the fiscal year ended July 31, 1903, but President Russell says in part:

We have paid the interest on first mortgage bonds	$164,400
And charged off to depreciation	52,844
Interest on borrowed money	57,553
Leaving a deficit of	141,164

Restated, it would appear that the charges against net earnings amounted to	$415,961
And the net earnings	274,797

Deficit for year	$141,164
Deficit at July 31, 1902, was	585,790
Deficit at July 31, 1903, per balance sheet	$726,954

The above figures make no provision for the sinking fund conditions of the first mortgage bonds, requiring payment of 1% on the amount outstanding July 30, 1897. This payment is not due, however, until February 1, 1904.

President Russell attributes the poor showing of the company to two causes, viz.: Cost of maintaining idle properties turned over by the reorganization committee, and lack of working capital. Efforts are being made to dispose of the idle property, which if carried out, would in a measure do away with the second difficulty by providing funds with which to operate the business. Facilities for a larger volume of business are at hand, and it is reported that this could be handled at very little increased cost for operations.

Stock.—Authorized, $12,000,000 ; issued, $11,960,860.

Dividends.—None paid.

Annual meeting, Third Tuesday in September.

Main office, New York.

Directors.—William Barbour, William R. Potts, James B. Clews, John Kean, Alfred R. Turner, Jr., Josiah C. Reiff, Thomas Russell, Joseph G. Taylor, E. Le B. Gardiner.

TENNESSEE COAL, IRON & RAILROAD COMPANY.

Chartered by the Legislature of Tennessee in 1860 under the name of Tennessee Coal & Railroad Company. Present name assumed in 1881. In September, 1892, a consolidation was effected with the De Bardeleben Coal & Iron Company, and the properties of the Cahaba Coal Mining and Excelsior Coal Companies were acquired.

The company owns half a million acres of coal, iron and limestone and timber lands in the States of Alabama and Tennessee, and its blast furnaces have an annual capacity of over 800,000 tons.

The company owns all the capital stock of the Alabama Steel & Shipbuilding Company, which concern has a daily capacity of 1,000 tons of steel billets and slabs. This property is operated by the Coal & Iron Company under lease and under guarantee of its bonds and 6% on the preferred stock.

General balance sheet, December 31, 1903:

Assets.

Coal, ore lands and other real estate	$26,047,005
Plants and equipment	9,188,632
Investments	273,971
Treasury securities	609,000
Cash	329,094
Bills and securities receivable	1,479,984
Supplies, etc.	2,087,742
Assets of bond sinking fund	46,706
Total	$40,062,135

Liabilities.

Common stock	$22,552,800
Preferred stock	248,300
Funded debt.,	11,858,000
Alabama Steel & Shipbuilding bonds	1,100,000
Alabama Steel & Shipbuilding preferred stock	440,000
Alabama Steel & Shipbuilding reserve, etc., funds	240,301
Current liabilities	1,888,572
Profit and loss, surplus	1,734,162
Total	$40,062,135

Income and profit and loss account for year ended and at December 31, 1903:

Net earnings after deducting all operating expenses, repairs, renewals, taxes, insurance, bad debts, etc.	$2,889,957
Miscellaneous income.	15,020
	$2,904,977
Interest on bonds and dividends on guaranteed securities.	739,521
Net profits	$2,165,456
Royalty and replacement funds	411,422
	$1,754,034
Dividend on preferred stock	19,864
Surplus for year and at December 31, 1903	$1,734,170

The surplus at December 31, 1903, amounting to $1,409,785, was written off against cost of property.

During the years 1901, 1902 and 1903, expenditures for property was $4,645,153 for the period, all of which was paid for out of earnings. During the same period the net debt decreased $564,409, and there was charged off for depreciation $4,351,077. The amount carried to surplus for the year after payment of dividend on the preferred stock is equivalent to about 7½% on the common.

Surplus for recent years after all charges and dividends was: 1901, $484,351; 1902, $1,409,785; 1903, $1,734,170.

The net profits of 1902 were more than double those of 1901, and 1903 shows an increase of 17% over 1902.

Stock.—Common: Authorized, $23,000,000; issued, $22,552,800. Preferred: Authorized, $1,000,000; issued, $248,300.

The preferred is 8% cumulative, but three-fourths was exchanged in 1900 for common, on the basis of 180% common for par in preferred, together with 54% accrued dividends. Back dividend was paid on all non-assenting stock.

Funded and guaranteed debt amounts to $13,206,300, calling for an annual payment of $737,340.

Dividends.—Preferred : 8% (see above).

Common : 1887, 1% ; 1900, 6% ; none since.

Main office. Birmingham, Ala.; New York office, 100 Broadway.

Annual meeting in May, at Tracy City, Tenn.

Directors.—Don H. Bacon, William Barbour, Albert B. Boardman, Henry R. Sloat, Joseph Dickson, Charles McCrery, Walker Percy, James Henry Smith, Frank S. Witherbee, Cord Meyer, S. L. Schoonmaker, Benjamin F. Tracy, James T. Woodward.

TEXAS & PACIFIC RAILWAY.

Organized under Act of Congress March 3, 1871, and general railroad laws of the State of Texas. The present corporation is the result of reorganization in 1888, without confirmation of foreclosure sale, thus preserving the original federal charter. The plan of reorganization provided for the retirement of all bonds subsequent to the Eastern Division first mortgage and creation of new first incomes.

Mileage operated at June 30, 1903, was 1,827 miles, of which 1,735 miles is owned, the balance being operated under trackage rights.

The line extends from New Orleans, La., via Dallas and Fort Worth, to El Paso, Texas, with parallel line between Texarkana and Ft. Worth in northern Texas, and branches.

The road is considered a Gould property. The Missouri Pacific holds a large interest in the stock, and the St. Louis & San Francisco owns all but $980,000 out of a total issue of $24,650,000 second consolidated income bonds.

General balance sheet, June 30, 1903 :

Assets.

Railroad, buildings. equipment. etc.	$87,405,560
New Orleans Pacific Railroad stock held to protect rights Louisiana Division	6,716.200
Securities owned.	686,108
Elevator property.	500,390
New equipment.	2,140.116
Gordon coal mine.	141,541
Materials, fuel, etc.	522,876
Cash on hand	351,133
Accounts collectible.	1,126,650
Land notes receivable	31,930
Miscellaneous.	231,662
Total.	$99,854,168

Liabilities.

Capital stock	$38,763,810
Funded debt, etc.	54,279,602
Equipment obligations, etc.	2,250,010
Vouchers and pay rolls	953,438
Interest due and accrued	319,702
Bills payable	1,625,000
Other accounts	316,501
Income account, surplus	1,346,106
Total	$99,854,168

Income and profit and loss account for year ended and at June 30, 1903:

Earnings:

Freight	$8,504,462
Passenger	2,494,545
Mail	269,683
Express	223,008
Miscellaneous	603,046
Gross income	$12,094,744

Transportation expenses:

Maintenance of way and structures	$1,518,098
Maintenance of equipment	1,395,265
Conducting transportation	5,011,663
General expenses	361,080
Total expenses	$8,286,106
Net earnings	$3,808,638
Other receipts	171,485
Total income	$3,980,123

Deductions from Income:

Interest on bonds	$1,473,354
Taxes	296,053
Interest and discount	408,949
Improvement account	273,264
Equipment account	568,121
Miscellaneous	21,660
Total	$3,041,401
Surplus for year	$938,722
Interest on second income bonds, 5%	1,161,900
Balance, debit to surplus	$223,178
Surplus, June 30, 1902	1,569,284
Surplus, June 30, 1903	$1,346,106

The results from operations for 1903 compared with 1902 are as follows: Gross earnings increased 7.63%, expenses increased 6.88%, net earnings increased 9.30%.

The per cent. of expenses to earnings was 68.51 against 68.99 in 1902, 68.26 in 1901, and 67.50 in 1900.

Stock.—Authorized, $50,000,000 ; issued, $38,763,810.

Funded debt.—Of the funded debt $24,650,000 is second mortgage 5% income bonds, non-cumulative. No foreclosure can be had under this mortgage unless default is made on the first mortgage. As above stated, nearly all of this issue is held by the Gould interests.

The balance of the funded debt calls for fixed interest payments, and is a first lien on the property.

Dividends.—None paid on stock.

Interest on income bonds : 1899, 1½% ; 1900, 4% ; 5% since.

Annual meeting, third Wednesday in March.

Main office, Dallas, Texas ; New York office, 195 Broadway.

Directors.—Russell Sage, A. Lawrence Hopkins, George J. Gould, Edwin Gould, Samuel Sloan, John T. Terry, Charles M. McGhee, C. E. Satterlee, Thomas T. Eckert, Howard Gould, Frank Jay Gould, Louis Fitzgerald, Winslow S. Pierce, John P. Munn, Robert M. Gallaway, L. S. Thorne.

TWIN CITY RAPID TRANSIT COMPANY.

Organized in June, 1891, under the laws of New Jersey, to succeed to the Minneapolis Street, the Minneapolis, Lyndale & Minnetonka, the St. Paul City Railway, and the Minneapolis & St. Paul Suburban Railway Companies.

The company has the exclusive right to operate street cars of and between the cities of St. Paul, Minneapolis and Stillwater.

The property consists of 253 miles of line with 80 pound "T" rail imbedded in concrete on the principal city streets, and is operated by water power. A large steam power plant however is under construction to meet increased requirements.

General balance sheet, December 31, 1903 :

Assets.

Roadway, etc., including securities in treasury	$31,820,072
Notes and accounts receivable	19,201
Cash	1,310,250
Materials and supplies	125,973
Total	$33,275,496

Liabilities.

Common stock..	$16,511,000
Preferred stock..	3,000,000
Funded debt...	12,637,000
Unpaid vouchers	115,493
Interest accrued not due	229,831
Bills payable..	559,284
Dividends payable..	206,388
Miscellaneous...	16,500
Total..	$33,275,496

Income account for year ended December 31, 1903:

Earnings:	
Passenger..	$4,042,230
Other..	21,709
Gross earnings...	$4,063,939
Expenses:	
General..	$165,675
Maintenance of equipment	211,298
Maintenance of way and structures........................	117,536
Operating power plants...................................	331,281
Insurance..	41,104
Injuries and damages.....................................	162,695
Legal expenses...	22,999
Car service...	825,462
Total expenses..	$1,878,050
Net earnings..	$2,185,889
Deduct, interest and taxes	731,041
Surplus for year...	$1,454,848
Dividends:	
Preferred, 7%..	$210,000
Common, 5%...	825,550
Total...	$1,035,550
Surplus after dividends..	$419,298
Surplus, December 31, 1902...	2,991,346
Transferred to credit of property account.............................	$3,410,644

President Thomas Lowry in his report states that any surplus shown hereafter will mean cash on hand or its equivalent, and that surplus earnings invested in property will be transferred to that account, thus explaining the disappearance of such usual balance sheet item. The gross earnings for the year show an increase over 1902 of 12.51%, and the percentage of expenses to earnings during the same period increased 1.06%.

Stock.—Common: Authorized, $17,300,000; issued, $16,511,000. Preferred: Authorized, $3,000,000; issued, $3,000,000.

The preferred stock is 7% cumulative.

Dividends.—Regular dividends (Q-J) have been paid on the preferred.

The first dividend of 1% on the common was paid in August, 1899; in 1900, 3%; in 1901, 3½%; in 1902, February, 2%; May, 1¼%; August, 1¼%; November, 1¼%; in 1903, 5%; in 1904, February, 1¼%.

Annual meeting, first Tuesday in May.

Corporate office, Elizabeth, N. J.; main office, Minneapolis.

Directors.—Thomas Lowry, C. G. Goodrich, Clinton Morrison, John Kean, J. Kennedy Tod, William A. Read, A. E. Ames.

UNION BAG & PAPER COMPANY.

Incorporated under the laws of New Jersey in 1899. It is estimated to do about 90% of the paper bag business of the United States.

In addition to its bag factories, the company owns pulp and paper mills, timber lands and water power. Its plants are located at Sandy Hill, N. Y., Hadley, N. Y., Ballston Spa, N. Y., Watertown, Mass., and Kankanna, Wis.

General balance sheet, January 31, 1904:

Assets.

Cost of properties	$26,911,085
Insurance, etc	30,367
Logs	481,936
Supplies, etc., at cost	244,789
Merchandise in hand or process	924,455
Accounts receivable	314,628
Investments	102,000
Cash	43,141
Total	$29 052,401

Liabilities.

Preferred stock	$11,000,000
Common stock	16,000,000
Loans on bills payable	915,000
Accounts payable	163,112
Extinguishment and depreciation funds	95,359
Surplus	878,929
Total	$29,052,401

Income account for 12 months ended January 31, 1904:

Profits for year.. $812,498

Dividend on preferred (7%)............................... $770,000
Depreciation, etc.. 38,013

Total.. $808,013

Surplus for year.. $4,485

The following is a summary of the profits earned and dividends distributed since the formation of the company:

	Profits earned.	Dividends paid.
Year ended February 28, 1900.......	$1,063,461	$577,500
Year ended February 28, 1901.......	813,570	770,000
11 months ended January 31, 1902 ..	932,228	770,000
Year ended January 31, 1903........	952,686	770,000
Year ended January 31, 1904........	774,484	770,000

Stock.—Issued as authorized (see balance sheet).

Funded debt.—The company has no funded debt, all the properties taken over being free from incumbrance.

Dividends.—7% on preferred since July 1, 1899, payable quarterly, January, April, July and October. No dividends yet paid on common stock.

Annual meeting.—Second Tuesday in April.

Corporate office, 15 Exchange Place, New Jersey; main office, New York.

Directors.—M. B. Wallace, Isaac H. Dixon, Chas. A. Dean, Albert H. Chatfield, Lucius G. Fisher, William H. Moore, Edgar G. Barrett, J. B. Hosford, George R. Sheldon, J. H. Moore, L. V. Walkley, Douglas W. Mabee, William H. Van Nortwick, David S. Walton and John H. Derby.

UNION PACIFIC RAILROAD COMPANY.

Organized under an act of the Legislature of Utah, January 22, 1897, for the purpose of reorganization of the Union Pacific Railway Company.

The company owns practically the entire capital stock of both the Oregon Short Line Railroad Company and the Oregon Railroad & Navigation Company, and operates same as part of the property reported on below. Through ownership of about $90,

000,000 stock of the Southern Pacific Company, the company exercises a strong working control over the operation of that company's lines, which are its direct connection at Portland and at Ogden. Over $80,000,000 of the capital stock of the Northern Securities Company is also owned. Title in both cases being vested in the Oregon Short Line. The company owns the entire capital stock of the Union Pacific Coal Company, and large interests in the Occidental & Oriental Steamship Company and Pacific Express Company.

The mileage operated at July 1, 1903, was 6,105 miles, of which all but 68 miles was owned by the combined companies.

The line with branches reaches from Omaha to Portland, Ore., Spokane, Wash., and Helena Mont., and to Frisco, in Southwest Utah; also from Kansas City to Denver.

Condensed general balance sheet, June 30, 1903, Union Pacific and auxiliary companies:

Assets.

Cost of railways, equipment, etc.	$358,659,788
Cost of extensions.	910,000
Stocks and bonds owned.	139,896,217
Trust funds	124,228
Agents and conductors	614,445
Cash.	1,908,559
Individuals and companies	444,841
Material, fuel and supplies	4,680,182
Traffic balances.	184,498
U. S. Government transportation.	974,831
Loans to Southern Pacific Company	15,396,119
Bills receivable	550,000
Dividends accrued to June 30 on Northern Securities stock.	618,689
Miscellaneous.	53,196
Advances for construction of new lines.	7,366,565
Due from sundry proprietary companies.	181,951
Advances for ocean steamships.	3,799,896
Rolling stock.	707,381
Unadjusted claims and accounts	462,879
Land contracts prior April 1, 1898.	372,248
Land contracts subsequent.	2,482,233
Total	$540,388,745

Liabilities.

Union Pacific Railroad Company common stock.	$108,770,900
Union Pacific Railroad Company preferred stock.	99,551,900
Outstanding stocks auxiliary companies.	44,886
Funded debt, after deducting bonds of auxiliary companies owned.	279,272,000
Coupons matured, not presented.	184,718
Coupons due July 1.	2,528,005
Interest accrued on bonds and loans.	1,511,570
Loans and bills payable.	14,250,000
Vouchers and pay rolls	3,330,931

Liabilities (continued).

Dividends payable July and October	$4,386,660
Unpaid dividends	22,436
Taxes assessed, but not due	719 847
Due to sundry proprietary companies	247,349
Trust accounts	275,711
Reserve for betterments and additions	500,000
Reserve for flood damages	500,000
Insurance fund	191,300
Replacement funds	113 809
Deferred payments on land contracts	2,854,481
Profit and loss	21,132,240
Total	$540,388,745

Condensed income and profit and loss account for year ended and at June 30, 1903 :

Earnings:

Passenger	$9,760,552
Mail, express, baggage	3,015,731
Freight	36,261,679
All other sources	1,178,287
Total rail lines	$50,216,248
Water lines	858,940
Gross earnings	$51,075,188

Expenses:

Maintenance of way and structures	$5,293,475
Maintenance of equipment	6,025,640
Conducting transportation	13,827,532
General expenses	1,256,356
Total rail lines	$26,403,003
Water lines	936,881
Total operating expenses	$27,339,884
Taxes	1,407,332
Total expenses and taxes	$28,747,216
Net earnings	$22,327,972

Additions to income:

Interest on bonds of companies other than O. S. L. and O. R. R. & N. Co	322,282
Dividends on Nor. Sec. Co. stock and companies other than O. S. L. and O. R. R. & N. Co	3,687,645
Rentals and other income	437,916
Total income	$26,975,816

Deductions from income :

Interest on funded debt	$11,551,124
Interest on loans	89,844
Sinking fund requirements	12,013
Miscellaneous expenses	22,722
Interest on O. S. L. R. R. Co. income bonds	23,470
Total	$11,699,173
Surplus for year	$15,276,642

Surplus for year......	$15.276,642
Dividend on U. P. common stock (4%)	$4,350.612
Dividend on U. P. preferred stock (4%)	3,982,064
Dividend on O. R. R. & N. stock (4%)............................	492
Appropriation for betterments and improvements......	2,000,000
Total...	$10,333,168
Balance carried to profit and loss	$4,943,474
Profit and loss balance forward*.................................... ..	16,188,766
Profit and loss June 30, 1903...........................·............	$21,132,240

* The balance shown last year was $21,361,692, which has been reduced by charging off net amount of unfunded discount and premium on capital issues.

Compared with the preceding year, average miles of road operated increased .89% ; gross earnings increased 7.53% ; operating expenses increased 13.02% ; taxes increased 2.74% ; net earnings increased 1.76% ; surplus applicable for dividends after all charges increased 5.33%. Surplus after payment of dividends increased 9.94%. Percentage of operating expenses to earnings increased from 50.92 to 53.53%. In 1901 this percentage was 53.61. This is chiefly found to be due to large charges for maintenance of equipment and cost of conducting transportation. The cost of maintenance of way was less than in the two preceding years. Such increased cost is said to be due to higher cost of both labor and material, and congestion due to increased traffic.

During the year above reported upon, capital expenditures amounted to $7,974,840 for extensions, ballasting, bridges, shops, real estate, equipment, etc., which was reduced to the net amount of $4,540,292 by appropriation from the year's surplus income, $1,000,000 ; charged to funds previously provided $1,043.775.76 ; proceeds from sale and lease of lands, $1,390,771.50.

Stocks.—Common—Authorized, $196,178,700 ; issued, $108,770,-900.

Preferred—Authorized, $100,000,000 ; issued, $99,551,900.

The preferred is 4% non-cumulative.

Dividends on common.—1898, none ; 1899, none ; 1900, 3½% ; 1901 to April, 1904, 4% yearly.

Dividends on preferred.—1898, 1½% ; 1899, 3½% ; 1900, 4% ; 1901 to April, 1904, 4% yearly.

Funded debt.—This liability was increased during the year $31,174,000, proportionately increasing the fixed charges. The increase is chiefly due to the sale of Oregon Short Line Railroad Company 4% participating bonds, previously held within the organization, and originally issued to take up Northern Pacific purchase money certificates. The funds obtained, however, having been used to repay loans and open accounts, resulted in a large saving in the total interest charges.

Annual meeting.—Second Tuesday in October.

Main office.—120 Broadway, New York.

Directors.—H. G. Burt, Winslow S. Pierce, James Stillman, Marvin Hughett, E. H. Harriman, Thos. T. Eckert, James H. Hyde, Otto H. Kahn, T. Jefferson Coolidge, Jr., George J. Gould, Oliver Ames, J. H. Schiff, Louis Fitzgerald, Chas. A. Peabody and H. H. Rogers.

THE UNITED STATES LEATHER COMPANY.

Formed under the laws of New Jersey February 25, 1893, and acquired the plants of a number of concerns engaged in the manufacture and sale of sole and belting leather.

The properties acquired represented tannery plants, saw mills, lands and railroads, together with the stocks of raw and finished material, tan bark, lumber, etc.

General balance sheet, December 31, 1903:

Assets.

Cash	$2,049,952
Due by customers	6,048,313
Bills receivable	140,897
Doubtful debts, value	5,926
Other debtors	144,548
Hides and leather	10,328,626
Bark at tanneries	1,915,974
Sundry personal property, etc	401,355
Advances to other companies	1,117,553
Drawbacks	457,713
Railroad mortgage	100,000
Tannery plants, etc	6,313,295
Stock of other companies	49,142,022
Bonds, Central Pennsylvania Lumber Company	10,000,000
Treasury stock	100,000
Good will, etc	62,832,300
Unexpired insurance	67,260
Total	$151,165,739

Liabilities.

Common stock..	$62,882,300
Preferred stock...	62,282,300
Bonds, less in treasury...................................	5,280,000
Accrued interest, etc.....................................	17,549
Current accounts...	334,394
For exchange, not due....................................	1,075,224
Bills payable...	1,450,000
Miscellaneous..	309,587
Surplus..	17,534,385
Total...	$151,165,739

Income account for the year is not available. The surplus account at December 31 for recent years is shown in the balance sheet, as below :

1900..	$4,540,870
1901..	5,460,880
1902	6,486,326
1903..	17,534,885

The large increase in surplus above shown in the year 1903, viz., $11,048,059, is chiefly due to re-appraisal of the subsidiary companies' timber and bark lands, which appears to have been added to the valuation of "stocks of other companies." This asset was increased during the year by $13,463,977.

" Advances to other companies," which during the three preceding years averaged about $13,500,000, shows a decrease during the year of $13,403,995, and is said to be due to the fact that the subsidiary companies were able to sell their bark at higher prices. They therefore did not call upon the United States Leather Company for as much money as in previous years.

A new asset appearing in the balance sheet is " Bonds of Central Pennsylvania Lumber Company, $10,000,000," and since the balance of the assets and liabilities are about on an average of previous years, this no doubt has a direct bearing upon such reduction of amounts due from subsidiary companies, the amount so realized either having been invested in the bonds or the bonds having been received in the reduction of the debt. The available surplus is largely represented by these bonds.

Stock.—Common : Authorized, $64,000,000; issued, $62,882,300. Preferred : Authorized, $64,000,000; issued, $62,282,300.

The preferred stock is entitled to 8% cumulative dividends.

Funded debt outstanding, $5,280,000 6% debentures, due May,

1913. Coupons, May and December. Annual interest charge being $316,800.

Dividends.—Preferred : 1895, 6% ; 1896, 1% ; 1897, 4% ; 1898, 4¾%; 1899, 5%; 1900 to May, 1904, 6% yearly.

None paid on the common.

At May, 1904, the overdue dividends on the preferred stock amounted to 39%.

The excess of current assets over current liabilities would indicate a fairly good financial condition as to working capital, and plans for the relief of the obligations to the preferred stockholders have been under consideration.

No liability is shown for the accrued dividends, which would amount to some $24,000,000.

Annual meeting, fourth Wednesday in February.

Main office, 26 Ferry Street, New York.

Directors.—James Horton, Edward R. Ladew, James R. Plum, Patrick C. Costello, Jerry Crary, Lewis H Lapham, Oscar B. Grant, John J. Lapham, Lyman F. Rhoads, Josiah T. Tubby, Samuel P. Davidge, Walter G. Garritt, William H. Humphrey, C. Sumner Horton, A. Augustus Healy, Charles H. Lee, Daniel T. Stevens, George W. Childs, Frank H. Goodyear, George A. Vail, Joseph H. Ladew, Edward C. Hoyt, Loring R. Gale. James H. Proctor, Edson G. Davidge, Eugene Horton, Theodore R. Hoyt.

UNITED STATES REALTY & CONSTRUCTION COMPANY.

Incorporated under the laws of New Jersey in August, 1902, and took over various real estate and building construction interests, its principal constituents being the George A. Fuller Company and the New York Realty Corporation.

The company also acquired a number of properties from the Central Realty Bond & Trust Company and some stocks of the Plaza Realty Company.

Consolidated balance sheet (all companies), June 30, 1903:

Assets.

Good will of sub. companies..	$37,041,006
Investments—Real estate $17,153,831, less underlying mortgages $8,638.304....	8,515,527
Interest in real estate, and securities in realty companies at cost or under..	2,483,393
Loans on mortgage...............................	4,183,500
Stocks and bonds at market value. June 30. 1903....................	1,873,985
Building plant, office furniture and materials, less depreciation.....	159,470
Expenditure on building contracts in progress, less payments received on account thereof....................................	1,617,185
Proportion of estimated profit on contracts in progress..............	862,147
Accounts receivable...	678,865
Cash...	4,824,676
Total..	**$62,239,753**

Liabilities*

Preferred stock...	$27,011,100
Common stock....... ....,.....	33,198,000
Outstanding stock of sub. companies...............................	41,000
Current accounts payable..	1,240,651
Accrued interest, taxes, etc...	145,039
Dividends declared, payable July 1, 1903............................	405,167
Surplus..	198,797
Total..	**$62,239,753**

*Contingent liabilities.—In addition to the ordinary liabilities in connection with building contracts, there are contingent liabilities estimated as follows: Loans and mortgages contracted to be made, $3,743,000 ; calls on stock not fully paid, $172,000 ; syndicate participations, $121,000. Such contingent liabilities if maturing into an obligation and set up in the balance sheet, would of course be offset by assets so created and therefore not affect the surplus.

Income account for the nine months ended June 30, 1903 :

Interest receivable........	$310,657
Income from investments:	
Real estate.......	98,423
Part interest in realty securities...................................	74,548
Stocks and bonds.....................	75,910
Profit on building contracts:	
Buildings completed...................................	230,071
Buildings in progress—estimated.	576,773
Profit on real estate investments....................................	228,800
Miscellaneous profits..	106,952
Total income..	**$1,702,134**
Deduct:	
Interest payable............................	$207,210
Expenses of management...	564,863
Total expenses..	**$772,073**

Net earnings.... .... $930,061
Profit from estimated increase in value of investments still held........ 487,625

Total income... ....$1,417,686

Dividend on preferred stock, 4½%........ ....$1,215,499
Dividend on outstanding stock, sub. companies....................... 3,390

Total..$1,218,889

Balance carried to surplus... $198,797

Stock.—Common—Authorized, $36,000,000 ; issued, $33,198,000.

Preferred—Authorized, $30,000,000 ; issued, $27,011,100.

The preferred stock is 6% cumulative.

The company has no funded debt.

Dividends.—On preferred—January, 1903, to July, 1903 inclusive, 1½% quarterly. The October, 1903, dividend was passed, and future profits from construction will be determined only on work completed.

A plan for reorganization of the company's financial obligations is under consideration.

Annual meeting.—First Tuesday in July.

Corporate office, Jersey City; New York office, 137 Broadway.

Executive committee.—James Stillman, Henry S. Black, Charles M. Schwab, Albert Flake, Robert E. Dowling, Hugh J. Grant, Henry Morgenthau.

Directors include Charles M. Schwab, John W. Gates, Charles Francis Adams, Cornelius Vanderbilt, etc.

UNITED STATES RUBBER COMPANY.

Organized under the New Jersey laws in 1892 for the purpose of combining numerous concerns engaged in the manufacture of rubber boots, shoes, etc.

The property of the following concerns was acquired :

American Rubber Company.

Boston Rubber Company.

Boston Rubber Shoe Company.

L. Candee & Company.

Goodyear Metallic Rubber Shoe Company.

Goodyear India Rubber Glove Manufacturing Company.

Lycoming Rubber Company.

Myer Rubber Company

National India Rubber Company.

New Brunswick Rubber Company.

New Jersey Rubber Shoe Company.

Para Rubber Shoe Company.

Woonsocket Rubber Company.

The company is supposed to control over 75% of the rubber boot and shoe business of the United States.

At one time it had some rubber tire manufacturing interests, which in 1899 it sold to the Rubber Goods Manufacturing Company.

Consolidated balance sheet, March 31, 1904, United States Rubber Company and its subsidiary companies:

Assets.

Property and plants	$47,716,005
Inventories, manufactured goods and materials	16,801,876
Cash	1,660,853
Bills and loans receivable	2,072,313
Accounts receivable	6,489,129
Securities owned	2,681,649
Miscellaneous assets	783,522
Total	$78,205,347

Liabilities.

Capital stock:	
Preferred	$23,525,500
Common	23,666,000
Boston Rubber Shoe Company debentures	4,800,000
United States Rubber Company funding notes	10,000,000
Fixed surpluses (subsidiary companies)	8,134,849
Loan accounts payable	1,622,000
Merchandise accounts payable	3,066,233
Deferred liabilities	430,664
Reserve for depreciation of securities	500,000
Reserve for dividend	352,882
Surplus	2,107,219
Total	$78,205,347

Consolidated Income and profit and loss account for year ended and at March 31, 1904, United States Rubber Company and subsidiary companies :

Gross sales, boots and shoes and miscellaneous......................	$64,553,237
Net sales, boots and shoes and miscellaneous......................	$33,396,919
Cost of goods sold...	28,987,863
Manufacturing profits....................................	$4,409,056
Freight, taxes, insurance, general and selling expenses............ ..	1,766,179
Operating profits....................................	$2,642,877
Other income....................................	187,330
Total income....................................	$2,830,207
Less :	
Interest and commission on funding notes and borrowed money.	$802,174
Interest on Boston Rubber Shoe Company debentures.	240.000
Interest allowed customers for prepayments.................	113.097
Total...................................	$1,185,271
Net income to surplus................................	$1,644,936
Deduction for bad debts, etc	$69,295
Reserve for depreciation of securities.........................	500,000
Reserve for dividend....................................	352,882
Total...................................	$922,177
Surplus for year.......................................	$722,759
Surplus April 1, 1903....	1,384,460
Surplus March 31, 1904....................................	$2,107,219

Compared with the preceding year the operations for the year above reported on shows the following results :

Increase in gross sales 24.4%.

Increase in total income $55,810, or 2%.

Net income to surplus shows an increase of 3.1%.

The surplus account has been increased from $1,384,460 to $2,107,219, after providing $500,000 for depreciation on securities and $352,883 as a reserve for preferred dividend of 1½% due June 15, 1904.

The books are examined by Haskins & Sells, certified public accountants, who append their certificate. This includes the statement that the quick assets, including inventories of raw material and manufactured goods on hand, exceed all the liabilities of the United States Rubber Company and its subsidiary companies other than capital stock, reserve and surplus accounts on March 31, 1904, to the extent of $9,290,329.34.

Funded debt.—The entire indebtedness of the United States Rubber Company and its subsidiary companies, excepting the $4,800,000 Boston Rubber Shoe debentures, was funded in 1902 into $12,000,000 5% notes.

From the earnings of the past two years $2,000,000 of these notes have been paid.

Dividends.—Common: 1894, none ; 1895, 2½% ; 1896, none ; 1897, 2% ; 1899, 2% ; 1900, 2% ; 1901, 1902, 1903 and 1904, none.

Preferred : 1894, 8% ; 1895, 8% ; 1896, 8%; 1897, 6%; 1899, 8%; 1900, 8% ; 1901, 1% ; 1902 and 1903, none ; June, 1904, 1½%.

Annual meeting, third Tuesday in May.

Corporate office, New Brunswick, N. J.; main office, 42 Broadway, New York.

Directors.—Walter S. Ballon, E. C. Benedict, Samuel P. Colt, E. S. Converse, H. E. Converse, Costello C. Converse, James B. Ford, J. Howard Ford, Francis L. Hine, Henry L. Hotchkiss, Lester Leland, Frederick M. Shephard, Francis Lynde Stetson John D. Vermeule.

UNITED STATES STEEL CORPORATION.

Incorporated under the laws of the State of New Jersey, February 5, 1901, and certificate amended April 1, 1901.

The corporation acquired practically all of the capital stocks of the undermentioned companies, and the financial operations of these companies are embraced in the statements of earnings and balance sheet :

The Carnegie Company.
Federal Steel Company.
National Tube Company.
American Steel & Wire Company of New Jersey.
National Steel Company.
American Tin Plate Company.
American Steel Hoop Company.
American Sheet Steel Company.
American Bridge Company.
Lake Superior Consolidated Iron Mines.
Shelby Steel Tube Company.

The properties owned at various plants December 31, 1903, were:

86 blast furnaces.
14 open hearth steel plants.
17 Bessemer steel plants.
6 steel rail mills.
57 bar, billet, etc., mills.
11 structural shape mills.
14 plate mills.
251 puddling furnaces.
59 merchant mills producing bar, iron and steel.
447 hot mills producing tin plate, etc.
24 rod mills.
22 wire plants.
21 tube plants.
26 bridge and structural plants.
24 complete foundries.
11 skelp mills.
16 miscellaneous armor, axle, etc., works.

Besides extensive iron ore mines in Lake Superior region; over 160,000 acres of coking, steam and gas coal lands; 20,000 coke ovens; railroads; 112 lake vessels, ore docks, etc.

The output of the combined properties in 1903 was:

Output.	Gross tons.
Iron ore	15,363,355
Pig iron, spiegel, etc.	7,279,241
Bessemer steel	6,191,660
Open hearth steel	2,976,300
Coke manufactured	8,658,391
Coal mined (not used for coke)	1,120,733
Finished products:	
Bessemer steel rails	1,934,315
Finished structural work	469,692
Plates and sheets	1,374,928
Wire and wire products	1,126,605
Bars, slabs, billets, etc.	493,292
Other finished products	2,236,758

Condensed general balance sheet, December 31, 1903:

Assets.

Property accounts	$1,357,394,469
Deferred charges to operations, explorations, stripping and developing, etc.	4,820,343
Trustees of sinking funds	497,051
Investments, outside property etc.	5,522,546
Current assets:	
Inventories	107,976,523
Accounts receivable	34,457,369
Bills receivable	3,139,457
Agents' balances	1,029,470
Sundry marketable stocks and bonds	5,985,509
Due from bankers (payable on demand)	12,822,900
Cash on hand subject to check	50,199,661
Total	$1,583,845,298

Liabilities.

Capital stock of United States Steel Corporation:
Common.. $508,302,500
Preferred... 360,281,100
Capital stock of sub companies not held by United States Steel
Corporation 109,114
Bonded and debenture debt:
United States Steel Corporation 50-year 5% bonds............... 298,319,000
United States Steel Corporation 10-60-year 5% bonds............ 152,902,500
Union Steel Company guaranteed bonds and other sub com-
panies' bonds... 99,819,535
United States Steel Corporation 10-60-year 5% bonds, issued and
sold, but not delivered 17,097,500
Mortgage and purchase money obligations........ 5,882,864
Current liabilities:
Current accounts payable and pay rolls...... 15,729,791
Bills and loans payable (sub companies) 4,429,484
Special deposits, due employees and others..................... 3,941,795
Reserve for expenses, convertible preferred stock.............. 783,560
Accrued taxes, not yet due....................................... 1,408,697
Accrued interest and coupons.................................... 6,942,393
Preferred stock dividend No. 11, payable February 15, 1904..... 6,304,919
Sinking and reserve funds:
Sinking, depreciation, improvement and replacement funds.... 20,584,281
Contingent operating funds....................................... 3,707,163
Insurance funds.. 2,524,368
Bond sinking funds and accretions................................ 8,678,051
Undivided surplus of United States Steel Corporation, etc.......... 66,096,682

Total.. $1,583,845,298

Income and profit and loss account for year ended and at
December 31, 1903, United States Steel Corporation and sub
companies.

Gross receipts.. $536,572,876
Manufacturing and operating expenses..... ....*............... 409,268 599

Balance... $127,304,272
Miscellaneous manufacturing, operating, gains and rentals received 1,720,043

Income.. $129,024,315

Other income :
Proportion net income properties owned, not included in above. $1,327,731
Interest and dividends.. 2,220,820

Total.. $3,548,551

Total income... $132,572,866

General expenses :
Administering, selling and general............................... 11,942,916
Taxes... 2,972,600
Miscellaneous... 393,917
Commercial discounts and interest............ 1,538,419

$16,847,852

Balance.. $115,725,013

Balance.........	$115,725,013
Interest charges :	
Interest on bonds and mortgages sub. companies...............	$5,756,488
Interest on bills payable, etc., sub. companies.................	797,373
Total.................	$6,553,861
Net earnings for year 1903.....................	$109,171,152
Deduct :	
Sinking funds on bonds of sub. companies.....................	$1,598,013
Depreciation and extinguishment funds........................	4,599,822
Extraordinary replacement funds..............................	9,297,531
Special fund for depreciation, improvements and construction.	10,000,000
Total.................	$25,495,366
Balance of net earnings.........................	$83,675,786
Deduct :	
Interest on United States Steel Corporation 50-year 5% bonds....	$15,195,850
Interest on United States Steel Corporation 10-60 year bonds...	3,886,946
Sinking fund on United States Steel Corporation 50-year bonds.	3,040,000
Sinking fund on United States Steel Corporation 10-60 year bonds.................	757,500
Total.................	$22,880,296
Balance.........................	$60,795,490
Less—Charged off for depreciation in inventory valuations, etc.....	5,378,838
Balance.........................	$55,416,652
Dividends on United States Corporation stock :	
Preferred, 7%..................	$30,404,173
Common, 2½%	12,707,563
Total.................	$43,111,736
Undivided profits or surplus for year..................	$12,304,916
Surplus December 31, 1902.........................	77,874,597
Total.....	$90,179,513
Less :	
Expense conversion preferred stock..................	$6,800,000
Charged off for expenditures made since April 1, 1901, from surplus for construction and for payment of capital liabilities..	17,234,129
Total.................	$24,034,129
Balance surplus December 31, 1903, per balance sheet..............	$66,096,682

Of the surplus as above shown $25,000,000 was provided in the organization, leaving $411,096,682 as the result of operations since April 1, 1901.

From August to December, 1903, the production of iron in the United States fell off 45% and the production of steel nearly 60%, whilst the price of billets fell off from $30 to $23. The effect on the leading concern interested in the trade should naturally be supposed to correspond in figures in which its own operations so largely contribute.

Compared with the year 1902, it is found that the net earnings for the entire year fell off about 18%, indicating that the earlier part of the year was about as prosperous as the preceeding periods.

With such marked contraction in the volume of business, combined with the sharp decline in the selling values, it is something to be wondered at that the showing for the year was so favorable, as to leave an undivided surplus equal to about an additional 2½% on the common stock.

That this result has not been reached through economies at the expense of the property is seen in the fact that \$34,785,191 was expended for repairs and replacements, \$21,845,413 being included in operating expenses and \$12,939.778 charged against funds provided for the purpose. This total amount exceeds similar expenditures for 1902 by \$5,628,180.

It should be observed that the surplus for the year is arrived at after providing for sinking funds, depreciation, etc., in the amount \$33,179,812. Further a charge of \$5,378,838 was charged off for depreciation in inventory valuations, etc. There is every indication that the accounts are prepared and stated in the most exact and conservative manner, in fact, the books are examined and passed upon by most eminent independent auditors.

The excess of current assets over current requirements, as seen in the balance sheet, shows the company to possess almost unlimited working capital, and places it in a very strong position financially. An interesting notice is included in the annual report to the employees, some 10,000 in number, who accepted the company's offer in 1902 to subscribe for the preferred stock, which is given below in full:

"EMPLOYEES' SUBSCRIPTION TO PREFERRED STOCK.

" The offer to the employees of this corporation and of the subsidiary companies to subscribe for the preferred stock of this corporation was renewed at the end of the year 1903 for the succeeding year, and resulted in subscription by 10,248 employees for 32,519 shares.

" In view of the decline in the market of the selling price of preferred stock of the corporation, which might naturally excite apprehension of possible loss to the employees who had subscribed under the offer of 1902, the finance committee of this corporation on September 30, 1903, issued to subscribers a circular letter as follows:

" 'The finance committee sees no reason to change its opinion as to the intrinsic value of the preferred stock subscribed for pursuant to the said circular, but of course it recognizes that the decline in the market or selling price naturally may occasion anxiety in the minds of the subscribers under the circular. Accordingly it deems it proper now to dispel apprehension of loss by the following additional offer or guaranty:

" 'The corporation will at any time during January or February, 1908, pay to every subscribing officer or employee who shall have retained his stock for the full period of five years, and otherwise complied with the terms of the circular, $82.50 per share for the stock, less the rebates and benefits he shall have been entitled to under the circular (not including benefits received on account of difference between interest and dividends, which he will in any event retain), provided he wishes to sell the stock for that price at that time.' "

Stock.—Common—Authorized, $550,000,000; outstanding, $508,-302,500.

Preferred—Authorized, $550,000,000; outstanding, $360,281,100. The preferred is 7% cumulative.

Originally $510,314,100 par value preferred stock was issued, but this amount has been reduced by exchange for 10-60-year bonds, issued for that purpose to the extent of $150,000,000. The plan contemplated exchanging $200,000,000 of the preferred stock, and since the stock draws 7 and the bonds only 5% interest the result on fixed charges may be easily seen.

Funded debt.—See balance sheet.

Dividends.—On preferred—1¾% quarterly, August, 1901, to May, 1904.

On common—1% quarterly, September, 1901, to September, 1903; inclusive; December, 1903, ½%; none since to May, 1904.

Annual meeting.—Third Monday in April.

Corporate office, Hoboken, N. J.; New York office, 71 Broadway.

Directors.—J. P. Morgan, Henry Phipps, Henry H. Rogers, Charles M. Schwab, Elbert H. Gary, George W. Perkins, Edmund C. Converse, James Gayley, Francis H. Peabody, Charles Steele, William H. Moore, Norman B. Ream, Peter A. B. Widener, James H. Reed, Henry C. Frick, William Edenborn, Marshall Field, Daniel G. Reid, J. D. Rockefeller, Jr.; William E. Corey, Robert Bacon, Nathaniel Thayer, John F. Dryden, Clement A. Griscom.

VIRGINIA-CAROLINA CHEMICAL COMPANY.

Formed under the laws of the State of New Jersey, September 12, 1895, to consolidate the southern fertilizer industries.

The company also acquired nearly all of the stock of the Southern Cotton Oil Company, whose properties it operates, and owns the largest phosphate property known.

General balance sheet, June 15, 1903:

Assets.

Cash	$1,913,556
Accounts receivable	3,918,835
Bills receivable	4,513,975
Merchandise inventory	5,637,456
Undivided earnings sub companies	3,383,475
Investments	27,689,879
Steamer, steam tugs, barges and lighters	20,250
Plants, pyrites and phosphate mines and lands	11,099,468
Brands, trade marks, good will, etc	3,348,900
Unearned insurance	75,034
Total	$61,600,827

Liabilities.

Capital stock:	
Preferred	$12,000,000
Common	27,984,400
Collatnral trust loan	7,000,000
Bills payable	4,794,260
Accounts payable	296,462
Due subsidiary companies	4,587,254
Contingent fund (bad debts)	200,000
Accrued interest on collateral trust	72,917
Undivided profits	4,665,534
Total	$61,600,827

Income and profit and loss account for year ended and at June 15, 1903 :

Gross profits	$3.231.377
Repairs and depreciation charged off	635,060
Net profits	$2,596.317
Interest on collateral trust	209,401
Net income	$2,386 916
Dividends :	
Preferred, 8%	960.000
Common, 4%	1.399,220
Total	$2,359,220
Balance surplus for year	$27,696
Undivided profits June 15, 1902	4,637,838
Undivided profits June 15, 1903	$4,665,534

The capacity of the plants during the past few years is said to have been increased some 33%, and with a view to utilizing the property to its fullest extent, the Directors report that increased tonnage was striven for during the year 1902–03, rather than profits. It was unfortunate that higher proportionate prices for raw material prevailed—presumably in the cost of cotton seed— but nearly 30% increase in tonnage is reported. The gross profits show a reduction of over 28%. However, full dividend was paid on the preferred stock, the usual 4% on the common, after which $27,696 was left to carry to undivided profits.

Stock.—Common—Authorized, $38,000,000 ; outstanding, $27,-984,400.

Preferred—Authorized, $12,000,000 ; Outstanding, $12,000.000.

The preferred is 8% cumulative and has preference in the distribution of assets.

The shareholders will vote on May 18, 1904, on authorizing $8,000,000 additional preferred stock to be offered to stockholders at par. This is to provide ·funds to reduce the floating debt and provide working capital.

Dividends.—On preferred, 8% quarterly (Q. J.), to April, 1904.

On common, 1896, December 1% ; 1897 to March, 1902, 4% yearly ; June, 1902 to June, 1903, 1¼% quarterly.

In September, 1903, the common dividends were suspended to provide for additional working capital.

Annual meeting.—First Wednesday after June 15.

Corporate office, Jersey City ; executive office, Richmond, Va.

Directors.—Samuel T. Morgan, E. B. Addison, S. W. Travers, S. Dabney Crenshaw, A. R. Ellerson, W. B. Chisholm, L. A. Carr, Henry Walters, J. William Middendorf, Samuel Spencer, James B. Duke, Fortesque Whittle and F. B. Dancy.

THE WABASH RAILROAD COMPANY.

Successor in 1889 to the Wabash, St. Louis & Pacific, which was sold under foreclosure.

The company operates 2,483 miles of rallroad extending from Detroit and Toledo to Chicago, St. Louis, Kansas City, Des Moines and Omaha. Quite recently the line has obtained entry, via the Wheeling & Lake Erie, a Gould line, to Pittsburg, at which point it has a contract with the Carnegie Steel Company to carry about 400,000 tons of steel yearly.

The property is controlled by the Gould-Rockefeller interests, and is considered to be the eastern outlet of the Missouri Pacific, that company owning about $14,000,000 out of $82,000,000 stock and voting debentures. Plans are under consideration for building an extension from Pittsburg to Baltimore, whereby the Wabash will obtain access to the Atlantic tidewater. A Gould syndicate has acquired the West Virginia Central & Pittsburg and the Western Maryland Railroad for this purpose.

General balance sheet, June 30, 1903 :

Assets.

Road, equipment. etc	$143,882.500
Supplies and materials	1,214,803
Cash on hand	987,035
Stocks and bonds	1,553,020
Accounts collectible	1,375,986
Bills receivable	53,239
Advances and miscellaneous	1,152,588
Equipment suspense account	583,030
Total	$150,832,203

Liabilities.

Common stock..	$28,000,000
Preferred ssock...	24,000,000
Bonds	91,949,000
Interest..	883,289
Vouchers and pay rolls...................................	2,738,406
Individuals and railroads................................	466,607
Taxes accrued..	386,337
Hospital account	5,183
Notes payable..	23,287
Equipment notes	583,030
Dividend on debenture bonds..............................	105,000
Sale debenture bonds, series " B ".......................	369,237
Equipment fund account...................................	311 960
Miscellaneous..	40,872
Profit and loss..	969,994
Total..	$150,832,203

Income and profit and loss account for year ended and at June 30, 1903 :

Earnings:	
Passenger..	$6,135,501
Freight	13,327,479
Mail, express, etc.................................	1,677,851
Gross earnings..	$21,140,831
Expenses :	
Maintenance of way, etc............................	$3,700,962
Maintenance of equipment	3,114,664
Transportation....................................	8,511,278
General	488,759
Total expenses...	$15,815,663
Net earnings...	$5,325,167
Investments, rentals, etc..............................	531,428
Total income...	$5,856,595
Deduct :	
Taxes	$664,703
Track and bridge rentals...........................	898,518
Additions and miscellaneous........................	852,711
Interest on bonds..................................	3,034,513
Total..	$5,450,445
Net income	$406,150
Dividend on preferred debenture "A"	210,000
Surplus for year.......................................	$196,150
Profit and loss balance, forward.......................	773,844
Profit and loss, June 30, 1903.........................	$969,994

Statistics of operations from 1899-1900 show a steady improvement in all departments of traffic, but the improvement is somewhat more marked in 1902-1903. Compared with 1901-1902 the year above reported on shows an increase in gross earnings of

10.9%, and in net earnings of 2.3%. Expenses, however, showing percentage to earnings of 72.67, 72.64 and 72.68 for the three preceding years, were 74.81% for the year ended June 30, 1903. Transportation expenses increased slightly less proportionately to the increased business, and the net increase is found to result from heavy charges for maintenance of way and maintenance of equipment. Had the track and equipment been in a badly run-down condition transportation expenses would have a tendency to increase; it would therefore appear that repair service charged out was somewhat in the nature of improvements, which, in view of prospective increase in traffic, is a very conservative policy.

Better rates for both passenger and freight business was obtained during the year and the revenue train load increased from 269 tons in 1899-1900 to 302 tons in 1902-1903.

Stock.—Issued as authorized (see balance sheet).

Funded debt includes 6% income debentures, $3,500,000 series "A" and $26,500,000 series "B," upon which interest is not compulsory. These debentures carry voting power.

Dividends.—None paid.

Interest on debentures.—None paid on series "B."

On series "A": 1890 to 1893, 6% yearly; 1894 and 1895, none; 1896, 1%; 1897 to 1899, none; 1900 to January, 1904, 6% yearly, (J & J).

Annual meeting, second Tuesday in October.

Main office, St. Louis; New York office, 195 Broadway.

Directors.—O. D. Ashley, Thomas H. Hubbard, Edgar T. Welles, James H. Hyde, Joseph Ramsey, Jr., George J. Gould, S. C. Reynolds, John T. Terry, Russell Sage, Winslow S. Pierce, Edwin Gould, Henry K. McHarg and Cyrus J. Lawrence.

WESTERN UNION TELEGRAPH COMPANY.

Organized under the laws of the State of New York in 1851, and adopted present name in 1856.

This company operates telegraph lines to every point of importance in the United States, but its wires are paralleled by the Postal Telegraph Company, and the two companies share a practical control of this business.

General balance sheet, June 30, 1903:

Assets.

Telegraph lines, stocks owned of leased telegraph companies that are merged in Western Union Company's system, franchises, patents, etc. $112,073,906
Stocks and bonds of leased telegraph companies received in exchange for collateral trust bonds 8,504,000
Stocks of not leased telegraph companies and other securities....... 11,459,416
Real estate. 4,765 131
Supplies and materials in supply departments...................... 498,011
Sundry accounts rec-ivable, etc.................................... 2,156,265
Cash in treasury and in hands of agents (since remitted to treasury). 2,678,015

Total $142,134,744

Liabilities.

Capital stock.. $97,370,000
Funded debt... 24,504,000
Gold and Stock Telegraph Company for stocks of other companies held through lease of that company until 1981 1,946,592
Sundry accounts payable, etc. (including dividend July 15. 1903) 3,696,244
Surplus of income prior to October 1, 1881, appropriated for construction and acquisition of telegraph lines and property (in excess of the $15,526,590 capital stock distributed in 1881 on account of such appropriations of income during the 15 years preceding). 1,598,184
Surplus of income subsequent to October 1, 1881 ($12,389,964), plus the proportion of surplus of income prior to October 1, 1881 ($629,760), that was not appropriated as above 13,019,724

Total $142,134,744

Income and surplus account for year ended and at June 30, 1903 :

Revenues... $29,167,687
Expenses... 20,953,215

Net revenue.. $8,214,472
Interest on bonds.. 1,077,700

Profits.. $7,136,772
Appropriated for dividends 4.868,050

Surplus for year... $2,268,722
Surplus July 1, 1902.... 10,751,003

Surplus June 30, 1903.. $13,019,725

President Clowry in his annual report states that there were added to the company's system during the year 402 miles of poles and 59,228 miles of wire, of which 47,000 was copper.

The number of messages transmitted was 69,790,866, being 415 983 more than for the preceeding year. This does not include leased wire or railroad messages, which probably amount to some 10,000,000 per annum.

The revenues for the year increased $1,094,591.70, at a net increase in expenses of only $172,448.86. After all payments and dividends, $2,268,721.73 was added to surplus account. This amounts to over 2% additional on the stock above the 5% paid.

Stoek.—In October, 1892, stock was increased from $86,199,852 to $100,000,000, and a stock dividend of 10% was authorized to represent surplus earnings invested in plant. Amount outstanding July 1, 1903, $97,370,000, of which $29,495 belongs to and is in the treasury of the company.

Bonded debt at July 1, 1903 :

Funding and real estate mortgage bonds, due May 1. 1950, 4½%....... $16,000,000
Collateral trust bonds, due January 1. 1938, against which bonds and
  stocks bearing the company's guarantee of interest or dividends
  at 6% per annum have been deposited with the trustee, 5%........   8,504.000

Dividends since 1886.—1887, 2%; 1888 and 1889, 5% yearly; 1890, 5¾%; 1891, 5%; 1892, 5% and 10% in stock; 1893, 5%; April, 1904, 1¼%, payable quarterly (1¼% Q.—J.).

Annual meeting.—Second Wednesday in October.

Main office.—195 Broadway, New York.

Executive committee.—Thomas T. Eckert, Robert C. Clowry, John T. Terry, Samuel Sloan, George J. Gould, Russell Sage, Edwin Gould, Louis Fitzgerald, Frank J. Gould, Jacob H. Schiff and James H. Hyde.

WHEELING & LAKE ERIE RAILROAD COMPANY.

Successor in 1899 to the Wheeling & Lake Erie Railway Company sold under foreclosure.

In April, 1901, a syndicate controlled by the Gould interests acquired control, and the line is operated in close harmony with the Wabash Railway, but under its own management.

Together with an extension known as the Pittsburg, Carnegie & Western Railway just completed, the Wabash obtains access to Pittsburg. A lease of these properties to the Wabash is looked for in the near future.

The Wheeling & Lake Erie Railroad Company owns a majority of the stock of the Pittsburg, Wheeling & Lake Erie Coal Company, which is leased to other parties for a term of 10 years from 1901.

Mileage operated 472 miles, extending from Toledo, Ohio, to Martin's Ferry, and Cleveland to Zanesville, Ohio, with branches.

General balance sheet, June 30, 1902 (last published):

Assets.

Cost of road and equipment	$49,671,640
Materials and supplies	221,367
Stocks and bonds owned	462,321
New equipment in suspense	1,969,297
Additions and improvements	635,476
Advances for construction	375,994
Consolidated bonds in treasury	266 000
Cash on hand	859,418
Due from agents	108,488
Due from U. S. P. O. department	8,697
Due from railroads and individuals	331,846
Due from Pacific Express Company	1,894
Miscellaneous	7,726
Total	$54,920,166

Liabilities.

Common stock	$20,000.000
1st preferred stock	4 986,900
2d preferred stock	11,993,500
Bonds outstanding	13,867,000
Bonds issued to treasury	266,000
Equipment trust obligations	1,969,297
Bills payable	450,524
Vouchers and pay rolls	560,694
Railroads and individuals	100,310
Interest due	28,780
Interest accrued, not due	184,796
Taxes accrued, not due	67,113
Miscellaneous	19,624
Profit and loss	425,627
Total	$54,920,166

Income and profit and loss account for year ended and at June 30, 1902:

Earnings:

Freight	$2,927,874
Passenger	446,304
Mail and express	61,290
Other sources	101,555
Gross earnings	$3,537,023

Operating expenses:

Conducting transportation	1,432,708
Maintenance of equipment	533,520
Maintenance of way and structures	522,973
General expenses	104,602
Total expenses	$2,593,803
Net earnings	$943,220

Net earnings...	$943.220
Deduct :	
Interest on bonds..	$572,296
Taxes..	129.562
Rentals and miscellaneous..	169.238
Total...	$871.096
Surplus for year..	$72,124
Profit and loss July 1, 1901..	353,503
Profit and loss June 30, 1902......................................	$425,627

The above report for 1901-02 is the last issued in annual form, but from periodical reports of earnings, it is found that the gross earnings for the year 1902-03 was $4,234,771, and net earnings $1,001,710, also that the net earnings for the nine months to March 31, 1903, was 19% in excess of the same period in 1902.

During the year above bituminous coal furnished 65% of the freight carried.

There was no change in the mileage operated as compared with the preceeding year. Total revenue tonnage increased nearly 1,000,000 tons or 37% ; number of passengers carried increased about 10%. The average distance travelled by each passenger was greater for the year, as the number of passengers carried one mile shows an increase of 17%. The results of previous improvements having in view present economies in operations are indicated by the average revenue train load, which in 1900 was 355 tons ; in 1901, 388 tons, and in 1902, 430 tons.

Stock.—Common—Authorized, $20,000,000 ; issued, $20,000,000.

1st preferred—Authorized, $5,000,000 ; issued, $4,986,900.

2d preferred—Authorized, $12,000,000 ; issued, $11,993,500.

The preferred stocks are 4% non-cumulative in the order of their preference.

Dividends.—None paid.

Annual meeting.—First Wednesday in May.

Main office, Cleveland ; New York office, 195 Broadway.

Directors.—George J. Gould, Edwin Gould, Cyrus J. Lawrence, Winslow S. Pierce, Alvin W. Krech, W. E. Connor, Joseph Ramsey, Jr., Myron T. Herrick, George A. Garretson, E. W. Oglebay, H. P. McIntosh, Robert Blickensderfer, Dan R. Hanna, William G. Mather and C. M. Spitzer.

WISCONSIN CENTRAL RAILWAY.

Successor to the Wisconsin Central Company, sold under foreclosure in 1899.

The line operated, in total 1,043 miles, extends from Chicago to Ashland, Wis., and to Minneapolis and St. Paul, with branches and spurs reaching the Lake Michigan and Lake Superior iron mines.

The stock has been held in a voting trust under an arrangement for five years, expiring July 1, 1904.

General balance sheet, June 30, 1903 :

Assets.

Road and securities	$49,187,861
Equipment	4,112,736
Material in private tracks	126,827
Company's stock in treasury	2,585,020
Stocks and bonds owned	60,034
Trustees	78,038
Sinking fund	81,987
Special improvement fund	29,070
Fuel, supplies, etc.	721,018
Agents and conductors	428,570
United States Post Office	31,318
Individuals and companies	194,007
Cash	1,376,912
Trust equipment and miscellaneous	592,067
Total	$59,605,466

Liabilities.

Preferred stock	$12,500,000
Common stock	17,500,000
Bonds	27,320,500
Vouchers and pay rolls	503,849
Interest on funded debt, accrued	551,614
Equipment renewal account	160,646
Sinking fund trustees	29,029
Accounts payable and miscellaneous	322,205
Profit and loss	717,622
Total	$59,605,466

Income and profit and loss account for year ended and at June 30, 1903 :

Earnings :

Freight	$5,024,477
Passenger	1,359,570
Mail, express and miscellaneous	267,815
Gross earnings	$6,651,862

Gross earnings........	$6,651,862
Expenses :	
Maintenance of way and structures.............................	$763,097
Maintenance of equipment..	721,615
Conducting transportation..........	2,459,098
General expenses	262,183
Total expenses...	$4,205,993
Net earnings..	$2,445,869
Other income	38,430
Total net income.................	$2,484,299
Deduct:	
Taxes accrued.................................	$234,291
Interest on bonds...	1,132,390
Rentals accrued..	392,434
Miscellaneous...	1.111
Total.....	$1,760,226
Surplus for year	$724,073
Surplus June 30, 1902...	632,049
	$1,356,122
Deduct:	
Appropriated by board for—	
Improvements	$424,638
New equipment	138,459
M. & S. E. Div. bonds sinking fund...........	10,543
Reserve to retire series "A" equipment trust bonds, maturing July 1, 1903... .	60,000
Appropriated for purchase of series "J," equipment trust bonds...	4,860
Total	$638,500
Balance profit and loss, June 30, 1903.............................	$717,622

President Whitcomb in his report calls attention to the following facts :

The commodities carried during the year as compared with the previous year show increases or decreases as under—

	Increase. Tons.	Decrease. Tons.
Products of agriculture..........................	161,307	....
Products of animals..............................	....	6,179
Products of mines	....	11,179
Products of forest	81,918	....
Manufactures....................................	9,423	....
Other commodities........................	76,104	....
An increase in all tonnage of	311,394 tons.	

And also states that the territory tributary to the company's lines is being rapidly settled and new industries constantly being planted.

Increase in gross earnings over the preceeding year was 10.10%; increase in expenses, 8.31%; increase in net earnings, 13.33%.

The per cent. of expenses to earnings was 63.23, against 64.28, 65.11, 63.52, for the three respective preceeding years.

Stock.—Common—Authorized, $17,500,000; issued, $16,147,876. Preferred—Authorized, $12,500,000; issued, $11,267,104.

The preferred is 4% non-cumulative. After 4% on both, each class shares equally in further dividends.

Funded debt, June 30, 1903, consisted of:

W. C. Ry. 1st general mortgage 4s, due July 1, 1949	$23,748,000
W. C. R. R. 1st series, due January 1, 1909	658,500
C. W. & M. R. R. 1st 6s of March, 1916	776,000
M. & L. W. R. R. 1st 6s of July, 1906	604,000
M. Term. purchase money 3½s, January 1, 1950	500,000
M. & S. E. Div. 4s of 1951	439,000
W. C. Ry. gold equipment trust 5%, dated 1902, due 1-10 yearly	595,000
The 1st general mortgage 4s are authorized for	$27,000,000

The unissued are reserved to retire underlying bonds.

Dividends.—None paid.

Annual meeting.— Second Tuesday in October.

Main office, Milwaukee, Wis.; New York office, 38 Broad Street.

Directors —John Crosby Brown, William L. Bull, James C. Colgate, Fred. T. Gates, Gerald L. Hoyt, E. W. Sheldon, Joseph S. Dale, Francis R. Hart, Henry F. Whitcomb, Howard Morris, and William F. Vilas.

Private Telegraph Code.

BUY STOCK.

Buy 10 shares	....	Abating
20	"	Abbess
30	"	Abbot
40	"	Abhor
50	"	Abide
60	"	Ability
70	"	Able
80	"	Abode
90	"	Abolish
100	"	Abound
150	"	Abrade
200	"	Abridge
300	"	Abridgment
400	"	Abroad
500	"	Abrogate
1,000	"	Abrogation

BOUGHT STOCK.

Bought 10 shares	....	Abrupt
20	"	Absent
30	"	Absolute
40	"	Absolve
50	"	Absorb
60	"	Abstain
70	"	Absume
80	"	Absurd
90	"	Abuse
100	"	Abut
150	"	Abutment
200	"	Academy
300	"	Academic
400	"	Acaulous
500	"	Accelerate
1,000	"	Acceleration

SELL STOCK.

Sell 10 shares	....	Acceding
20	"	Accent
30	"	Acclaim
40	"	Accord
50	"	Accost
60	"	Accrue
70	"	Accurate
80	"	Accuse
90	"	Ace
100	"	Access
150	"	Achieve
200	"	Acid
300	"	Acidify
400	"	Acidulate
500	"	Acidulous
1,000	"	Acme

SOLD STOCK.

Sold 10 shares	....	Acorn
20	"	Acquire
30	"	Acquit
40	"	Acrostic
50	"	Acting
60	"	Actor
70	"	Actress
80	"	Active
90	"	Actuary
100	"	Acumen
150	"	Acute
200	"	Adage
300	"	Adamant
400	"	Adaptability
500	"	Adder
1,000	"	Addle

COMMODITIES.

Wheat.................................. ....Ally
Corn.................... ....Almoner
Oats..Aloft
Pork.................... ....Aloud
Lard...Alpha
Ribs..Alpine
Cotton...Amass

Buy —— bushels —— wheat.....................Amative
Sell ——   "   ——   "   ....Amatory
Buy ——   "   —— corn   ....Amazon
Sell ——   "   ——   "   ....Amber
Buy ——   "   —— oats   ....Ambition
Sell ——   "   ——   "   ....Amble
Buy —— barrels —— pork   ....Amboy
Sell ——   "   ——   "   ....Ambrosia
Buy —— tierces —— lard   ....Ambush
Sell ——   "   ——   "   ....Amends
Buy —— lbs.   —— ribs   ....Amherst
Sell ——   "   ——   "   ....Amiable
Buy —— bales —— cotton ....Amidst
Sell ——   "   ——   "   ....Ammon

Bought —— bushels —— wheat..................Amnesty
Sold   ——   "   ——   "   ....Amorous
Bought ——   "   —— corn   .... Amply
Sold   ——   "   ——   "   .... Amplify
Bought ——   "   —— oats   ....Amsden
Sold   ——   "   ——   "   ....Amuse
Bought —— barrels —— pork   ....Anacosta
Sold   ——   "   ——   "   ....Anagram
Bought —— tierces —— lard   ... .Analect
Soid   ——   "   ——   "   ....Andes
Bought —— lbs.   —— ribs   ....Anecdote
Sold   ——   "   ——   "   ....Angel
Bought —— bales —— cotton..................Angola
Sold   ——   "   ——   "   ....Anger

LIST OF SECURITIES.

Amal. Copper.............Babbler
Am. Car & Foundry.......Babe
  " Cotton Oil...........Baboon
  " Sugar Refining.......Badge
  "   " pref... .Badger
Atchison, T. & S. F.......Baker
  "   " pref ....Balcony
Baltimore & Ohio.........Bald
Brooklyn Rapid Transit..Ballad
Chesapeake & Ohio.......Ballot
Cleveland, C. C. & St. L...Bamboo
Chicago Gt. Western.....Band
  " Ind.& Louisville..Bandage
  " Mil. & St. Paul....Banner
Colorado Fuel & Iron.....Bannock
Delaware & Hudson......Banquet
Erie ....Baptist
Louisville & Nashville . Baronet
Manhattan .. ..Barracks
Metropolitan St. Ry......Barrow
Mexican Central.........Barshot
  " National........Barrel
Missouri, Kans. & Texas..Barter
  "   " pref ..Base
Missouri Pacific...........Basin
National Lead...........Basket
New Jersey Central.......Bath
New York Central........Bather
Norfolk & Western.......Battle
Northern Pacific..........Bawl
  "   " pref......Bawling

Ontario & Western........Bay
Pacific Mail...............Beacon
Pennsylvania Railroad....Bear
People's Gas of Chicago...Beam
Pittsburg, C. C. & St. L....Beard
Pressed Steel Car.........Beast
Reading..................Beauty
  " 1st pref............Beautiful
  " 2d pref............Beautify
Republic Steel............Beaver
  "   " pref........Becalm
Rock Island..............Bedding
Standard Rope & Twine...Bedew
Southern Pacific..........Beech
  " Railway.........Beef
  "   " pref......Beetle
Tennessee Coal & Iron....Beeves
Union Pacific.............Behave
  "   " pref.........Behavior
U. S. Leather.... ....Beget
  " pref..........Behalf
  " Rubber..... ....Behest
  " Steel common.......Behind
  "   " pref..........Before
Wabash...................Behold
  " pref.............Beholden
Western Union............Bells
Wisconsin Central.........Bellman
Wheeling & Lake Erie....Bestir
  "   " 1st pref .Bestired
  "   " 2d pref..Bestiring

NUMERALS.

1-16..Cab
⅛..Cabbage
¼..Cabin
⅜..Cabal
½..Caboose
⅝..Cackle
¾..Cackling
⅞..Cactus
1 ..Cadence
1⅛..Cadet
1¼..Cajole
1⅜..Calabash
1½..Caldron
1⅝..Caleb
1¾..Caliber
1⅞..Calico
2 ..Caliph
2⅛..Calm
2¼..Calmly
2⅜..Calmness
2½..Calomel
2⅝..Calumet
2¾..Cambric
2⅞..Cameo
..Camp
3⅛..Camped
3¼..Camping
3⅜..Camphene
3½..Camphor
3⅝..Canary
3¾..Candid
3⅞..Candidly
4 ..Candidate
4⅛..Candling
4¼..Candor
4⅜..Cane
4½..Canebrake
4⅝..Canine
4¾..Canker
⅞..Cannibal

5 ..Canopy
5⅛..Canon
5¼..Canvas
5⅜..Capable
5½..Caper
5⅝..Capital
5¾..Capsize
5⅞..Capstan
6 ..Capsular
6⅛..Capsule
6¼..Captain
6⅜..Captivate
6½..Captivity
6⅝..Capor
6¾..Captured
6⅞..Carat
7 ..Caravan
7⅛..Carbon
7¼..Carbonate
7⅜..Carboy
7½..Carbuncle
7⅝..Carcass
7¾..Carding
7⅞..Cardinal
8 ..Careful
8⅛..Careless
8¼..Caress
8⅜..Carmine
8½..Carnal
8⅝..Carnally
8¾..Carnival
8⅞..Carousal
9 ..Carouse
9⅛..Carousing
9¼..Carpenter
9⅜..Carpet
9½..Carpeting
9⅝..Carriage
9¾..Carry
9⅞..Cartoon

10 ..Cartridge
10⅛..Cascade
10¼..Casmate
10⅜..Cashmere
10½..Casing
10⅝..Castigate
10¾..Castle
10⅞..Castor
11 ..Casual
11⅛..Casually
11¼..Catacomb
11⅜..Catalogue
11½..Catcher
11⅝..Catchup
11¾..Catgut
11⅞..Cathartic
12 ..Cathedral
12⅛..Catholic
12¼..Catheter
12⅜..Catnip
12½..Caucus
12⅝..Caustic
12¾..Caution
12⅞..Cautious
13 ..Cavalry
13⅛..Cavern
13¼..Cavity
13⅜..Cayenne
13½..Cedar
13⅝..Celebrate
13¾..Celestial
13⅞..Cement
14 ..Cemented
14⅛..Cementing
14¼..Censure
14⅜..Censuring
14½..Census
14⅝..Center
14¾..Centipede
14⅞..Centralize

15 ..Centrally
15⅛..Century
15¼..Chafe
15⅜..Chafing
15½..Chagrin
15⅝..Chain
15¾..Chained
15⅞..Chaining
16 ..Chairman
16⅛..Chaise
16¼..Chalked
16⅜..Challenge
16½..Chamber
16⅝..Champagn
16¾..Champion
16⅞..Chance
17 ..Chancing
17⅛..Chandler
17¼..Changeful
17⅜..Chanting
17½..Chaos
17⅝..Chapel
17¾..Chaplain
17⅞..Chaplet
18 ..Chapter
18⅛..Character
18¼..Charade
18⅜..Charcoal
18½..Charlotte
18⅝..Charity
18¾..Chastise
18⅞..Chastity
19 ..Chat
19⅛..Chatting
19¼..Chatty
19⅜..Chattel
19½..Cheapen
19⅝..Cheapness
19¾..Checkmat
19⅞..Cheek

20 ..Cheerful	25⅝..Churning	31¼..Clemency	36⅞..Cobbling
20⅛..Cheerfully	25¾..Chyle	31⅜..Clergical	37 ..Cobweb
20¼..Chemical	25⅞..Cigar	31½..Clergy	37⅛..Cock
20⅜..Chemist	26 ..Cima	31⅝..Clerking	37¼..Cockade
20½..Chemistry	26⅛..Cinnabar	31¾..Clever	37⅜..Cockney
20⅝..Cherub	26¼..Cinnamon	31⅞..Cleverly	37½..Cod
20¾..Cherubim	26⅜..Circle	32 ..Client	37⅝..Codfish
20⅞..Chest	26½..Circuit	32⅛..Cliff	37¾..Codger
21 ..Chestnut	26⅝..Circulate	32¼..Climate	37⅞..Coddle
21⅛..Chick	26¾..Circus	32⅜..Climb	38 ..Coffee
21¼..Chicken	26⅞..Cistern	32½..Climber	38⅛..Coffin
21⅜..Chide	27 ..Citadel	32⅝..Climbing	38¼..Cogent
21½..Chiding	27⅛..Citizen	32¾..Clinch	38⅜..Cognac
21⅝..Chief	27¼..Citrine	32⅞..Clinics	38½..Cohabit
21¾..Chieftain	27⅜..Citron	33 ..Cloak	38⅝..Cohabiting
21⅞..Chilblain	27½..Civic	33⅛..Cloaked	38¾..Cohesion
22 ..Child	27⅝..Civilian	33¼..Clock	38⅞..Collapse
22⅛..Childhood	27¾..Civility	33⅜..Clodpate	39 ..Collapsing
22¼..Childish	27⅞..Civilize	33½ Clodpoll	39⅛..Colleague
22⅜..Childless	28 ..Claimant	33⅝..Clog	39¼..Collide
22½..Children	28⅛..Clam	33¾..Clogged	39⅜..Colliding
22⅝..Chilly	28¼..Clamor	33⅞..Clogging	39½..Collusion
22¾..Chimney	28⅜..Clang	34 ..Cloister	39⅝..Colonist
22⅞..China	28½..Clap	34⅛..Closely	39¾..Colony
23 ..Chinese	28⅝..Clapboard	34¼..Closet	39⅞..Color
23⅛..Chink	28¾..Clarify	34⅜..Clothe	40 ..Colored
23¼..Chisel	28⅞..Clarion	34½..Clothing	40⅛..Colorless
23⅜..Chiseled	29 ..Claritude	34⅝..Cloud	40¼..Column
23½..Chivalry	29⅛..Clashing	34¾..Cloudy	40⅜..Combat
23⅝..Cholic	29¼..Clasp	34⅞..Cloven	40½..Combatant
23¾..Choose	29⅜..Class	35 ..Clown	40⅝..Combine
23⅞..Chorus	29½..Classical	35⅛..Clownish	40¾..Combining
24 ..Chosen	29⅝..Clatter	35¼..Club	40⅞..Comedian
24⅛..Chowder	29¾..Clavicle	35⅜..Clubbed	41 ..Comely
24¼..Christen	29⅞..Claymore	35½..Clubber	41⅛..Comet
24⅜..Christened	30 ..Clean	35⅝..Clubman	41¼..Comfort
24½..Chronic	30⅛..Cleaner	35¾..Clumsy	41⅜..Comforted
24⅝..Chub	30¼..Cleanest	35⅞..Cluster	41½..Comforting
24¾..Chubby	30⅜..Cleanly	36 ..Clutch	41⅝..Coming
24⅞..Chuckle	30½..Cleansed	36⅛..Coach	41¾..Comma
25 ..Chuckling	30⅝..Clearer	36¼..Coachman	41⅞..Command
25⅛..Chunam	30¾..Clearness	36⅜..Coagulate	42 ..Commander
25¼..Church	30⅞..Cleaver	36½..Coax	42⅛..Commanding
25⅜..Churl	31 ..Cleft	36⅝..Coaxing	42¼..Commend
25½..Churlish	31⅛..Clement	36¾..Cobble	42⅜..Commit

65 ..Cram	70⅝..Crudely	76¼..Cursing	81⅞..Daring
65⅛..Cramp	70¾..Crudeness	76⅜..Cursory	82 ..Dark
65¼..Cramping	70⅞..Cruel	76½..Curtain	82⅛..Darker
65⅜..Crane	71 ..Cruelly	76⅝..Curtained	82¼..Darkened
65½..Craning	71⅛..Crumb	76¾..Curvet	82⅜..Darkest
65⅝..Cranium	71¼..Crumble	76⅞..Cushion	82½..Darkness
65¾..Crank	71⅜..Crusade	77 ..Custody	82⅝..Darling
65⅞..Cranky	71½..Crusader	77⅛..Custom	82¾..Dash
66 ..Crape	71⅝..Crust	77¼..Cuticle	82⅞..Dashaway
66⅛..Crash	71¾..Crusted	77⅜..Cutlass	83 ..Dashboard
66¼..Crashing	71⅞..Crusting	77½..Cyclops	83⅛..Dasher
66⅜..Crate	72 ..Crutch	77⅝..Cymbal	83¼..Dashing
66½..Crater	72⅛..Cube	77¾..Cypress	83⅜..Dastard
66⅝..Cravat	72¼..Cubic	77⅞..Dab	83½..Dastardly
66¾..Crave	72⅜..Cuckoo	78 ..Dabbling	83⅝..Date
66⅞..Craven	72½..Cucumber	78⅛..Dabchick	83¾..Datum
67 ..Crawfish	72⅝..Cuddle	78¼..Dabbler	83⅞..Daughter
67⅛..Crawl	72¾..Cuddy	78⅜..Daddy	84 ..Daunt
67¼..Crawled	72⅞..Cudgel	78½..Daffodil	84⅛..Daunted
67⅜..Crawling	73 ..Cuff	78⅝..Dainty	84¼..Daunting
67½..Crayon	73⅛..Culinary	78¾..Dallas	84⅜..Dauntless
67⅝..Cream	73¼..Culprit	78⅞..Dalliance	84½..Dauphin
67¾..Creamy	73⅜..Culture	79 ..Dally	84⅝..Dawn
67⅞..Create	73½..Cultured	79⅛..Dalton	84¾..Dawning
68 ..Created	73⅝..Cultivate	79¼..Damage	84⅞..Daze
68⅛..Creating	73¾..Culverts	79⅜..Damaged	85 ..Dazed
68¼..Creature	73⅞..Culverin	79½..Damaging	85⅛..Dazzle
68⅜..Credible	74 ..Cunning	79⅝..Damask	85¼..Deacon
68½..Credit	74⅛..Cup	79¾..Damp	85⅜..Deaconry
68⅝..Creditor	74¼..Cupping	79⅞..Damped	85½..Deaden
68¾..Credulous	74⅜..Cupid	80 ..Damper	85⅝..Deadly
68⅞..Cricket	74½..Cupidity	80⅛..Damping	85¾..Deaf
69 ..Crimson	74⅝..Cupola	80¼..Damsel	85⅞..Deafness
69⅛..Cripple	74¾..Curable	80⅜..Damson	86 ..Deal
69¼..Crisp	74⅞..Curate	80½..Dance	86⅛..Dealer
69⅜..Crispness	75 ..Curator	80⅝..Dancer	86¼..Dealing
69½..Critic	75⅛..Curbing	80¾..Dancing	86⅜..Dealt
69⅝..Critical	75¼..Curdle	80⅞..Dander	86½..Dean
69¾..Croup	75⅜..Curfew	81 ..Dandruff	86⅝..Deanery
69⅞..Croupade	75½..Curious	81⅛..Dandy	86¾..Dearth
70 ..Crow	75⅝..Curly	81¼..Danger	86⅞..Debar
70⅛..Crowbar	75¾..Curling	81⅜..Dangerous	87 ..Debarred
70¼..Crowed	75⅞..Currant	81½..Dapper	87⅛..Debase
70⅜..Crowing	76 ..Curricle	81⅝..Darby	87¼..Debate
70½..Crude	76⅛..Curry	81¾..Dare	87⅜..Debating

87½..Debauch	93⅛..Deformity	98¾ Detest	104⅜..Dirempt
87⅝..Debtor	93¼..Defraud	98⅞..Develop	104½..Direness
87¾..Debility	93⅜..Defunct	99 ..Development	104⅝..Dirge
87⅞..Decade	93½..Degrade	99⅛..Device	104¾..Dirgelike
88 ..Decamp	93⅝..Degree	99¼..Devil	104⅞..Dirk
88⅛..Decant	93¾..Delayer	99⅜..Devilish	105 ..Disbody
88¼.Decanter	93⅞..Delegate	99½..Devote	105⅛..Disbowel
88⅜..Decent	94 ..Delegation	99⅝..Devotion	105¼..Discipline
88½..Decently	94⅛..Delight	99¾..Devour	105⅜..Discord
88⅝..Declare	94¼..Delighted	99⅞..Devoured	105½..Discorded
88¾..Decoct	94⅜..Delightful	100 ..Devoted	105⅝..Discourse
88⅞..Decoction	94½..Dell	100⅛..Dexter	105¾..Discover
89 ..Decorate	94⅝..Delphic	100¼..Dexterity	105⅞..Disdain
89⅛..Decorator	94¾..Delta	100⅜..Dexterous	106 ..Disfigure
89¼..Decorum	94⅞..Deluge	100½..Diadem	106⅛..Disfiguring
89⅜..Decorus	95 ..Delusion	100⅝..Dials	106¼..Disgrace
89½..Decreed	95⅛..Delusive	100¾..Dialogue	106⅜..Disguise
89⅝..Decrepid	95¼..Delve	100⅞..Diameter	106½..Disgust
89¾..Dedicate	95⅜..Demand	101 ..Diamond	106⅝..Disgusting
89⅞..Deed	95½..Democrat	101⅛..Dictate	106¾..Dislike
90 ..Deeded	95⅝..Demolish	101¼..Dictation	106⅞..Dislocate
90⅛..Deepen	95¾..Demon	101⅜..Dictator	107 ..Dismal
90¼..Deepened	95⅞..Demur	101½..Dictatorial	107⅛..Dismayed
90⅜..Deface	96 ..Dentist	101⅝..Dictionary	107¼..Dismiss
90½..Defame	96⅛..Dentistry	101¾..Digest	107⅜..Disorder
90⅝..Default	96¼..Denial	101⅞..Digestion	107½..Dispel
90¾..Defaulted	96⅜..Departed	102 ..Dignify	107⅝..Display
90⅞..Defeat	96½..Depot	102⅛..Dignified	107¾..Displayed
91 ..Deference	96⅝..Deprive	102¼..Dikes	107⅞..Dispute
91⅛..Deferential	96¾..Deputation	102⅜..Dim	108 ..Dissipate
91¼..Defect	96⅞..Deputy	102½..Dimly	108⅛..Dissolved
91⅜..Defection	97 ..Desert	102⅝..Dimension	108¼..Distemper
91½..Defective	97⅛..Deserter	102¾..Diminished	108⅜..Distend
91⅝..Defense	97¼..Desertion	102⅞..Dimple	108½..Distill
91¾..Defensive	97⅜..Design	103 ..Dingy	108⅝..Distillery
91⅞..Deficient	97½..Designer	103⅛..Dinner	108¾..Distinct
92 ..Defile	97⅝..Desk	103¼..Diploma	108⅞..Distinction
92⅛..Deflect	97¾..Desolate	103⅜..Dipsas	109 ..Distinguish
92¼..Deflected	97⅞..Despot	103½..Diptote	109⅛..Distress
92⅜..Define	98 ..Despotism	103⅝..Direct	109¼..Distressing
92½..Defining	98⅛..Destiny	103¾..Direction	109⅜..Distribute
92⅝..Definition	98¼..Destination	103⅞..Director	109½..Distribution
92¾..Defy	98⅜..Destroy	104 ..Directrix	109⅝..District
92⅞..Defiant	98½.Detailed	104⅛..Dire	109¾..Distrib
93 ..Deform	98⅝..Detective	104¼..Direful	109⅞..Ditch

110 ..Divan	115⅝..Dreadful	121¼..Duck	140..Eclipse
110⅛..Division	115¾..Dream	121⅜..Duckling	141..Economy
110¼..Divorce	115⅞..Dreamer	121½..Duel	142..Economist
110⅜..Divorcing	116 ..Dreaming	121⅝..Dueling	143..Eddy
110½..Divulge	116⅛..Dreampt	121¾..Duelist	144..Eddying
110⅝..Divulged	116¼..Dress	121⅞..Dug	145..Eden
110¾..Divulging	116⅜..Dressed	122 ..Dugout	146..Edge
110⅞..Doctor	116½..Dresser	122⅛..Dulcet	147..Edged
111 ..Doctored	116⅝..Dressing	122¼..Ducify	148..Edging
111⅛..Doctoress	116¾..Drew	122⅜..Dumb	149..Edict
111¼..Document	116⅞..Dribble	122½..Dummy	150..Edify
111⅜..Dodge	117 ..Dribbling	122⅝..Dump	151..Edifying
111½..Dodging	117⅛..Drift	122¾..Dumpish	152..Edit
111⅝..Dogma	117¼..Drifted	122⅞..Dumpling	153..Editing
111¾..Dogmatic	117⅜..Drifting	123 ..Dunce	154..Editor
111⅞..Dolphin	117½..Drill	123⅛..Dungeon	155..Editress
112 ..Domain	117⅝..Drilled	123¼..Dued	156..Educate
112⅛..Domestic	117¾..Drilling	123⅜..Duplex	157..Educating
112¼..Dominion	117⅞..Drink	123½..Durable	158..Education
112⅜..Domino	118 ..Drinking	123⅝..Duration	159..Effecting
112½..Donate	118⅛..Drive	123¾..Dusk	160..Effectual
112⅝..Donated	118¼..Driven	123⅞..Dusky	161..Effigy
112¾..Donkey	118⅜..Driving	124 ..Dutiful	162..Egg
112⅞..Doom	118½..Dromedary	124⅛..Duty	163..Eggshaped
113 ..Donor	118⅝..Drop	124¼..Dwarf	164..Eggshell
113⅛..Dough	118¾..Dropped	124⅜..Dwarfed	165..Eject
113¼..Doughty	118⅞..Dropping	124½..Dwell	166..Ejection
113⅜..Dowel	119 ..Dropsy	124⅝..Dwelled	167..Elaborate
113½..Dowager	119⅛..Dropsical	124¾..Dwelling	168..Elapse
113⅝..Dower	119¼..Drove	124⅞..Dynasty	169..Elapsed
113¾..Downed	119⅜..Drown	125 ..Eagle	170..Elapsing
113⅞..Downy	119½..Drowned	126 ..Earnest	171..Elastic
114 ..Drab	119⅝..Drowning	127 ..Earnestly	172..Elasticity
114⅛..Drafted	119¾..Drudge	128 ..Earth	173..Elate
114¼..Drag	119⅞..Drudgery	129 ..Earthly	174..Elating
114⅜..Dragged	120 ..Drug	130 ..Easterly	175..Elation
114½..Dragging	120⅛..Druggist	131 ..Eastward	176..Elbow
114⅝..Drake	120¼..Druid	132 ..Eat	177..Elbowed
114¾..Dram	120⅜..Drum	133 ..Eaten	178..Elder
114⅞..Drama	120½..Drunk	134 ..Eating	179 Elderly
115 ..Dramatic	120⅝..Drunkard	135 ..Eaves	180..Elect
115⅛..Drank	120¾..Dry	136 ..Ebony	181..Electoral
115¼..Dray	120⅞..Dryness	137 ..Echo	182..Electing
115⅜..Dread	121 ..Ducal	138 ..Echoed	183..Electrical
115½..Dreaded	121⅛..Duchess	139 ..Echoing	184..Electricity

238

185..Elegant	450..Embellish	4.000..Enchant	400,000..Equinox
186..Elegantly	500..Emblem	5.000..Endure	500,000..Equip
187..Elephant	600..Embrace	6,000..Energy	1,000,000..Erect
188..Elevate	700..Embrocate	7,000..Engage	2,000,000..Erection
189..Elevation	800..Emerald	8,000..Engine	3,000,000..Ermine
190..Elixir	900..Emerge	9,000..Engrave	4,000,000..Eruption
191..Elocution	1,000..Emerging	10,000..Enjoy	5,000,000..Escort
192..Elope	1,100..Emetic	15,000..Enlarge	6,000,000..Esquire
193..Eloping	1,200..Eminent	20,000..Enlist	7,000,000..Essence
194..Elopment	1.250..Emissary	25,000..Enlighten	8,000,000..Establish
195..Elude	1,300..Emit	30,000..Ensue	9,000,000..Estimation
196..Eluding	1,400..Emotion	40,000..Enter	10,000,000..Esteem
197..Emanate	1,500..Emotional	50,000..Enterprise	20,000,000..Eternal
198..Emanating	1,600..Emperor	60,000..Entertain	30,000,000..Eternity
199..Embalm	1,700..Emphasis	70,000..Entrance	50,000,000..Evacuate
200..Embalming	1,800..Emphatic	80,000..Entreat	60,000,000..Evade
250..Embargo	1,900..Empire	90,000..Environs	70,000,000..Eventful
300..Embark	2,000..Empress	100,000..Epicure	80,000,000..Exalt
350..Embarking	2,500..Emulate	200,000..Epigram	90,000,000..Excavate
400..Embassy	3,000..Enamel	300,000..Epsom	100,000 000..Excel

REGARDING ORDERS.

Buy at market ....Fact
Sell   "   "   ....Factory
Buy " opening...Faculty
Sell "   "   ....Fade
Close at —— per cent. profit...Fagot
Stop loss at —— ....Faith
Keep order good until cancelled ....Falcon
  "   "   for day only ....Fame
Cancel all orders ....Family
  "   "   "   in —— ....Famous
  "   "   "   for buying...Fan
  "   "   "   " selling..Fancy
  "   "   "   in letter of —— ....Farce
  "   "   "   " telegram of —— ....Farcial
Refer to letter of —— ....Farm
  "   telegram of —— ....Farming
Order too late for market, will keep for next day...................Fashion
  "   "   "   will await further advices regarding it...Fawn
Mistake in your telegram...Feast
  "   our   "   ....Feasting
Please repeat..Feathers
Reduce limit to —— ....Fed
Advance   "   —— ....Feeble
Buy in short —— ....Fellow
Your letter of —— received...Fence
Sell long —— ....Ferns
Grain market closed ....Fervent
Stock   "   "   ....Festival
Cotton   "   "   ....Fetch
Impossible to execute at your limit..................................Fiddle
Wire instructions ....Fifer
Please give positive order...Figs
Regard orders as cancelled ....Filbert

REGARDING THE MARKETS.

How does market look ? ....Gable
  "   "   ——   "   ....Gaff
Wire opinion of —— ....Gainer
  "   opening price of —— ....Gallery
  "   closing   "   —— ....Gallant
  "   price of —— ....Gallop
Do you advise buying —— ? ....Galvanic
  "   "   selling —— ?...Galvanize
What do you advise ?...Gamest

240

Market steady ....Gangway
"   "   and dull................   ....Gaping
"   strong ....Garden
"   "   and indications favor higher prices....................Garland
Appears safe to buy ....Garlic
"   "   hold...Garment
Would buy on reaction...Garret
Market oversold ; rally seems probable.............................Garter
Rally apparently due...Gate
Market weak...Gather
"   looks like selling lower......................................Gaudy
Appears safe to sell...Gauntlet
Would sell on rally..Gay
Market overbought ; looks like a sale ....Gem
Reaction apparently due...Gentle
Believe a purchase on all reactions.................................Ginger

REGARDING TELEGRAMS.

Wire fully as possible..Hall
"   in cipher...Hallway
"   "   plain language..Ham
Wire answer promptly..Hamlet
Will wire soon as practicable..Hamper
Please repeat..Handsome
Should this be too late for to-day's market, give attention to-morrow. Hanks

MARGINS AND REMITTANCES.

Please forward further margin and wire reply promptly, stating
  amount and form of remittance ....Kedge
Mailing check for —— ....Keel
Expressing —— dollars......   ....Keenly
Deposited —— dollars to your credit with —— ....Keg
Require —— dollars ....Kennel
Unless you remit further margin at once, must close all or part of
  holdings ....Kersey
Deposit —— dollars to our credit with —— ....Kettle
Require —— per cent. margin.......................................Kidney
Margin insufficient..Kindle
Draw on me through —— ....King
Have drawn on you for —— ....Kingdom
Cannot act without margin first in hand ....Kinglike
What is amount of credit ?..Kingly
Your present credit is —— ....Kinsman
At market figures your margin is —— ....Kitchen
Send funds by wire..Koran

BOND INVESTMENTS.—United States Government Bonds.

BONDS.	Denominations.	Interest payable.	Date of Closing Transfer Books for Registered Issues.	Approximate Price June 14, 1904
TWO'S. Due 1930.				
Registered........	$50, 100, 500, 1000, $5000, 10000, 50000	Jan., April	Nov. 30, Feb. 28	105
Coupon..........	$50, 100, 500, 1000	July, Oct.	May 31, Aug. 31	105½
THREE'S Due 1908-18.				
Registered........	$20, 100, 500, 1000, $5000. 10000	Feb., May	Dec. 31, Mar. 31	106¼
Coupon..........	$20, 100, 500, 1000	Aug., Nov.	June 30, Sep. 30	106¾
FOUR'S Due 1907.				
Registered........	$50, 100, 500, 1000, $5000, 10000, 20000, $50000	Jan., April	Nov. 30, Feb. 28	106½
Coupon..........	$50, 100, 500, 1000	July, Oct.	May 31, Aug 31	107½
FOUR'S. Due 1925.				
Registered........	$50, 100, 1000, 5000, $10000	Feb., May	Jan. 15, April 15	133
Coupon..........	$50, 100, 500, 1000	Aug., Nov.	July 15, Oct. 15	133½
3,65/100's District of Columbia. Due 1924				
Registered........	$1000, 5000	Feb., Aug.	Jan. 21	119
Coupon..........	$50, 500	Feb., Aug.	July 21	
FOUR'S. Philippine. Due				
Registered........	$1000, 10000	Feb., May / Aug., Nov.	Jan. 15, April 15 / July 15, Oct. 15	110⅞

Following is a list of carefully selected bond investments. They include, in our opinion, the issues best suited to the private investor, all being high class as to the security offered and having an active market upon the New York Stock Exchange. This enables the holder to at all times determine the value of his investment and realize quickly upon the same. Description of the properties securing these bonds may be found elsewhere in this book. Persons who wish a more detailed description of any individual bond than is here shown can receive same by request at any of our offices.

BOND.	Maturity	Interest Date.	Denominations.	Form: R-Registered C-Coupon Cx-Coup. but may be registered as to principal.	Approximate Price June 1, 1904.	Yield per Cent.
Atch T & S F genl mtg 4s.........	1995	A & O	$500 etc.	Cx & R	101½	3.95
Baltimore & Ohio prior gold 3½s..	1925	J & J	500 "	"	95¼	3.93
Baltimore & Ohio gold 4s.........	1948	A & O	500 "	"	101⅝	3.97
B & O S W Div 3½s...............	1925	J & J	500 "	"	91	4.25
B R T, Bkn U El 1st gold 4-5s.....	1950	F & A	1,000	Cx	104¼	*
B R T, Kings Co El 1st gold 4s.....	1949	F & A	1,000	"	86½	4.80
Brooklyn Union Gas 1st con 5s....	1945	M & N	1,000	"	112½	4.36
Central of Georgia co 5s.........	1945	M & N	1,000	Cx & R	107½	4.65
Chesapeake & Ohio 1st con 5s.....	1939	M & N	1,000	"	115¼	4.18
Chic & Alton R R ref gold 3s.	1949	A & O	1,000 "	"	83¼	3.80
C B Q, Gt Nor-Nor Pac col tr 4s...	1921	J & J	1,000 "	C & R	94⅞	4.60
Chic & Eastern Ill genl con 1st 5s.	1937	M & N	1,000 "	"	116¼	4.15
Chic R I & Pac Ry genl gold 4s....	1988	J & J	1,000 "	Cx & R	104	3.84
C C C & St L genl gold 4s.........	1993	J & D	1,000	"	98½	4.25
Denver & R G 1st con gold 4s.....	1936	J & J	500 "	"	99¼	4.10
Detroit City Gas gold 5s	1923	J & J	1,000	Cx	97½	†
Erie 1st con g prior lien 4s	1996	J & J	1,000	Cx & R	98½	4.13
Laclede Gas (of St L) 1st gold 5s..	1919	Q—F	100 "	Cx	107¾	4.30
L & N unified gold 4s..............	1940	J & J	1,000 "	Cx & R	100¾	4.00
Manhattan Railway 4s	1990	A & O	1,000 "	"	103¼	3.85
Metropolitan genl col tr 5s........	1997	F & A	1,000 "	"	113	4.51
Metropolitan Third Ave 1st con 4s	2000	J & J	1,000 "	Cx	94¾	4.32
M K T 1st gold 4s..................	1990	J & D	500 "	"	98½	4.12
Mo Pacific 1s con gold 6s..........	1920	M & N	1,000	"	120¼	4.35
Mo Pacific 1st col gold 5s..........	1920	F & A	1,000	"	108	4.50
Mo Pacific St L & I M con ry l 5s..	1931	A & O	1,000	"	114⅞	4.14
National of Mexico p l 4½s........	1926	J & J	500 "	"	102½	4.43
N Y C genl mtg 3½s	1997	J & J	1,000 "	Cx & R	100	3.50
N Y C, L S col tr 3½s.............	1998	F & A	1,000 "	"	90½	3.98
N Y Gas E L H & P 1st col tr g 5s	1948	J & D	1,000	"	105½	4.83
do purchase money 4s	1949	F & A	1,000	Cx	93	4.33
Nor & West Ry 1st con g 4s.......	1996	A & O	500 "	Cx & R	98⅞	4.12
Nor Pac p l g 4s	1997	Q—J	500 "	"	104¼	3.87
Nor Pac genl lien 3s...............	2047	Q—F	500 "	"	72¼	‡
Penn R R convert g 3½s..........	1912	M & N	500 "	Cx	95	4.27
Reading genl 4s..................	1997	J & J	1,000 "	Cx & R	99¼	4.12
Rio G Western 1st g tr 4s.........	1939	J & J	1,000 "	Cx	96¼	4.31
So Pac, C P 1st ref guar g 4s......	1949	F & A	500 "	Cx & R	100¼	4.13
So Ry 1st con g 5s................	1994	J & J	1,000 "	"	115⅞	4.33
Texas & Pac 1st g 5s..............	2000	J & D	1,000	Cx	116⅛	4.50
U P R R ry & l g g 4s..............	1947	J & J	500 & 1,000		104⅞	3.85
U P 1st lien con g 4s..............	1911	M & N	1,000 etc.	Cx & R	96⅞	4.56
U P, Ore Ry & Nav con g 4s.......	1946	J & D	1,000	Cx	100½	4.06
U P, Ore Ry 1st g 6s..............	1922	F & A	1,000	"	124	4.37
U P, Ore 4s and participating.....	1927	F & A	1,000 "	Cx & R	94¾	4.47
United R R of S F tran sink f 4s ..	1927	A & O	1,000	"	78¼	5.65
Wabash 1st g 5s..................	1939	M & N	1,000	Cx	115½	4.17
Western Union F & R E g 4½s....	1950	M & N	1,000 "	C & R	102	4.43
W & L E R R Co 1st con 4s........	1949	M & S	1,000	Cx	90	4.58

* Rate changes February, 1905. † Redeemable any time at 110.

‡ Land receipts under certain conditions may be used to redeem at par.

Bonds in the following list are not considered of as high a grade as the above. They offer, however, excellent security combined with good speculative possibilities.

BOND.	Maturity	Interest Date.	Denominations	Form: R-Registered C-Coupon Cx-Coup. but may be registered as to principal.	Approximate Price June 1, 1904.	Yield per Cent.
Atch T & S F adjustment 4s......	1995	A & O	500 etc.	Cx & R	91½	4.52
Atlantic Coast Line 1st 4s........	1952	M & S	1,000 "	"	95	4.14
Ches & Ohio g 4½s................	1992	M & S	1,000	Cx	104¼	4.35
Chic & Alton Ry g 3½s...........	1950	J & J	1,000	Cx & R	79½	4.68
Cnic R I & P R R 4s...............	2002	M & N	1,000 "	"	69	5.05
Chic R I & P R R C T 5s..:.......	1913	M & S	1,000	Cx	80	*
C C C & St L Peoria & E inc 4s....	1990	April 1	1,000	C	58½	†
Colo F & I con deb 5s	1911	F & A	1,000	Cx & R	73	‡
Colo So 1st g 4s...................	1929	F & A	1,000	Cx	83¾	5.05
Consol Tob g 4s...................	1951	F & A	50 "	Cx & R	60	8.07
Erie 1st con genl 4s..............	1996	J & J	1,000	"	85½	4.80
Erie Penn Col Trust 4s	1951	F & A	1,000 "	"	89¾	4.65
Int Paper 1st con 6s..............	1918	F & A	1,000	Cx	108	§
Kansas City So 3s	1950	A & O	1,000 "	Cx & R	70	4.55
Lack Steel 1st con 5s.............	1923	A & O	1,000	Cx	98	‖
Mex Cent con g 4s................	1911	J & J	1,000	Cx & R	64½	14.10
Mex Cent 1st inc 3s..............	1939	July 10	1,000	Cx	12½	†
M K & T 2d g 4s..................	1990	F & A	500 "	"	77½	5.38
Mo P, St L & I M, U & Ref 4s.....	1929	J & J	1,000	"	88½	4.40
Natl of Mex con 4s	1951	A & O	500 "	"	74	5.60
N & W, Poco Coal joint 4s........	1941	J & D	1,000	Cx & R	91½	4.59
Reading, Jersey Central col 4s....	1951	A & O	1,000	"	93½	4.40
St L & S F ref g 4s................	1951	J & J	1,000 "	"	82	5.13
St L & S F, K C F S & M ref 4s....	1936	A & O	1,000 "	"	79⅞	5.30
St L & So W 1st g 4s	1989	M & N	1,000	Cx	93	4.26
St L & So W con g 4s..............	1932	J & D	1,000	Cx & R	65¾	7.90
Seaboard Air Line 1st mtg 4s.....	1950	A & O	1,000 "	"	70½	5.85
Seaboard Air Liue col tr ref 5s....	1911	M & N	1,000	Cx	98	5.30
So P, Cent P col 4s	1949	J & D	500 "	Cx & R	90¼	4.57
So P, S A & A P guar 1st 4s.......	1943	J & J	1.000	"	81½	5.10
Toledo, St L & W 50-yr g 4s........	1950	A & O	1,000 "	"	70½	**
U S Steel, C T 2d 5s.............	1963	M & N	500	"	73¼	††
Wabash deb B's 6s.............	1939	J & J	1,000		57	‡‡
Wisconsin Central 1st genl g 4s...	1949	J & J	1,000	Cx	90½	4.60

* Redeemable at 102½.   † Income.   ‡ Redeemable at 105.
§ Redeemable at 105 after 1907.
‖ Redeemable at 107½ and convertable into stock after 1906.
** Redeemable at par after 1925.   †† Redeemable in 1913 at 110.
‡‡ Interest payable if earned.

All quotations subject to change according to market.

STOCK FLUCTUATIONS IN PAST YEARS.

Stocks and Par Value.	1894.	1895.	1896.	1897.	1898.	1899.	1900.	1901.	1902.	1903.
Amalgam. Copper. $100	......	......	......	......	......	......	99½ Nov	130 Jun	79 Feb	75⅝ Mar
	......	......	......	......	......	......	89¾ Dec	60½ Dec	53 Nov	33⅝ Oct
Amer. Car & Foundry .. 100	......	......	......	......	......	21⅞ May	25⅜ Nov	35 Jun	37 Sep	41¾ Jan
	......	......	......	......	......	10⅝ Dec	12½ Jan	19 Jan	28¼ Apr	17¼ Nov
American Cotton Oil.... 100	34¾ Aug	30½ May	19 Jan	26⅞ Sep	39¾ Aug	46 Nov	37½ Apr	35½ Jun	57 May	46¼ Feb
	21½ Dec	14 Dec	8 July	9½ May	15½ Mar	30 Dec	30 Jun	24 Mar	30½ Jan	25¼ Aug
do do pfd.... 100	79½ Sep	79⅞ May	69 Feb	80½ Sep	90⅜ Aug	97 Nov	100 Apr	91½ Jan	99½ Apr	98 Feb
	63 Jan	59 Dec	37 Aug	52¼ Feb	66 Mar	87¼ Jan	88¾ Sep	85 Apr	86 Feb	82 July
American Ice........... 100	......	......	......	......	......	41¼ Sep	49½ Apr	41⅜ Mar	28½ Mar	11¾ Jan
	......	......	......	......	......	31 Dec	27½ Jun	25¾ Oct	9½ July	4 Oct
do do pfd.... 100	......	......	......	......	......	85 Sep	78½ Feb	77¾ Mar	67 Jan	42¼ Jan
	......	......	......	......	......	72¾ Dec	60½ Jun	62 Oct	32 July	16½ Oct
American Linseed Oil... 100	......	......	......	......	......	16⅜ Nov	16¼ Feb	30⅛ July	27¾ May	19¾ Jan
	......	......	......	......	......	8¾ Jun	6 Nov	5⅛ Jan	14 Dec	5 July
do do pfd.... 100	......	......	......	......	......	61 Dec	60 Feb	66 July	58 Mar	48½ Jan
	......	......	......	......	......	44¼ Jun	34½ Dec	31 Jan	39½ Dec	23½ Nov
American Locomotive... 100	......	......	......	......	......	......	......	33⅞ Nov	36⅞ Apr	31⅝ Feb
	......	......	......	......	......	......	......	22½ Aug	26 Nov	10½ Oct
Amer. Smelt. & Ref..... 100	......	......	......	......	......	59 Apr	56½ Dec	69 Apr	49⅝ May	52⅞ Feb
	......	......	......	......	......	30 Dec	34½ Jun	38½ Oct	37 Nov	36¾ Oct
do do pfd.... 100	......	......	......	......	......	94½ Apr	99 Nov	104⅞ Jun	100⅛ Jun	99½ Feb
	......	......	......	......	......	77½ Dec	85 Jun	88 Feb	87½ Nov	80¼ Oct
†American Spirits....... 100	......	15¼ Oct	14⅞ Nov	15⅞ Aug	15⅜ Jun	15½ Mar	4 Feb	2½ Mar	......	......
	......	13 Nov	4½ Aug	6¼ Nov	6½ Jan	3 Dec	1½ Sep	2 Jan	......	......
do do pfd.... 100	......	49 Oct	33¼ Nov	36 Aug	41¾ Aug	41⅛ Mar	14 Sep	......	......	......
	......	45½ Oct	15⅛ Oct	15 Dec	16 Mar	29½ Jun	14 Sep	......	......	......
American Sugar 100	114⅞ Aug	121⅜ Jun	126⅝ Apr	159½ Sep	146⅛ Aug	182 Mar	149 Dec	153 Jun	134½ July	134⅜ Jan
	75⅝ Feb	86½ Jan	95 Aug	109⅛ Mar	107½ Mar	123¼ Jan	95¼ Mar	103⅛ Dec	113 Nov	107⅛ Oct
do do pfd.... 100	109⅝ May	107 Aug	105½ Jun	121½ Sep	116 Jan	123 Mar	118 July	130 July	122 Aug	123 Dec
	79¾ Jan	90¼ Jan	92¼ Aug	100¼ Jan	103 Mar	110 Jan	107 Mar	111 Dec	115 Jan	116 Aug
*Anaconda 25	......	......	......	......	......	70 Apr	54⅞ Apr	54¼ Apr	142 Jan	125½ Feb
	......	......	......	......	......	31½ Dec	37⅞ Jun	28¼ Dec	80 Dec	58 Oct
At., Top. & Santa Fe.... 100	16 Mar	23⅝ Sep	18 Nov	17 Sep	19⅝ Dec	24⅞ Feb	48¾ Dec	91 Jun	94⅛ July	89⅞ Jan
	3 July	3½ Jan	10½ Aug	9⅛ Apr	10¼ Apr	17 May	18⅝ Jan	42¼ Jan	74¼ Jan	54 Aug
do do pfd.... 100	......	36½ Sep	28⅛ Feb	35½ Sep	52½ Dec	68⅛ Aug	89⅛ Dec	108 May	106⅛ Sep	103½ Jan
	......	16 Dec	14⅛ Aug	17 Apr	22⅞ Mar	50⅝ Jan	58¼ Jan	70 May	95½ Jan	84⅜ Aug
Baltimore & Ohio 100	81½ Apr	66¾ Sep	44 Jan	21⅛ Sep	72¾ Dec	61½ Apr	89⅞ Apr	114½ May	115¾ Aug	104 Jan
	58⅜ Dec	32½ Dec	10½ Sep	9 July	12⅜ Jan	43⅞ Jun	55¼ Jan	81¾ Jan	92⅝ Dec	71⅝ Sep

* Prior to 1902 price quoted in dollars per share, since then upon per cent. basis.

† See note page 000.

Stocks and Par Value.		1894.	1895.	1896.	1897.	1898.	1899.	1900.	1901.	1902.	1903.
Brooklyn Rapid Transit	$100	......	......	25 1/8 Apr	37 5/8 Dec	78 7/8 Dec	137 Apr	88 7/8 Dec	88 7/8 Apr	72 1/8 Apr	71 1/8 Feb
		......	......	18 Aug	18 5/8 Jan	35 Mar	61 Dec	47 1/8 Sep	55 7/8 Oct	54 3/4 Nov	29 1/2 Sep
Canada Southern	100	53 3/4 Aug	57 1/2 Aug	51 3/4 Feb	62 1/8 Sep	58 Dec	70 Jan	61 1/4 Dec	89 Nov	97 May	78 1/2 Jan
		47 Jan	42 Dec	40 3/4 Aug	44 1/8 Jan	44 1/2 Mar	46 1/4 Dec	47 5/8 Feb	54 1/8 Jan	71 Dec	57 1/2 Sep
Canadian Pacific	100	73 1/2 Jan	62 1/2 Sep	62 3/4 May	82 Dec	90 1/2 Jan	99 1/2 May	99 3/4 Feb	117 1/2 May	145 1/4 Sep	138 3/4 Feb
		58 Dec	33 Mar	52 Jan	46 1/2 Mar	72 Apr	84 5/8 Mar	84 3/4 Sep	87 May	112 1/4 Jan	115 5/8 Oct
Central R. R. of N. J	100	117 3/4 Mar	116 1/2 Sep	110 Nov	103 1/4 Jan	99 Dec	126 3/8 Nov	150 1/2 Dec	196 5/8 Dec	196 Apr	190 Jan
		87 1/2 Dec	81 1/2 Feb	87 1/2 Aug	68 1/4 May	84 1/2 Nov	97 Jan	115 Jan	145 3/4 Jan	165 Nov	153 Oct
Ches. & Ohio	100	21 7/8 Aug	23 5/8 May	18 1/2 Nov	37 1/8 Aug	26 3/8 Dec	31 7/8 Dec	42 3/4 Apr	52 5/8 May	56 7/8 Aug	53 1/2 Jan
		16 May	12 1/2 Dec	11 Aug	15 5/8 Mar	17 1/4 Mar	23 3/4 May	24 Jun	29 May	43 Nov	27 1/4 Nov
Chic. & Alton	100	146 1/2 Nov	170 Sep	164 Nov	170 Mar	172 Dec	175 1/2 Mar	42 Dec	50 1/2 Apr	45 3/8 July	37 1/4 Jan
		130 Feb	147 Jan	146 Aug	147 July	150 Mar	168 Jan	§31 Oct	27 May	29 1/2 Dec	18 1/2 Sep
Chic. Gt. Western	100	......	......	10 3/8 Jun	20 3/8 Aug	18 Aug	20 5/8 Jan	18 Dec	27 Nov	34 5/8 Sep	29 5/8 Jan
		......	......	4 Oct	3 5/8 Jun	9 1/2 Feb	10 1/2 Dec	9 7/8 Sep	16 Jan	22 Dec	13 Aug
Chicago Gas	100	80 Jun	78 1/2 Jan	78 3/4 Nov	103 3/4 Aug	112 Nov	*	*	*	*	*
		58 3/4 Jan	49 7/8 July	44 5/8 Aug	75 3/8 Feb	86 1/2 Mar	*	*	*	*	*
Chi., Ind & Louisv	100	......	......	......	13 Aug	11 July	19 Nov	29 Apr	52 7/8 Dec	80 May	......
		......	......	......	8 Oct	7 Feb	7 3/4 Jan	14 Jan	23 Jan	49 1/4 Jan	......
do do pfd	100	......	......	......	38 1/2 Sep	38 1/2 July	52 1/2 Nov	64 Dec	77 3/4 Sep	90 May	......
		......	......	......	26 Nov	23 Apr	31 Jan	45 1/4 Jan	58 3/4 Jan	75 Jan	......
Chi., Mil. & St. Paul	100	67 3/8 Sep	78 7/8 Sep	80 Nov	102 Sep	120 3/4 Dec	136 1/8 Sep	148 1/4 Dec	188 May	198 3/4 Sep	183 1/4 Jan
		54 1/4 Jan	53 7/8 Mar	59 7/8 Aug	69 1/4 Apr	83 1/4 Apr	112 Dec	108 1/2 Jun	134 May	160 Jan	133 1/4 Aug
do do pfd	100	123 1/2 Mar	130 Sep	131 Dec	146 Sep	166 1/2 Dec	179 Sep	187 1/2 Dec	200 May	199 1/2 Oct	194 1/4 Jan
		116 Jan	114 3/4 Mar	117 1/2 Aug	130 1/2 May	140 Apr	165 Dec	169 1/2 Jan	175 May	186 Jan	168 Aug
Chic. & Northwest	100	110 3/8 Jun	107 1/2 Oct	106 3/4 Apr	132 1/2 Sep	143 1/4 Dec	173 Sep	172 3/4 Dec	215 May	271 Apr	224 1/2 Jan
		96 1/4 Dec	87 3/8 Mar	85 1/8 Aug	101 3/4 Apr	113 1/4 Mar	141 1/4 Jan	150 1/4 Jun	168 1/8 Jan	204 1/8 Jan	153 Sep
do do pfd	100	145 Apr	151 Nov	152 Dec	165 1/2 Sep	191 1/2 Nov	210 7/8 Sep	220 Dec	248 Apr	274 1/2 Apr	250 Jan
		135 1/2 Jan	137 Feb	140 3/4 Aug	153 Jan	163 Jan	188 Jan	195 1/8 May	207 Mar	230 Jan	190 Aug
Chic. Rock Island & Pac.	100	72 3/8 Apr	84 3/8 Aug	74 7/8 Feb	97 1/4 Sep	114 7/8 Dec	122 1/8 Jan	122 1/8 Dec	175 1/4 Jun	206 Sep	200 1/8 Jan
		58 1/2 Oct	59 Dec	49 1/4 Aug	60 1/4 Apr	80 Mar	100 Dec	102 Jun	116 7/8 Jan	152 Jan	132 Oct
Chi., St. P., M. & Om.	100	41 3/8 Apr	46 Aug	49 3/4 Dec	89 1/2 Sep	94 Dec	126 1/2 Sep	126 Nov	146 3/4 Nov	170 1/2 Apr	162 Jan
		32 Dec	28 3/4 Mar	30 1/2 Aug	47 Jan	65 Mar	91 Feb	110 Oct	125 Mar	140 Feb	117 July
Chicago Terminal	100	......	......	......	......	9 5/8 Mar	25 1/4 Mar	14 7/8 Dec	31 Apr	24 7/8 Aug	19 7/8 Jan
		......	......	......	......	4 1/2 Jan	7 1/2 Jan	8 1/8 Oct	10 1/2 Jan	15 Dec	8 Aug
do do pfd	100	......	......	......	......	37 1/2 Aug	56 1/2 Mar	39 3/4 Apr	57 1/2 Apr	42 Apr	36 Jan
		......	......	......	......	22 1/2 Jan	31 1/4 Dec	26 1/2 Oct	28 3/4 Dec	29 Dec	15 Sep
C. C. C. & St. L.	100	40 Aug	50 Aug	39 1/2 Feb	41 1/2 Sep	47 1/2 Aug	64 3/8 Nov	76 Dec	101 Nov	108 3/8 Aug	99 3/8 Jan
		31 Jan	28 Dec	19 1/2 Aug	21 1/2 Jun	25 Mar	42 1/2 Jan	55 Jun	73 May	93 Nov	66 Aug
do do pfd	100	88 May	97 Aug	90 1/2 Feb	86 1/2 Sep	97 Dec	108 Dec	118 Dec	124 Nov	124 1/4 Nov	119 Jan
		78 Jan	82 Jan	73 Aug	63 Jun	77 1/2 Mar	94 May	103 1/8 Jun	115 3/4 Jan	118 Jan	112 Dec

* Succeeded by Peoples' Gas Co. § New stock.

Stocks and Par Value	1894.	1895.	1896.	1897.	1898.	1899.	1900.	1901.	1902.	1903.
Col. Fuel & Iron........$100	27½ Apr / 21 Jan	41½ Sep / 20½ Dec	34¼ Feb / 14⅝ Aug	27⅞ Sep / 15¼ Jun	33⅞ Dec / 17 Mar	64 Sep / 30½ Feb	56½ Sep / 29¼ Feb	130½ Jun / 41¾ Jan	108⅝ May / 73¼ Aug	83½ Jan / 24 Nov
Colorado Southern...... 100					8⅜ Dec / 6¼ Jan	8⅞ Jan / 4⅜ Sep	8¾ Dec / 5 Jan	18 Apr / 6⅝ Jan	35¼ Sep / 14⅛ Jan	31¼ Jan / 10 July
do do 1st pfd. 100					50¾ Dec / 45⅜ Nov	58⅝ Mar / 43⅜ Sep	47½ Mar / 20½ Mar	60 Dec / 28¾ Apr	70½ Aug / 59¼ Jan	72 Jan / 44½ Aug
do do 2d pfd. 100					20 Dec / 14¾ Nov	25 Mar / 12½ Dec	20½ Dec / 14 Sep	28¾ Apr / 10½ Jun	45⅜ Aug / 18⅝ Jan	44¼ Aug / 18 Oct
Consolidated Gas........ 100	140 Apr / 111 July	161¼ Dec / 126 Jan	168 Nov / 133 Aug	241½ Sep / 136½ Jan	205½ Jun / 164 Oct	223¾ Mar / 163 Jun	201 Nov / 164 Sep	238 Apr / 187 Jan	230¼ Apr / 205 Dec	222 Jan / 164 Aug
Corn Products........... 100									38⅞ Mar / 26¾ Dec	35 Mar / 15½ Nov
Delaware & Hudson...... 100	144½ Apr / 119¾ Oct	134⅞ Sep / 118 Dec	129⅝ Feb / 111½ Aug	123 Sep / 99⅝ Apr	114½ Feb / 93 Nov	125¾ Jun / 100½ Jan	134½ Dec / 100½ Jan	185¼ Apr / 105 May	184½ May / 153½ Nov	183⅞ Feb / 149 Aug
Del., Lack. & Western.. 50	174 / 155¼ Oct	174 Oct / 154 Dec	166 Aug / 138 Aug	164 Aug / 146½ May	159 Feb / 140 Oct	194½ Oct / 157 Jan	194¾ Dec / 171½ Sep	258 Dec / 188¼ Jan	297 Nov / 231 Nov	276½ Feb / 230 July
Denver & Rio Grande... 100	13 Nov / 8¼ July	14 Sep / 10 Dec	14 Feb / 10 Aug	14¾ Aug / 9¼ Apr	21½ Apr / 10 Apr	25⅜ Apr / 15⅞ Dec	34 Apr / 16⅞ Dec	53¼ May / 29½ Jan	51¾ Dec / 33⅝ Dec	43 Oct / 18 Oct
do do pfd 100	37⅝ Nov / 24 Jun	55½ Sep / 32¾ Jan	51 Feb / 37 Aug	50½ Aug / 36 Apr	71⅜ Dec / 40 Apr	80 Apr / 63 Dec	87 Apr / 64½ Dec	103¾ Jun / 80 Jan	90¾ Aug / 85⅛ July	90½ Feb / 62 Nov
Des Moines & Ft. Dodge. 100	7¾ Jun / 5½ Jan	11 Jun / 5½ Feb	9½ Jun / 5 Aug	14¾ Aug / 7 Apr	23½ Dec / 8⅞ Apr	23½ Jan / 12½ Dec	21 Jun / 12 Jun	45 Jan / 18 Jan	53⅝ July / 39 Feb	47¼ Jan / 12 Sep
*Distilling Co. of Amer.. 100							6¼ Mar / 4 Jun	10½ Oct / 6⅞ Nov	4 Dec / 4 Oct	
do do pfd.... 100							20⅞ Nov / 12 July	34½ Nov / 23¼ Sep	45 Oct / 32½ Aug	
*Distillers' Sec. Corp'n... 100									33 Dec / 27 Dec	34¾ Jan / 20 July
Dul., South S. & Atlantic 100	8 Apr / 4 Nov	9 Jun / 2⅜ Mar	6 Jan / 3⅜ July	6¾ Nov / 3 Apr	3½ Dec / 2⅝ Aug	8 Nov / 3 Apr	6¾ Jun / 4 Feb	12½ Jun / 4½ Feb	23⅜ Aug / 10 Jan	19¼ Sep / 7 Aug
do do pfd.... 100	19 Apr / 13 Aug	16¾ Jun / 5¼ Mar	14¼ Apr / 10¼ Nov	10¼ Aug / 6½ May	8¼ Aug / 5 Apr	17¼ Nov / 7¾ Jan	22¼ Dec / 13⅝ Jan	22½ Sep / 13⅝ Feb	35¾ Sep / 18⅝ Jan	28⅜ Feb / 7 Aug
Erie.................. 100			17¾ Nov / 10¼ Aug	19 Sep / 11⅛ Apr	16¼ Feb / 11 Apr	16¼ Jan / 10 Dec	27⅞ Dec / 10⅜ Jan	45½ Jun / 24½ Feb	44⅝ Jan / 28⅝ Dec	42⅝ Jan / 23 Aug
do 1st pfd............ 100			41¾ Mar / 27 July	46⅝ Sep / 27 Apr	43⅜ Feb / 29¼ Apr	42 Jan / 27⅞ May	63⅜ Dec / 30⅜ Jan	75 Dec / 45½ May	75¾ Jan / 60½ Dec	74 Feb / 35 Aug
do 2d pfd............. 100			25 Mar / 13 Aug	25⅝ Aug / 15½ May	21⅛ Feb / 15½ Apr	22½ Jan / 15⅜ Apr	43¼ Dec / 15 Sep	59¾ Jan / 32¾ Dec	63¼ Jan / 44⅜ Dec	62⅜ Apr / 44⅛ Feb
General Electric...... 100	45¼ Mar / 30⅝ Jan	41 Sep / 20 Dec	39½ Aug / 20 July	41⅜ May / 28⅜ Ja)	50½ Dec / 20¼ Mar	132 Nov / 95⅜ Jan	200 Nov / 120 Jan	289¾ Dec / 183⅜ Jan	334 Apr / 170½ Oct	204 Feb / 136 Sep

* American Spirits succeeded by Distilling Co. of America in 1899. Distilling Co. of America succeeded by Distillers' Securities Corporation in 1902.

Stocks and Par Value.		1894.	1895.	1896.	1897.	1898.	1899.	1900.	1901.	1902.	1903.
Glucose Sugar	$100	......	......	......	......	72½ Dec	76¾ Mar	60 Nov	65 May	51½ Jan	......
		......	......	......	......	65 Dec	37 Dec	44 May	37 Oct	39⅜ Jan	......
Great Northern pfd	100	106 Apr	134 Jun	122 Nov	141 Sep	180 Jun	195 Apr	191½ Dec	208 Mar	203 Dec	209 Jan
		100 Jan	100 Jan	108¼ Mar	120 Jan	122 July	142¼ Jan	144¾ Jun	167½ May	182 May	160 Oct
Hocking Valley	100	......	......	......	......	......	37⅝ Sep	42⅞ Dec	75½ Dec	103 Sep	106½ Feb
		......	......	......	......	......	22 July	30½ Jan	40½ May	66 Jan	63 Sep
do do pfd	100	......	......	......	......	......	66¼ Sep	74¾ Dec	88½ Dec	98⅜ Dec	99¼ Mar
		......	......	......	......	......	53½ Dec	58 Jan	69¾ Jan	81⅛ Jan	77 Oct
Illinois Central	100	95¼ Sep	106 Sep	98 Jan	110¾ Aug	115⅜ Dec	122 Jan	132¾ Dec	154¾ Jun	173½ Sep	151 Jan
		82¾ Dec	81⅛ Jan	84⅛ Aug	91½ Apr	96 Apr	105½ Dec	110 Jun	124 May	137 Jan	125⅛ July
International Paper	100	......	......	......	......	67 Dec	68½ Jan	26⅞ Nov	28 Mar	23⅝ Mar	19⅞ Jan
		......	......	......	......	48 Sep	17 Dec	14½ Mar	18½ May	16½ Dec	9 July
International Power	100	......	......	......	......	......	......	......	100½ May	199 Apr	73 Jan
		......	......	......	......	......	......	......	54⅞ May	49 Dec	23 Nov
Iowa Central	100	11¾ Apr	11½ Jun	10¼ Feb	13½ Sep	11½ Dec	15¾ Aug	27⅜ Dec	43¾ Jun	51¾ Aug	48 Jan
		6 Jan	5⅜ Jan	5½ Aug	6 Apr	7¼ Mar	10¼ Mar	11⅞ Jan	21 Jan	35⅛ Dec	16 July
do pfd	100	39¾ Apr	38 Sep	38 Apr	41¾ Sep	42½ Dec	62¼ Aug	58 Mar	87½ July	90⅜ Apr	77⅜ Jan
		23¾ Jan	19 Jan	19 July	23 Jun	25 Apr	40 Dec	39 Sep	48 Jan	65 Nov	30½ Oct
Lake Erie & Western	100	19¼ Aug	28 July	22½ Feb	22½ Sep	23½ Aug	24 Dec	52 Dec	76½ Nov	71½ Jan	53 Jan
		13⅞ Jan	15¼ Feb	12⅛ Aug	13 May	12 Oct	14¾ Jun	20⅛ Mar	39¾ Jan	40 Dec	23½ Nov
do do pfd	100	74 Sep	85 Jun	75 Feb	79⅞ Sep	83 Aug	85 Dec	115 Dec	135½ Sep	138 Feb	118 Feb
		63 Jan	61 Dec	55½ Aug	58¼ Apr	53 Oct	60 Jan	83¼ Feb	108⅛ Jan	120 Oct	89 Nov
Lake Sh. & Mich. So	100	139 Aug	153½ July	156 Dec	181 Sep	215 Dec	208 Jan	240 Dec	355 Nov	340 Apr	334 Jan
		118¾ Jan	134½ Jan	134¾ Jan	152 Jan	170¾ Jan	196½ Jan	197 Jan	230 Apr	328 Jun	275 Dec
Long Island	50	100 Jan	88¼ Jan	84 Jan	55 Jan	59½ Aug	84½ Feb	89⅛ Dec	90 Dec	91⅞ May	83 Jan
		85½ Nov	83 Nov	40½ Dec	38 Dec	40 Jan	45 Dec	47½ Jan	67 Jan	73 Dec	49 Dec
Louisville & Nashville	100	57⅜ Sep	66⅛ Sep	55⅝ Feb	63⅞ Sep	65¼ Dec	88⅜ Oct	89 Dec	111¾ Jun	159½ Aug	130½ Jan
		40⅞ Jan	39 Dec	37⅛ Aug	40⅛ Apr	44 Apr	63 Mar	68¾ Sep	76 May	102⅛ Jan	95 Sep
Manhattan	100	127⅜ Apr	119⅞ May	113½ Feb	113 Sep	120¼ Jan	133⅜ Apr	116⅞ Dec	145 Dec	157⅛ Dec	155½ Jan
		102¼ Nov	95 Dec	73¼ Aug	81¾ May	90 Oct	85¼ Dec	84 Jun	83 May	128 Mar	126¼ Sep
Metropolitan	100	122 Apr	115 Nov	112[illegible] Nov	132⅛ Dec	194¾ Dec	251⅜ Mar	180 Feb	177 Jun	174 Feb	142⅞ Jan
		96½ Jan	81 Apr	78½ Aug	99¼ May	125¼ Mar	190⅜ Jan	146⅞ May	150 May	135 Dec	99⅞ Sep
Mexican Central	100	9⅜ Apr	14 Sep	12⅜ Feb	9½ Jun	7 Dec	17¼ Apr	17⅜ Dec	30 May	31⅛ Mar	29 Mar
		5⅝ Jan	5¾ Jan	6½ Aug	5 Aug	4¼ Apr	5⅞ Jan	10½ Jan	12¾ Jan	20⅝ Dec	8½ Nov
*Mexican National	100	......	4 May	2⅛ Feb	2¾ Aug	1½ May	6⅛ Sep	5 Mar	15¼ Nov	20¾ Mar	......
		......	⅞ Dec	¾ May	1 Nov	⅞ Dec	1 Jan	2⅝ Sep	3⅝ Jan	14⅛ Jan	......
Michigan Central	100	100⅜ Feb	103 Jun	97⅞ Feb	111⅞ Sep	118 Dec	116 Jan	115 Jun	180 Nov	192 Apr	135 Jan
		94 July	91¾ Mar	89 Aug	90 Jan	99½ Mar	110 Oct	104 Jan	107¼ Mar	150 Mar	102 May
Minn., St. P. & S. Ste. M.	100	......	......	......	6 Dec	7 Mar	37½ May	27 Apr	36¼ Nov	84 Nov	79½ Feb
		......	......	......	6 Dec	6½ Mar	8¾ Jan	14 Sep	15 May	36½ Jan	42 Aug

* Succeeded by National R. R. of Mexico.

Stocks and Par Value.		1894.	1895.	1896.	1897.	1898.	1899.	1900.	1901.	1902.	1903.
M., St. P. & S. Ste. M., pfd.	$100	......	......	......	......	......	72 May	69 Apr	94¾ Nov	137 Sep	134¼ Feb
		......	......	......	......	......	39 Feb	47 Nov	49 Apr	90 Jan	109½ Jun
Missouri, Kans. & Tex ..	100	16⅝ Apr	19 Jun	14¾ Nov	16⅞ Sep	14¼ Jan	14⅞ Jan	17⅛ Dec	35⅜ Apr	35¾ Sep	30⅛ Jan
		12 Jun	9¼ Dec	9¼ Aug	10 Apr	10 Apr	9½ Dec	9 Sep	15 Jan	22½ Dec	15½ Oct
do do pfd.	100	27⅛ Apr	40 Sep	31⅛ Feb	42 Sep	41 Jan	45¼ Aug	47½ Dec	68⅝ Apr	69¾ Sep	63½ Feb
		18⅞ Jun	18¼ Dec	16 July	24¾ Apr	28¾ Mar	28⅜ Dec	25⅝ Sep	37 May	51 Dec	33 Oct
Missouri Pacific..........	100	32½ Apr	42½ Sep	29¾ Apr	40¼ Sep	46¼ Dec	52½ Apr	72½ Dec	124½ Jun	125½ Sep	115⅞ Feb
		18¼ Jan	18⅝ Mar	15 Aug	10 May	22 Mar	33 Dec	38⅜ Jan	69 Jan	99½ Jan	85¾ Aug
National R. R. of Mex...	100	......	......	......	......	......	......	......	......	20⅜ Aug	24¾ May
		......	......	......	......	......	......	......	......	14 Dec	17⅛ Mar
National Lead..........	100	44⅞ Aug	37½ Sep	28⅝ Apr	47 Sep	39⅝ Aug	40½ Jan	28¼ Feb	25½ Jun	32 Sep	29½ Feb
		22 Jan	17½ Dec	16 Aug	21⅞ Feb	26¼ Mar	22½ Dec	15⅞ Aug	15 Mar	15½ Jan	10½ Nov
do do pfd...	100	92½ Aug	94½ Aug	92¾ Nov	109¾ Sep	114½ Dec	115 Jan	106½ Feb	93⅞ Jun	95 Aug	95 Feb
		68 Jan	73 Dec	75 Aug	88⅜ Feb	99½ Apr	103½ Dec	83 Aug	74¾ Dec	78⅛ Jan	75 Oct
New York Central......	100	102½ Aug	104⅝ Aug	99⅛ Feb	115½ Sep	124⅞ Dec	144¾ Mar	145⅜ Dec	174¼ Nov	167¾ July	156 Jan
		95¼ May	90 Dec	88 Aug	92½ Feb	105 Mar	120 Dec	125⅝ Jun	139⅜ Jan	147 Nov	112⅝ July
New York, Chi. & St. L.	100	16¾ Apr	18¼ May	15 Jan	17⅝ Sep	15⅝ Jan	19¾ Jan	24½ Dec	57⅞ Sep	57¼ July	45 Jan
		13 Dec	10 Dec	9 Aug	11 Feb	11¾ Apr	11½ Dec	11 Jun	16 May	40 Nov	19½ Sep
do do 1st pfd. ..	100	75½ Feb	75 Dec	80 Jan	81½ Sep	76 Jan	85 Oct	110 Dec	120 Sep	124½ Jan	118 Jan
		62 July	65 Apr	67½ July	67⅝ Feb	73 Feb	65 Mar	75 Jun	97 Mar	110½ Nov	100 Oct
do do 2d pfd....	100	34¼ Apr	34¼ May	35⅝ Apr	43½ Sep	40¼ Jan	41 Jan	58¼ Dec	95 Sep	100 Aug	87 Jan
		25 July	20 Dec	20 Aug	24 Feb	28 Mar	29 Dec	29 Jun	47 Mar	80 Nov	50 Sep
N. Y., N. H. & H........	100	197 Dec	218 Jun	186 Feb	185½ Sep	201 Dec	222 Apr	215¾ Jan	217 Jun	255 Apr	225¼ Jan
		178 July	174 Dec	160 July	160 Feb	178¼ Jan	198 Jan	207¾ Sep	206½ Feb	209½ Jan	187½ May
N. Y., Ont. & Western..	100	17¾ Sep	19¼ May	16⅝ Nov	20½ Sep	19⅛ Dec	28⅞ Mar	32¼ Dec	40½ May	37⅝ Sep	35¼ Feb
		14 Jun	11¾ Dec	11⅛ Aug	12¾ Apr	13¾ Apr	18⅜ Jan	18¼ Jun	24 May	25¼ Dec	19 Sep
North American........	100	5⅝ Mar	7 May	6½ Feb	6⅛ Aug	14¼ Jan	17⅜ Nov	22¾ Dec	109 Jun	134 Sep	124½ Jan
		2¾ Jun	2¾ Jan	3½ Aug	3⅝ Apr	7¾ Dec	6⅞ Jan	13⅝ Jan	73½ Feb	88 Jan	68 Sep
Norfolk & Western......	100	9½ Sep	6½ May	12¾ Nov	17¼ Sep	19⅜ Dec	28⅝ Aug	45¾ Dec	61⅜ Nov	80¾ Oct	76¼ Feb
		4 July	1¼ Dec	⅛ Apr	9 Apr	11½ Apr	17⅜ Mar	22⅝ Jan	42 Jan	55 Jan	53¾ Nov
do do pfd.....	100	17 Dec	19⅜ Jan	19¾ Nov	48½ Dec	63⅞ Dec	74¼ Aug	83 Dec	92¼ Nov	95 Sep	93½ Feb
		26¾ Sep	8 Dec	4⅛ May	22½ May	42½ Mar	61⅜ Jan	67 Jan	82 Feb	90 Feb	85 Aug
Northern Pacific........	100	6¼ Mar	8⅛ May	14⅜ Dec	22⅜ Dec	61½ Aug	57½ Aug	86½ Dec	1000 May	......	......
		3½ Jun	2½ Jan	12¼ Dec	11 Apr	35½ Jan	42⅝ Jan	45¾ Sep	77¼ Jan	......	......
do do pfd.....	100	23⅜ Mar	27 May	36 Nov	61¼ Dec	78 Nov	81½ Jan	91½ Dec	113¼ May	......	......
		12½ May	10⅞ Dec	30½ Dec	32⅛ Jan	65½ Mar	68 Dec	67 Sep	84¼ Jan	......	......
Pacific Coast..............		......	......	......	......	48½ Sep	54 Nov	62 Nov	78 Dec	81½ Sep	72 Jan
		......	......	......	......	34¾ Jun	38 May	46 May	52 Feb	65 Dec	39¾ Sep
Pacific Mail.........	100	24 Nov	34½ Sep	31 Feb	39¼ Sep	46 Dec	55 Jan	57 Nov	49½ Nov	48½ Jan	42¾ Jan
		13½ May	20 Jan	15¼ Aug	24 Jan	21 Apr	35 Dec	25¾ Jun	30½ May	37 Nov	17 Aug

Stocks and Par Value.	1894.	1895.	1896.	1897.	1898.	1899.	1900.	1901.	1902.	1903.
Pennsylvania........... $50	52⅛ Apr	57¼ Sep	54¾ Apr	59⅜ Sep	61¾ Dec	70 Jan	140½ Dec	161½ Apr	170 Sep	157⅝ Jan
	48 Jan	48¾ Jan	49¾ Aug	51⅜ May	55⅜ Apr	61 Jan	124⅜ Sep	137 May	147 Jan	110¾ Nov
Peo. Gas & Coke Co.....100	......	......	......	97⅝ Dec	112 Nov	129½ Apr	111½ Apr	120½ Jun	107 July	108⅜ Feb
	......	......	......	91 Nov	86½ Mar	90½ Dec	81⅝ Oct	95¾ Jan	98¼ Jan	87¾ Sep
Pitts., C. C. & St. L. 100	21¼ Sep	22¼ May	18¼ Feb	39½ Dec	63⅞ Dec	88 Jan	80½ Jan	81 Dec	105½ Sep	94 Jan
	10½ July	12 Dec	11 Aug	11½ Mar	38⅞ Jan	43 May	49¾ Sep	57 Jan	80½ Jan	55 Sep
do do pfd..... 100	54 Sep	60⅞ Sep	59 Feb	70½ Oct	84½ Dec	100 Aug	94 Jan	113 Dec	128 May	115 Jan
	41 Oct	43⅛ Jan	40⅛ Aug	44⅛ Jun	57 Mar	80 Feb	78 Jun	88 Jan	113 Mar	90 Oct
Pressed Steel Car....... 100	......	......	......	......	......	61 Aug	58¾ Jan	52 Jan	63½ Oct	65¾ Jan
	......	......	......	......	......	44¾ Jun	32½ Sep	30 Mar	39 Jan	22½ Nov
do do pfd..... 100	......	......	......	......	......	91 Sep	89⅛ Nov	89 Apr	96½ Oct	95 Feb
	......	......	......	......	......	75 Dec	70¾ Sep	72½ Mar	82¾ Feb	62½ Nov
Reading.................. 50	23⅜ Mar	22⅝ Sep	31¾ Nov	29¼ Sep	23⅝ Jan	25 Jan	26 Dec	58 Dec	78½ Sep	69¼ Jan
	13⅛ Dec	4⅝ Dec	2⅜ Jan	16¾ Apr	15½ Mar	15½ Dec	15 Sep	24½ Jan	52¼ Mar	37½ Nov
do 1st pfd.......... 50	......	......	......	57¾ Sep	54⅜ Dec	68½ Apr	71⅞ Dec	82⅞ Dec	90¼ Sep	89⅞ Feb
	......	......	......	38½ Apr	36 Mar	42¼ Dec	49 Jan	65 May	79⅞ Mar	73 Sep
do 2d pfd 50	......	......	......	35⅞ Sep	29 Jan	38¼ Mar	39⅛ Dec	64½ Dec	80⅞ Sep	81 Jan
	......	......	......	22½ Apr	17¾ Oct	22¼ Dec	23⅝ Sep	38 Jan	60 Jan	55¾ Nov
Republic Steel 100	......	......	......	......	......	33⅞ Sep	27½ Feb	24 Jun	24¾ Sep	22⅝ Feb
	......	......	......	......	......	16½ Dec	8¾ Jun	11¾ Sep	15⅝ Jan	5⅝ Nov
do do pfd 100	......	......	......	......	......	79 Aug	70¾ Feb	82 Apr	83⅜ Sep	80⅜ Feb
	......	......	......	......	......	60⅛ Dec	49 Aug	55¼ Jan	68 Jan	36¾ Nov
*Rio Grande Western... 100	16⅜ Nov	19⅞ Jun	18½ Feb	25½ Sep	32 Aug	44 Nov	80 Dec	85 Mar	......	......
	15 Feb	15 Apr	16 Feb	14¾ Jan	23 Feb	25½ Jan	43¼ Jan	65 Feb	......	......
do do pfd... 100	......	46¼ May	46¼ Feb	61½ Dec	69¼ Aug	90½ Nov	95¼ Dec	108 Jun	......	......
	......	30 Mar	39 Jan	25 May	50¼ Mar	66 Jan	80 Jan	93 Feb	......	
Rock Island Co. of N. J...100	......	......	......	......	......	......	......	......	50⅛ Dec	53⅝ Jan
	......	......	......	......	......	......	......	......	33½ Dec	19¼ Aug
do do pfd....100	......	......	......	......	......	......	......	......	85½ Nov	86 Jan
	......	......	......	......	......	......	......	......	71 Nov	55¾ Sep
St. Louis & San Fr...... 100	......	......	5½ Dec	9 Aug	9¼ Nov	14⅞ Feb	24⅛ Dec	56½ Dec	85½ July	90½ Feb
	......	......	4 Dec	4 Apr	6 Mar	8½ Dec	8⅝ Jun	21½ Jan	55 Jan	56 July
do do 1st pfd. 100	......	......	37 Dec	59⅜ Dec	70 Nov	75½ Jan	78 Dec	88 Mar	89 Aug	88 Feb
	......	......	34¼ Dec	37 Jun	52½ Mar	64 May	64 Sep	75 July	77 Dec	68 Aug
do do 2d pfd.. 100	......	......	14⅛ Dec	27½ Dec	35 Nov	44⅞ Jan	55 Dec	76¼ Jun	80⅜ July	24⅞ Jan
	......	......	12 Dec	12 Apr	22½ Feb	28½ Dec	31¼ Jun	53⅛ Jan	65½ Dec	13 Oct
St. Louis South W 100	5½ Apr	9¼ Sep	5¾ Feb	7 Aug	7⅝ Dec	18¼ Aug	18½ Dec	39½ Apr	39 Aug	12 Jan
	3 July	4⅛ Dec	2⅞ Aug	1 Apr	3¾ Jan	16¾ Jan	8¾ Jun	16 May	24½ Dec	30 Aug
do do pfd... 100	11 Apr	19⅞ Sep	13 Feb	14⅜ Sep	18 Dec	40⅜ Aug	45½ Dec	71 Jun	80 Sep	66 Jan
	7 July	8 Dec	6½ Aug	3½ Apr	7¾ Mar	17 Jan	21⅞ Jun	41½ Jan	55¼ Mar	24 Aug

* Nearly entire issue absorbed by D. R. G. & Col. So.

Stocks and Par Value.	1894.	1895.	1896.	1897.	1898.	1899.	1900.	1901.	1902.	1903.
Standard Rope & T. $100	.....	.....	12¼ Nov / 8½ Dec	11¾ Jan / 2¾ Dec	10½ Aug / 3¼ Jan	15¼ Nov / 6½ Sep	10¼ Jan / 4½ Mar	8½ Jun / 3½ Mar	8¾ May / 4 Jan	6½ Feb / 3½ Sep
Southern Pacific...... 100	25 Mar / 17¼ July	20⅜ Aug / 16¼ Apr	22¼ Jan / 14 Nov	23⅜ Sep / 13¼ Jan	35 Dec / 12 Apr	44¼ Nov / 6½ Sep	45⅜ Dec / 41⅜ Jun	63⅝ Jun / 29 May	81¼ Sep / 56 Dec	68¼ Mar / 38⅜ Sep
Southern Railway Co... 100	14⅞ Sep / 10⅜ Nov	14⅞ May / 11¾ Dec	11¾ Nov / 6⅜ Aug	13¼ Sep / ...	10¾ Apr / 7 Apr	14¼ Oct / 10 May	23⅜ Jun / 10⅝ Jan	33¾ Jun / 18 Jan	41⅛ Dec / 28 Dec	36⅜ Sep / 16½ Oct
do do pfd... 100	45¼ Sep / 33¼ Aug	44⅛ July / 7 Dec	33¼ Feb / 15¼ Aug	38⅝ Sep / 22⅞ Apr	43¾ Dec / 25⅝ Mar	58⅝ Nov / 40⅞ Jan	104⅝ Feb / 49¼ Jun	94¾ Nov / 67¼ Jan	89¼ Apr / 74⅜ Dec	63⅛ Oct / 96 Feb
Tenn. Coal & Iron...... 100	20⅞ Aug / 14 Oct	46⅝ Sep / 13¼ Jan	34¼ Feb / 13 Nov	35⅜ Apr / 17 May	38¾ Mar / 17 Mar	126 Sep / 36 Jan	104 Feb / 46 Oct	75⅞ Jun / 40⅞ Mar	74½ Dec / 48¾ Apr	68⅜ Mar / 25¾ Nov
Texas & Pacific......... 100	10⅞ Aug / 7 Jan	14⅜ Sep / 5 Dec	12 Nov / 5 Aug	15 Aug / 8 Apr	20⅛ Dec / 8⅞ Mar	25⅝ Mar / 12¼ Jan	26¾ Dec / 13⅜ Jan	53¼ May / 23¼ Jan	54⅜ Sep / 37 Dec	49⅜ Feb / 20¼ Aug
Twin City............. 100	.....	.....	5 Aug	14¾ Dec / 9¼ Dec	36½ Dec / 16½ Jan	72 Apr / 34 Jan	13⅜ Jan / 61½ July	105⅝ Dec / 23¼ Jan	37 Dec / 107 Jan	12¼ Jan / 79 Jan
Union Bag & Paper..... 100	.....	.....	.....	14¾ Dec / 9¼ Dec	.....	73 Apr / 10 Dec	25 Feb / 10 Jun	65⅜ Jun / 12 Apr	178 Feb / 11½ Nov	79 Oct / 15 Jan
do do pfd.... 100	.....	.....	.....	.....	.....	17¼ Nov / 38 Jan	77¾ Feb / 12 Apr	19⅛ Jun / 12 Dec	11½ Apr / 85 Apr	4½ July / 79¾ Jan
Union Pacific........... 100	22½ Mar / 7 July	17½ May / 4 Dec	12¼ Nov / 3½ Jan	27¾ Oct / 4½ Apr	36½ Feb / 23 Mar	89 Mar / 71 Dec	50¼ May / 77¾ Feb	65 Apr / 33 May	72 Jan / 85 Aug	-5¾ Jan / 79¾ Jan
do do pfd.... 100	11⅜ Aug / 8 Dec	24½ May / 7 Feb	11⅞ Feb / 5⅙ July	10 Aug / 6¼ May	81⅜ Dec / 38⅝ Jan	81⅛ Dec / 38⅜ Jun	81⅛ May / 43⅜ Jan	133 May / 76 May	113¼ Aug / 93½ Dec	104⅝ Aug / 65⅜ Aug
U. S. Leather........... 100	68¾ Apr / 52¼ Jun	9¾ May / 60⅞ Feb	60⅞ Feb / 41⅞ Aug	72 Sep / 50 Apr	75½ Sep / 53¾ Mar	85⅜ Jan / 64½ Apr	85⅜ Dec / 70½ Jan	99½ May / 81⅝ Jan	95 Aug / 95 Mar	95¼ Feb / 83⅝ Aug
do do pfd.... 100	45¼ Dec / 33¼ May	58 Jun / 21 Dec	29 Jan / 14½ Aug	25¼ Apr / 10 Jun	48½ May / 14½ Mar	40⅞ Nov / 37⅞ Dec	19 Jan / 7¼ May	16⅝ May / 7¼ May	14¾ Apr / 11⅛ Apr	88¾ Mar / 15¼ Feb
U. S. Rubber........... 100	99 Dec / 80 Jan	98½ Jun / 75 Dec	14½ Jan / 65 Oct	76¾ Jan / 50 July	113¼ Dec / 60 Mar	53 Jun / 121 July	7¾ Jun / 104¾ Jan	83¾ Aug / 60½ May	91¼ Sep / 70⅝ Jan	96¾ May / 71½ Oct
do do pfd..... 100	.....	.....	.....	.....	.....	64½ Nov / 57 Apr	79¼ Jan / 65 Jun	34 Jan / 44 Jan	70⅛ Jan / 19½ Apr	71½ Feb / 19⅛ Feb
U. S. Steel............. 100	.....	.....	.....	.....	.....	37⅞ Jan / 121 July	65 Jun / 44 Jan	12½ Oct / 85 Jan	19½ Apr / 14 Jan	19⅛ July / 7 Feb
do pfd............. 100	.....	.....	.....	.....	.....	99¾ Dec	104¾ Jan / 74½ Dec	85 Jan / 47 Oct	14 Jan / 64 Mar	58 Feb / 30¼ Nov
Wabash............... 100	8½ Apr / 5¾ July	10¼ Sep / 5 Dec	8 Nov / 4½ Aug	9¾ Sep / 4⅝ Mar	9½ Aug / 6¼ Mar	8⅝ Jan / 6½ Dec	14 Dec / 6½ Mar	47 Apr / 55 Apr / 24 May	64 Mar / 44¾ Dec	30¼ Dec / 10 Nov
do pfd.... 100	18⅝ Apr / 12¼ Jan	20⅜ Sep / 12¾ Jan	10¾ Feb / 11 Aug	23⅜ Sep / 11¼ Apr	24¼ Aug / 14¼ Mar	25½ Apr / 19 May	25 Dec / 27 Jan	1017⅛ Apr / 24 May / 69 May / 26 Jun	29¾ Feb / 95¾ Dec / 79 Dec	38⅝ Feb / 89¾ Mar / 49¾ Jan
Western Union....... 100	92½ Sep / 80⅞ Jan	95⅜ Sep / 82½ Dec	90¼ Nov / 72¼ Aug	96¾ Apr / 75¾ May	95⅞ Sep / 82¼ Aug	98¼ May / 82 Dec	88½ Jan / 77½ Jun	100¼ May / 81 Jan	97¼ Aug / 87 Dec	32¼ Feb / 16⅝ Oct / 55¼ Feb / 27½ Sep / 93 Jan / 80¼ Sep

Stocks and Par Value.	1894.	1895.	1896.	1897.	1898.	1899.	1900.	1901.	1902.	1903.
Wheeling & Lake Erie ..$100	14⅜ Aug / 9 July	18¼ Jun / 6⅞ Dec	13¼ Feb / 5¼ Aug	6½ Jan / ½ Jun	6¼ Dec / ¾July	13 Aug / 7⅞ Dec	13½ Dec / 8 Jun	22 Jun / 11⅜ Jan	28¾ Oct / 17 Jan	27½ Feb / 12 July
do 1st pfd. 100	51½ Apr / 32½July	54⅞July / 29 Dec	40¾ Feb / 20⅝ Aug	29 Jan / 2⅝ Apr	30¾ Dec / 8 July	64 Jan / 45 Dec	58½ Apr / 44½ Sep	60½ Mar / 36 May	66 Apr / 49½ Jan	62 May / 40¼ Nov
do 2d pfd. 100	......	......	......	......	......	32⅞ Sep / 21¼ Dec	33⅛ Mar / 21⅝ Jun	36 Mar / 24 May	42⅜ Sep / 28 Jan	38½ Feb / 20 Sep
Wisconsin Central...... 100	9 Apr / 1½July	8 Sep / 2¼ Jan	4½ Feb / 1½ Jun	4⅜ Aug / 1 Jun	3¾ Jan / 1 Jan	21 Nov / 13½ May	20¾ Mar / 10 Sep	26 Jun / 14½ Jan	30⅜ Sep / 19¼ Jan	29¼ Feb / 14½ Oct
do pfd ... 100	35 Apr / 25 July	......	......	8 Sep / 1¾ Apr	6¾ Jan / 3 Jan	59 Aug / 44 Dec	57 Apr / 30 Sep	49¾ Apr / 38½ Jan	57¾ Aug / 39½ Jan	55½ Feb / 33 Nov